Newlon

The men who made Mexico

LAS ANIMAS HIGH SCHOOL LIBRARY

THE MEN WHO

MADE MEXICO

THE MEN WHO MADE MEXICO

CLARKE NEWLON

ILLUSTRATED WITH PHOTOGRAPHS

DODD, MEAD & COMPANY

NEW YORK

Map of Mexico by Donald T. Pitcher

Copyright © 1973 by Clarke Newlon

All rights reserved

ISBN: 0-396-06778-6
Library of Congress Catalog Card Number: 72-12543

Printed in the United States of America
by The Cornwall Press, Inc., Cornwall, N. Y.

For Betty

ACKNOWLEDGMENTS

I am indebted to two estimable members of Washington's Mexican colony for the help they gave me on source material for this book and for helping me untangle some of the many complexities of their country's history.

His Excellency Rafael de la Colina, Ambassador to the Organization of American States and senior member of Mexico's diplomatic corps, belongs in the book as ᴛ.ᴀe subject of one of its chapters. Rather than this, however, he preferred the role of advisor and critic, and to contribute a commentary. Ambassador de la Colina began his distinguished career in Mexico's foreign service as consul to a number of North American cities. His first assignment as Ambassador Extraordinary and Plenipotentiary was in 1948 in Washington and later he served his country in this same capacity in Canada and Japan. From 1953 to 1959 he was Mexico's permanent representative to the United Nations; earlier he had helped draft that organization's first International Bill of Rights. In a speech made on that occasion, he said:

"Each nation, however small and unimportant it may appear, is a person in international law and as such, the proud possessor of certain inalienable rights. All of these juridical entities are equal before the law, but each one has distinct cultural traits and historical traditions that set it apart from all others. Each is endowed with spiritual values that must be cherished and preserved."

The Ambassador's assignments to special committees and organizations, his international awards and honors, and the list of his own writings fill a column in *Who's Who in America*. Himself a distinguished history scholar, the Ambassador was amiably exacting on detail and accuracy, right down to the nuances of phraseology. He was especially critical when he caught me mangling the title of one of his own Spanish ancestors.

Yolanda Sanchez is the attractive and talented Washington correspondent of Telesistema, Mexico's national television and radio system. Since she is on the screen and air five times each week with her contribution to Telesistema's nightly nation-wide newscast, Yolanda is probably the best known young woman in Mexico. She also is a former newspaper reporter and helped organize the International Association of Journalists and became its first president. IAJ held its second successful Congress in Mexico City in November of 1972 under her direction.

Yolanda was knowledgeable and greatly helpful with her suggestions in the business of selecting subjects for the more contemporary part of this book and in the labors of research and collecting of material on the people chosen.

COMMENTARY

With genuine interest I have read your manuscript contain-
ing several chapters of the biographical book you are writing
on Mexican leaders who, in one way or another, have influenced the history of my country or who have left a lasting
imprint on the thoughts, beliefs, and actions of its people. I
think that your project deserves unstinted praise. A book of
this type for the general public and especially for the schools,
is sorely needed. The scant knowledge in the United States
concerning events and personalities in its neighbor to the
south is regrettable. Your book will help fill this void.

Furthermore, the growing numbers of Mexican-Americans
and their increased weight in the political and economic life
of the United States makes your work doubly useful. I am
certain that they will find in it a readily available source of
information concerning the aspirations and achievements of
a great nation in its relentless search for freedom and justice.

Now that so many minorities of diverse ethnic origins are
looking back to their cultural roots, a book like yours will
enable the Mexican-Americans to know better the country
of their ancestors and to take justifiable pride in their rich
heritage.

Although I do not share some of your judgements and my

point of view as a Mexican citizen differs from yours, particu-

larly in regard to events involving the United States, on the basis of the chapters that I have read, I consider in general your treatment to be both interesting and sympathetic.

—RAFAEL DE LA COLINA
   Ambassador to the Organization
   of American States

CONTENTS

xi

MEXICO AND THE MEXICANS

MAN HAS LIVED in Mexico more than forty thousand years and most probably arrived there by slow stages over the Bering Strait "land bridge" before the frequent earthquakes of the area permitted it to sink beneath the arctic waters. The time is reasonably well established; man may have arrived earlier, but certainly no later. The Bering Strait route to the American continent is conjecture and one of several theories, but the most plausible one.

These early settlers, following the game as the ice receded, were Mongolian in appearance, their hair coarse and black, their faces flat and beardless, and their eyes heavy-lidded, their stature short but no longer stooped. They were primitive (but so were men in other parts of the world forty thousand years ago) and they were just entering the Stone Age, when man began to grow his food instead of killing it.

Pushing southward and across what is now the border between the United States and Mexico, they established over the next three hundred-odd centuries three great kingdoms. One of these, the Inca, was in Peru. The other two were in Mexico—the Aztec and the Maya—and it is from those two civilizations, and their tribal forebears, that most of today's Mexicans claim ancestry. Along, of course, with the Spanish

1

who conquered, exploited, and colonized both the Aztecs and the Mayas, and the Incas, too.

The Aztec is certainly the most studied and the most written about of any Indian tribe in America, possibly because it was the first to fall before the muskets and cannon of the Spanish *conquistadores*. But, actually, the Aztecs were late arrivals on the Mexican scene. Other tribes—Toltec, Huastec, Olmec, Zapotec, Mixtec, Xochicalco, and Tabasco, among them—had been in the area of Central Mexico for hundreds and even thousands of years before the Aztecs even arrived at the lakes of Anáhuac, the site of today's Mexico City.

They did not call themselves Aztecs, of course, but Tenochas, and they had come from the north seeking land.

They arrived in 1168, a date which is fully established by historians from the Aztec ideographic "picture history" and synchronized with modern calendars. They had come, they said, from the fabled land of Aztlan, and from this the Spanish derived the name Aztec by which they have been known since. Their language was Nahuatl.

They brought with them their own gods, and a passion for human sacrifice in which they tore the hearts from living victims to appease these gods. At times these sacrifices may have included a ritual cannibalism.

When the Aztecs arrived at Anáhuac they were probably not less than one thousand in number and certainly not more than five thousand. They had come from the north—probably most recently from what is now Arizona—and they were searching for a place they would be able to recognize. It would be marked, according to tribal oracle, by a three-branched bayonet cactus (with two open blossoms) on which would be perched an eagle holding a live serpent in his claws.

They found the three symbols at Anáhuac, and these became so much a part of national legend that today the cactus, the eagle, and the serpent appear on the great shield of Mexico. The Aztecs were reluctantly accepted by the much more culturally advanced Toltecs, who found their human sacrifice addiction barbaric but admired the beauty of their women and the daring bravery of their warriors.

And well they might have been wary. Within two centuries the Aztecs had virtually assimilated the Toltecs by conquest, marriage, and wife-stealing. They had adopted many of the Toltec gods, though subjugating them to their own great Huitzilopochtli. They had moved into and absorbed the Toltec culture and language, and were completely in charge of the city they had adopted, greatly enlarged and renamed Tenochtitlán, meaning "cactus on a rock."

They also, as time went on, assimilated or subdued other tribes. By the time the Spanish arrived in 1519 to provide the other side of the Mexican ancestry, the Aztecs pretty well controlled an empire stretching from the Pacific Ocean to the Gulf of Mexico, and from the high central plateau dominated by the twin volcanic peaks of Popocatepetl and Ixtacihuatl, to Guatemala. They ruled some two million people. More specifically, they exacted tribute from them in the form of food and other products, and sacrificial victims for which their need was endless.

Some of the Aztec wars, by prearrangement, were "flower wars," where killing was not permitted but the taking of prisoners for sacrifice was. Both the Aztecs and the Mayas in all fighting preferred to capture rather than kill.

The Aztecs had but one grain—corn—and their lives revolved around it. They cleared land by cutting and burning trees and brush. The earth was crudely cultivated with a sharpened and fire-hardened stick and the corn planted in early spring. Beans and squash were usually planted simultaneously so that their vines could climb on the cornstalks.

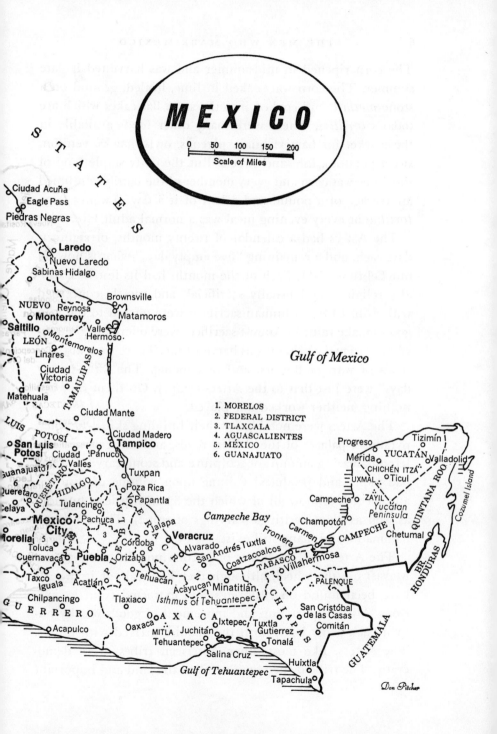

MEXICO

0   50   100   150   200
Scale of Miles

1. MORELOS
2. FEDERAL DISTRICT
3. TLAXCALA
4. AGUASCALIENTES
5. MÉXICO
6. GUANAJUATO

Gulf of Mexico

Campeche Bay

Gulf of Tehuantepec

Don Pitcher

The corn ripened in midsummer and was harvested in late summer. The corn was soaked in lime, hulled, ground on a stone *metlatl,* and cooked into the same flat cakes which are today's *tortillas.* There were many other foods available in the market for barter: quail, pigeons, owls, hawks, venison, sweet potatoes, fish, and sweets. But the daily staple food of the Aztec was corn and every member of the family consumed an average of a pound and a half of it a day. Twenty large *tortillas* at every evening meal was a normal adult fare.

The Aztecs had a calendar of twenty months, of eighteen days each, and a remaining "five empty days" what is now on our February 7-11. Each of the months had its festivals, usually religious and usually sacrificial, and mostly concerned with rain. In April human sacrifices were offered to the rain god to make rain; in August sacrifices were offered to the rain god *not* to make rain—it was harvest time. There were also festivals of war, of flowers, and of dancing. The "five empty days" were just that to the Aztecs—empty. On them they did nothing, neither worked nor played.

The Aztecs were notable for their building skills—temples, pyramids, palaces of the nobles, roads, and causeways. They left an amazing amount of sculpture and stone carving. They had paper and produced volume upon volume of histories and records (almost all of which the Spanish priests burned) as well as *glyph* writings (carvings of stone). These weren't flammable and many still exist.

The Aztecs had no beasts of burden nor did they (or the Mayas) use the wheel, although they knew about it; wheels have been found on children's toys extracted from excavations. All transportation and movement of goods was by human back or by boat, until the Spanish arrived with horses. The Aztecs, like most other American tribes, were democratic. The tribe owned or controlled the land and important decisions were made by ballot. Leaders were elected, though thereafter were inclined to rule by divine right. Every Indian was born into a clan and automatically became a member of it by the simple process of birth. But even if that clan happened to be the lowest in the social structure, the peasant farmer, it was still possible for any member to move out of it by demonstrating special skills. There was a professional military class, though every Aztec male became a warrior when there was need of him. Wars, in fact, were usually timed to follow the harvest. Teachers, scribes, merchants, and priests were also in strata of their own. A girl could move out of a clan through marriage.

The Aztec were monogamous, at least in theory. The boy married at twenty, usually, and the girl at sixteen, and marriages were almost always arranged by parents or a marriage broker. Children were plentiful and a man could divorce a wife who did not produce them. It was not illegal to be a bachelor in the Aztec society (as it was in the Inca) but it was impractical. *Tortillas* had to be cooked twice a day and the preparation took two hours. There had to be a woman around to do it.

The Mayas occupied what is today the Mexican state of Yucatán (often called "the giant thumb protruding into the Gulf of Mexico") plus present-day areas of Campeche, Tabasco, and Quintana Roo, the eastern half of Chiapas, all of British Honduras (now more often called Belize), and the western part of Honduras.

Their beginning dates back probably to about the year 2,000 B.C. and although almost nothing is known factually about them until the tenth century (A.D.) they have become classified by history as the intellectuals of the Indian tribes by a process of deduction.

Their total population (by the tenth or eleventh century)

was probably about three million. They did not call themselves Mayas; nobody knows what they really did call themselves. But they were builders of cities, temples, and great pyramids almost unparalleled in the history of that time. They produced a calendar by which through complicated computation they could trace their history back more than three million days. They painted, and on their multicolored frescoes, murals, and pottery which have been found in the literally hundreds of Mayan ruins, archaeologists have found human faces in expressions and attitudes depicting most of the human emotions: hate, love, scorn, wit, laughter, passion.

Like the Aztecs, they built great courts for games played with a rubber ball and on which they wagered enormous sums. They wrote and produced plays. And, again like the Aztecs, they danced ceremonially and for fun to the rhythmic (if tuneless) beat of drums, the piping of reeds, and the *umpahs* of the conch shell.

The Mayas also had but one grain, corn. They were almost constantly at war with neighboring tribes, usually to produce the prisoners needed for sacrifice to the ceaseless demands of the rain god. The Mayan territory was alternately blessed and cursed (and still is) by either too little or too much rain, and it took many blood stains on the altars to insure that the corn fields were neither too wet nor too dry. They had other food, of course, including the wild game which they hunted with arrows and spears and short swords studded with razor-sharp obsidian, a black flaky stone, and tracked with barkless dogs. Unlike the Aztecs, they were not landlocked; they cruised thousands of miles along the coast on hunting and trading expeditions, or in war parties. But their main food was corn, the *tortilla*. Without it they went hungry.

The Mayas held to one wife or husband, normally, and produced lots of children. The heads of the newly born

Mayan male children were placed between two lightly pressured planks to give them the flat, almost wedge-shaped form which was so much admired. There was also a great reverence for crossed eyes (many of the Mayan gods have them) and mothers frequently suspended a small ball between the eyes of the child to turn his eyes inward. Both Aztec and Maya women often filed their front teeth. They also pierced the nose for the insertion of an ornament and sometimes imbedded a semiprecious stone (normally topaz) in the side of the left nostril.

The Aztecs and the Mayas had one major god in common—the mystical, once human, and greatly revered Quetzalcoatl. Both had acquired, inherited, or adopted him from the Toltecs. According to legend, Quetzalcoatl was an early priest and ruler who had been conceived by virgin birth when his mother swallowed a piece of jade. Quetzalcoatl ruled the widespread Toltec nation for two decades, including what was later the Aztec capital, and also Tula, the Maya city in Yucatán. According to the legend he lost a civil war and fled to the coast where he set sail on the open sea with a vow to return on the day (by Aztec reckoning) of 1-Reed, the sign under which he had been born.

After conquering and absorbing the Toltecs, the Aztecs adopted Quetzalcoatl, whose symbol was a serpent's head wreathed in quetzal plumes, as their own and raised him to an equal level with their ranking deity, Huitzilopochtli. The Mayas also put the god of the plumed serpent very high in the ranks of their gods, whom the Spanish later found to be "numberless."

The Quetzalcoatl prophesy thus was known and perhaps accepted generally throughout Mexico, that is, the Aztec regions and the Mayan territory. And when Christopher Columbus on his fourth and last voyage came in contact with the Mayas, the word spread from tribe to tribe and mile over mile to Tenochtitlán.

Seventeen years later Hernán Cortés landed at Veracruz and began his march inland. The year was 1519 by the modern calendar and the year of 1-Reed by the Aztec calendar, the year Quetzalcoatl had vowed to return from the east in the guise of a white god. Thus, when Cortés appeared at the causeway entrance of Tenochtitlán, the ruler Moctezuma did not know whether to fight him as an enemy or welcome him as a returning god. He chose the latter course, then changed his mind, and it was the vacillation which probably cost him his empire.

After Columbus reported his discovery of the thickly settled land of the Mayas "with masonry houses and people who cover their persons in cotton garments," the Spanish made several ill-prepared attempts toward conquest, all of which were repulsed. The Aztecs were destined to fall first.

Cortés looked over the inhospitable mangrove swamp shores of Maya land as he sailed by and continued on to Veracruz. There he landed his 555 men and sixteen horses, burned his boats so there could be no turning back, and marched inland toward the city of Tenochtitlán of which the coastal Indians told fabulous stories. On the way he persuaded the Tlascaltecs, from whom the Aztecs had long extracted tribute, to be his allies.

His march through the jungle, mountains, and desert to what is now Mexico City is still one of the most incredible feats in history. The Aztecs never knew how few the Spanish were in numbers. It was their first contact with gunpowder and men on horseback. And after two years, during which time Cortés was welcomed, then thrown out and later laid siege to the city, tricked, captured, tortured, and finally

killed Moctezuma, he and his *conquistadores,* with their Tlas-
caltec allies, had destroyed the Aztec empire. Along with it
they destroyed the city of Tenochtitlán so completely that no
vestige of it remained a few years later.

In 1524, with the Aztecs subdued, Cortés made another famous march through the swamps of lower Mexico and across
Yucatán, meeting little resistance throughout his wide path,
but did not remain. In 1527 Francisco de Montejo, with a
force of 380 men and 57 horses, landed first in Yucatán and
later in Chetumal, Quintana Roo, and was driven off both
times. He finally resigned in favor of his son, who succeeded
where the father had failed, and after a terrible slaughter of
stubbornly resisting Mayas, established his capital city of
Mérida and completed the conquest of Mexico in 1546.

After the conquest, the Spanish soldier, and later the settler and the official, mingled his blood with the Indians
through countless marriages or less formal unions which resulted in children and the *mestizo,* part Indian, part Spanish. With the *mestizo,* as the country became colonized, was
the Spaniard, the man or woman actually born in Spain, and
the Creole, the man or woman of pure Spanish parentage but
born in Mexico. Later an intermingling of Negro blood was
added to the *mestizo* strain largely along the coastal areas, and
today the terms "Spaniard" and "Creole" are rarely used.
All are Mexicans.

The imposition of the Spanish language, however, was
total. After the conquest of the Aztecs the Spaniards combined the language of Tenochtitlán—Nahuatl—with other
local tribal languages and simply overwhelmed them with
Spanish. Many Indian words went into the language, of
course, but today the Spanish language is not only the language of the country, it is the *native* language.

Among the earliest and most effective of Mexico's colonizers was the Church. Mexico was named a bishopric in 1527 when the Pope designated Fray Juan de Zumárraga as the first Bishop and Protector of the Indians of Mexico. The earliest of the church orders to arrive were the Franciscans, who established monasteries at Huexotzinco, Teccoco, Tlaxcala, and Mexico City. They were followed closely by the Dominican and Augustinian orders. The year 1531 saw a miracle of the Blessed Virgin of Guadalupe come to pass when the Virgin appeared at the present site of the basilica of Guadalupe, just north of Mexico City, and caused flowers to grow out of a rock.

The Church was a two-sided coin to the Indian. On one hand it destroyed his temples, persecuted his priests, and imposed on him a new god with very strange creeds. On the other hand it tried hard to protect him against exploitation and virtual slavery at the hands of the *encomendero,* who was granted a certain number of Indians to work his land—and who theoretically was supposed to treat the Indians as his "children," to protect and educate them, but usually forgot. According to Victor Alba, in his book *The Mexicans,* there was never a color barrier with the Spanish and the Indian. To the Indian, for instance, the priest was Spanish and not a "white man." And to the priest the Indian was not inferior but merely "different." Perhaps this was true of the Church, but it is difficult to believe it was also true of the Spanish grandee who could barely tolerate his own son (of a Spanish wife) if the boy was born in Mexico and not in Spain.

Mexico gave Mother Spain great riches although, as history knows, they were not really a blessing. In the eighteenth century, Spain took one-third of the silver in the world from the state of Guanajuato. One fortunate nobleman, who had been granted the mines of Pachuca, was made richer by the incredible sum of five hundred million pesos.

In turn, Spain gave Mexico the horse and the pack animal and the wheel. The Spaniards built cities and established a school system. The University of Mexico, opened in 1551, is the oldest institution of higher education on the American continent. They also gave Mexico a copy of their own bureaucratic government administration, a mixed blessing.

The first Viceroy of Mexico was Antonio de Mendoza, in 1535, and there were a total of sixty-one in all, during the next almost three centuries. During those centuries the Spanish rulers faced the constant threat of rebellion at some level. The Indians rebelled against the tax levies of goods and forced labor, and the blacks rebelled against slavery. In 1598 the Tepic miners arose against their masters, and in 1680 the Indians of Tehuantepec revolted and for eight years controlled much of the Tehuantepec isthmus.

By the beginning of the nineteenth century the Spanish government had begun conscripting her Mexican colonists for service in the Spanish armies for the first time. The rulers of Spain were never very bright psychologically, but this came at a time when the fresh breezes of freedom from tyranny, whether on or offshore, were sweeping the Western world. The Americans to the north had successfully broken away from English rule and the French had successfully opted for *liberté, égalité,* and *fraternité,* if on a somewhat tenuous basis. The works of Montesquieu, Voltaire, Rousseau, and others were being smuggled into Mexico despite the vigilance of the Inquisition, and the intellectuals were reading them avidly. Mexico, as the century turned the corner into 1800, was ready at virtually every level for the rebellion against Spain which was just in the offing.

MIGUEL HIDALGO

IN THE EARLY 1800s there were some five million people in the colony which was known as New Spain—*gachupines, criollos, mestizos,* and Indians.

At the top were the *gachupines,* the men and women who were Spanish and had been born in Spain. They numbered about ten thousand.

Next in the ascending order of the Mexican hierarchy came the *criollos,* or Creoles; that is, men and women of pure Spanish blood but who had been born in New Spain. There were half a million, perhaps a few more, of these.

The *mestizos* were the Mexicans of mixed blood, part Spanish and part Indian, with often, especially in coastal areas, an admixture of Negro. And there were still a fair number of pure Indians. The *mestizos* and Indians numbered something over four million.

The caste system which controlled these four segments of Mexican society was rigidly structured. For some reason, almost unaccountable to the average person today, there was a vast social gap between the *gachupin* and the *criollo.* Only the *gachupin* (the word means "wearer of spurs") could—or did—hold such high offices in the Church as prelates, bishops, and archbishops. All of the provincial governors were appointed by the King of Spain and all were *gachupines,* and this held true for almost every high office or official position in Mexico. Consequently, a *gachupin* father would go to almost any length to have his wife sent back to the mother country to bear his children. Intermarriage between the *gachupin* and the *criollo* did happen, of course, but was not encouraged by the *gachupin* parents.

The *criollo* could become a doctor or a lawyer; he could hold all offices, except the highest, that is, he could be a bishop but not an archbishop. He could become an artisan (carpenter or mason), he could be a merchant, he could own land, and (in rare instances) become wealthy; he could study for the priesthood, as thousands of *criollos* did.

The *mestizos* made up the large laboring classes: the farmers, herdsmen, miners, servants—the hewers of wood and the carriers of stone. Sometimes they were indentured or bound to their jobs by contract; more often they were bound there simply because they had to eat and the economics of the country didn't permit them to move about.

At the bottom of the ladder was the Indian—even below the relatively small number of Negro slaves in Mexico. Frequently he was indentured or a virtual slave, forced to work in the mines or on the great haciendas of the *gachupin* or *criollo,* for both were slave-owners. The fact that the *criollo* resented the *gachupin* didn't make him any kinder to those beneath him in the social ladder—the *mestizos* and the Indians.

One of the many *criollos* who studied for the priesthood was Miguel Gregorio Antonio Hildalgo y Costillo Gallaga Mandarte y Villasenor, known more simply in Mexican history as Miguel Hidalgo. As a priest, Hidalgo was, to a small extent, responsible for some relaxation in the stern dogma of the Catholic Church in the schools of his day and, as the first of the revolutionary liberators of his country, occupies an important niche in the history of Mexico.

But in either role he seems oddly miscast. In another age, another world, Miguel Hidalgo would have been a great liberal thinker, a philosopher, a writer, perhaps. He was a very human person, given to such traits as spending more money than he made. He loved a joke and was possessed of a puckish sense of humor which at times got him in hot water. He was prey to all of the frailties of the flesh which afflict ordinary mortals, and when they resulted in temptations, he more often than not indulged them. He was *simpático*.

As a teacher, Hidalgo was successful in replacing doctrines and books which enabled his aspiring students to the priesthood to encounter a more generous and less demanding God. As a priest in his own parish, Hidalgo preferred to relegate many of the strictly religious duties to subordinates while he concerned himself with the physical and cultural welfare of his flock. As a military strategist he was sadly out of place.

He was probably one of the better educated men in the world of his day, both through formal training and through his own voracious reading. He read in French, Italian, and English, and was an expert on the Indian languages of Mexico as well. Like many other priests of the time, Hidalgo liked good living, appreciating both fine food and wine. He was fond of music for listening and for dancing, but his greatest pleasure, and doubtless his greatest talent, was in the discussion of ideas; nothing pleased him as much as getting together with a group of his peers (who were all too few in that day) and debating a new ideology, a new political concept, an original belief which had just been advanced. It was in such company that he was most brilliant.

Miguel Hidalgo was born in 1753 on the Hacienda San Diego Corralejo in the Bajío district near Guanajuato, the second of five sons. (His mother died bearing the fifth when Miguel was eight years old). His father, Don Cristóbal Hidalgo, was a Creole *(criollo)*, as was his mother, and as all four of his grandparents had been. Don Cristóbal was overseer of the large estate which comprised the hacienda and was himself well-to-do by *criollo* standards, being the owner of several horses, a sizable herd of cattle, and five slaves. The slaves were listed on the tax rolls of the day as being Negro and mulatto.

Along with the other sons, Miguel received a rudimentary education from his father, and when he was twelve was sent with his older brother, José Joaquin, to the San Francisco Javier school at Valladolid. This was a Jesuit school and due to the influence of several innovative and, for that day, radical teachers, had a far more advanced curriculum than any comparable school in Mexico. Normally the studies would have been limited to law, rhetoric, and theology. To these the Jesuits added modern languages, history, physics, mathematics, philosophy, and geography. Two years after Miguel and his brother enrolled there, the Jesuit order was expelled from Mexico by the Church for just such innovations and modern thinking, and the school was closed. Miguel had been a brilliant student, possibly the most outstanding of his class, and in these two years he had acquired a taste for learning; moreover, his instructors had instilled in him an intellectual curiosity which influenced his thinking and behavior thereafter.

After a summer spent with his father and brothers in the country, where, according to at least one biographer, he taught the *mestizo* children of a neighboring village to read and write, Miguel and his brother were enrolled in the autumn of 1767 by their father in the College of San Nicolás Obispo, also at Valladolid. His career there was again brilliant as he made his way through a formidable study course which included advanced Latin grammar and literature, Greek, French, Italian, and at least three Indian languages, physics, and more rhetoric. In 1770 he went (still with his brother, José) to college briefly at the University of Mexico where he earned a B.A. degree and where eight years later he was ordained a priest. This was on September 8, 1778.

He had taken a degree in theology, presented a thesis on the Otomí language, won several scholarships and scholastic honors, was president of his class and several literary societies, had acquired a reputation for brilliance from his teachers, and the popular nickname of "El Zorro" ("The Fox") from his classmates. He had also been suspended briefly for breaking out of his room via the window one night to participate in a student escapade.

Miguel Hidalgo was twenty-six when he was ordained, and he had studied the languages of the Indians with the intention of working with them, probably the Otomí tribe, on whose language he had focused most of his attention. Instead, however, the young priest stayed on at San Nicolás Obispo as a teacher.

Hidalgo remained at San Nicolás for the better part of twelve years, serving the school in various positions and finally, in 1790, as rector or head of the college. This position brought him both prestige and money, enough of the latter to buy three small haciendas. One of these, Xaripeo, he retained through much of his life and it brought him both pleasure and problems. On it he raised bulls for the *corrida*. He loved the bullfights, but the avocation was not profitable and consequently he was continually having financial troubles with the property. Brilliant as he was in many things, Hidalgo was notably (almost notoriously) inept at handling money, a trait which plagued him throughout much of his life.

In 1792 he abruptly resigned his position at San Nicolás Obispo and was assigned the curacy of Colima, a small town almost due west of Mexico City. Why he left is uncertain. Records show that the college had a considerable surplus when he took charge and a considerable deficit when he left, but this was simply put forward as an indication of misman-agement, never a hint of dishonesty. One historian felt that Hidalgo simply wanted to get into parish work. It is more probable, however, that his abrupt departure was due to the revisions he made in the college curriculum, the new courses he introduced, and the innovations he established. At San Francisco Javier he had seen the Jesuits expelled; now he was feeling the reactionary power of the Church himself.

He remained at Colima about eight months and was reas-signed to San Felipe, forty miles northwest of Guanajuato, in 1793, this time because the Church wanted a tough-minded representative there and Hidalgo was selected as the best man for the post, despite other deficiencies. Here he re-mained ten years, probably the best ten of his life. A neigh-boring priest and intellectual, José Martín García Carras-quedo, joined him in organizing the small "literary" groups which Hidalgo so loved. Both clerics read easily in French and together they explored the plays of Racine and Molière and, more important to the thinking of Hidalgo, of the French philosopher Jean Jacques Rousseau. The great French revolutionary writer wrote that men were born free, were equal in a state of nature, and should be allowed to create their own destinies. There was, he said, no divine right of royalty, and governments based on strength grew out of man's exploitation of the greed of others. The French literary atmosphere in Hidalgo's home grew so pronounced that friends gave it the name of "Franchia Chiquita" or Little France.

In San Felipe, Hidalgo also was able to indulge his passion for music. As the *cura* of the parish, he was one of the more important citizens of the community and his comfortable home was able to accommodate the musical evenings he frequently organized and at which the working-class *mestizos* of San Felipe were equally welcome with the more elite *criollos*. Such entertainments usually began with chamber music and ended with dancing; Hidalgo was fond of both. These affairs entailed providing food and drink for his guests, and the priest often found it difficult to make ends meet in San Felipe, pay the deficit at his hacienda, and debts he had left at the college. But he was popular at all intellectual and financial levels in his parish and must have been a pleasant man to know, a good companion.

In the summer of 1800 accusations against Hidalgo were made to the Holy Office of the Spanish Inquisition with a resultant investigation of the priest's professed beliefs and his manner of life. Inquisition had been established by Ferdinand and Isabella in 1478, some fourteen years before the Spanish Queen sponsored the first voyage of Columbus. Originally supposed to seek out Jews and Moors whose conversion to the Catholic faith was insincere, it rapidly became a method of "thought police" which threatened every Spaniard. The brutal tortures of the Inquisition were established by its first chief, the notorious Tomás de Torquemada. An innocent statement could be (and often was) twisted by enemies into an indication of heresy or lax morals and used to haul the victim up before the inquisitors. Originally under the control of the crown, the Inquisition was turned over to the Church in the sixteenth century and remained in force until abolished in 1820. It was never as strong or as ubiquitous in the New World as in the Old, but it did maintain a "branch office" in Mexico City.

The accusations made against Hidalgo were widely varied (from moral laxity to owning a copy of the Koran) but were chiefly important for his statements about the Church, about various Church officers including some of the former Popes, and about Church doctrine. Actually, the same puckish humor which had endeared him to his classmates and which led him later to distribute candy to his executioners, was probably the chief cause of his trouble, although he certainly read forbidden books and ascribed to beliefs the Church did not condone, and his personal moral code might have raised eyebrows today.

In the "literary hours" which he and Padre García Carrasquedo organized in San Felipe, they frequently entertained visiting priests, and Hidalgo, purely mischievously, delighted in making provocative statements. The result was lively arguments which sometimes shocked visitors, and it was a costly form of fun. Two of his guests eventually filed information with the Mexican Holy Office of the Spanish Inquisition.

The investigation dragged on for a year, and while it was eventually suspended and filed away to gather dust for nine years, Hidalgo was relieved of his assignment in San Felipe and, after a considerable period of idleness, was sent in 1803 to the parish previously occupied by his brother, José Joaquin, who had died two years previously. It was named Nuestra Señora de los Dolores, and as Our Lady of the Sorrows, the name became the inspiration for the battle cry, the *Grito de Dolores,* of the revolution which would begin there seven years later.

It was August of 1803 and just a few days after Hidalgo had observed his fiftieth birthday when he arrived in Dolores with an entourage which included a younger brother, two half sisters, and two of his illegimate daughters. (While it was not unusual at that time for a priest to ignore his vows of chastity, Hidalgo was more than ordinarily open about it, and freely acknowledged his parenthood.)

From the description of a friend which history has retained, Hidalgo, when he entered the scene at Dolores, was a rather fair man, with blue-gray eyes. His shoulders sagged a little and he was bald with a fringe of white hair. His costume was as traditional as his looks—a long black coat, a suit of knee breeches, waistcoat and jacket, and a large round hat. He carried a heavy walking stick.

Dolores was a town of some fifteen thousand persons on the edge of a fertile plain to the east of Guanajuata and, from Hidalgo's point of view, desirable in that it produced a sizable revenue for the Church of about nine thousand pesos annually.

As in San Felipe, he found it useful to delegate many of the parish affairs to subordinates and continued the parties and excursions into the country and the musical evenings for which he had become famous. Frequently here the guests were the Indians and the *mestizos* and when there was conversation it was more of practical things and technical matters. Hidalgo had decided, from whatever cause, to dedicate himself to a program of industrialization which would improve the economic lot of his parish.

It seems reasonable to place Dolores as the turning point in the life of Hidalgo, his changeover from a revolutionary thinker to a revolutionary activist. The people there were poor and insignificant in the eyes of the *gachupines,* who made the rules by which they lived. Half the town could have been wiped out by a disaster and Mexico City probably would not have cared—if it had known. But this was true also of other Mexican towns that Hidalgo had lived in, and he had not been notably moved to improve the lives of the people there in any material sense.

In any event, having decided to do something about liberating his charges in Dolores from the captivity of a one-industry economy—agriculture—Hidalgo proved to be something of a genius in both of the major undertakings he attempted, pottery and leather.

On a lot some two hundred feet square which belonged to the Church, he helped his parishioners construct a simple factory which became the *alfarería* or pottery works. It had large windows to make it light and airy, and they also opened onto covered patios which Hidalgo hoped to use for other purposes. The clay of the land near Dolores proved ideal to be fashioned into bowls and cups and plates, some covered with intricate designs, all under the direction of the priest, who had made himself into a master craftsman, experimenting with metals and glass to obtain different and varied colors and designs for the potter's wheel. So well did Hidalgo do his work that the pottery of Dolores soon came to enjoy a reputation as the most desirable of the region and it was much in demand at the markets throughout the entire area.

The leather industry was secondary to the pottery works, but was certainly successful and, in making it so, Hidalgo evolved tanning methods for the hides of cattle and horses that were forerunners to those employed today.

These, of course, were quite legitimate industries and, had word of them reached officials of the Church (as they most likely did not) would have brought praise for the man responsible. Two other ideas Hidalgo had for the welfare of his flock were less legitimate in the eyes of the government of New Spain—the growing of grapes for wine and of mulberry trees to feed silkworms.

The production of wine then (as now) was a major industry in the mother country of Spain and she had no wish to see a colony competing, even for its own use. If the colonists wanted wine, let them buy it from Spain. This was true also of the cultivation of mulberry trees to feed silkworms and manufacture silk. That too was an industry of Spain. So, the making of both wine and silk was forbidden in Mexico, except when special permission could be obtained by petitioning the crown in Madrid. There is some documentary evidence that Hidalgo actually planted grapes and produced wine, planted mulberry trees, fed silkworms, and produced silk—and then petitioned the crown. But his production of wine was small and consumed locally, while the silk went into gifts for the wives of relatives, so neither industry was important to the community. (Nor to Madrid, apparently; his petition was never answered.) More important to his parish were other crafts and trades to supplement the pottery and leather industries—beekeeping, weaving, and olive oil production. The apiaries were quite successful and the honey sold in the markets was a considerable source of income to the people of Dolores.

None of these activities in Dolores, all of which were genuinely beneficial to the people of the town, prevented Hidalgo from keeping abreast of the times and of continuing the intellectual friendships he had formed over the preceding years. Historian Hugh M. Hamill, Jr., writes: "Hidalgo was given to secular peregrinations all through the central part of Mexico. The frequency of his visits to Guanajuato is well known, for that rich mining capital was the home of many of his most intellectual friends. He also spent considerable time in San Miguel. Well before 1800 he was often there in the company of the sons of a wealthy merchant, Domingo Narciso Allende. One of these sons was Ignacio Allende, a captain of the Queen's Cavalry regiment stationed in his native city."

Though neither of them dreamed of it at the time, Hidalgo was destined to play a large part in the life of Ignacio Allende, who became his second-in-command and later preceded him before a firing squad. Another close friend in that area who also shared in the revolutionary leadership and its fateful conclusions was Juan de Aldama of San Miguel.

In addition to Hidalgo's journeys, he was the central figure of a large group of friends, the magnet around which they clustered. For every home he visited there were a dozen guests in his own house. It was inevitable that in the talks (often preceded by music, dancing, and varied entertainment) that the possibilities of revolution should have been discussed, for it was a time of revolt. The United States had successfully freed itself from the English rule of George III. France still struggled with her own search for liberty. There was a sweet smell of freedom in the air.

Mexico, actually, had seen half a dozen uprisings against the constituted authority of the colony, some spontaneous, some planned, none successful. The Corn Riot of 1692 was the direct result of a rain-ruined crop and a hungry populace trying to get at the royal granary. The year 1799 saw the Conspiracy of the Machetes, a badly organized scheme by a badly organized group of lower grade Creoles to stir up a rebellion and then distribute machetes for the slaughter of the *gachupines*. It failed in the early stages through betrayal.

The most serious, and the one which almost certainly led to Hidalgo's Querétaro revolt, was the Valladolid Conspiracy. It was set for December 21, 1809, and included among its conspirators Ignacio Allende and others who later joined Hidalgo. It is probable that Hidalgo knew of the Valladolid Conspiracy simply because so many of his friends were involved, but he was not a participant. The plan of the conspiracy was denounced and the leaders arrested and tried. Their defense—that with Napoleon's brother on the Spanish throne they wanted to save New Spain from the fate of Old Spain, that is, a takeover by the French—was successful and they were not punished.

After the Valladolid Conspiracy the Querétaro Conspiracy followed as a natural sequence. The stated motives were not —at that time—freedom from Spain, although there are indications that Hidalgo revised his thinking later to favor the theme of Mexico for the Mexicans. It started out as a movement to reform the present government, remove the *gachupines* from control, and free the working classes from the many tyrannies then in practice, including indenture and slavery. The basic plan for the revolt was written by Dr. Manuel Iturriaga, a canon of the cathedral in Valladolid and a long-time friend of Hidalgo, but there were dozens of others who had a hand in the organization.

There were Captains Allende and Aldama, of course, and a lieutenant from their regiment, Mariano Abasolo, who also had been involved in the Valladolid plot. There was José María Chico, who became a cabinet minister in the government Hidalgo planned later, and Miguel Domínguez. Domínguez had been born in Guanajuato and, although three years younger, studied with Hidalgo at San Nicolás, where the two began a friendship which lasted through the years. He was a lawyer with a reputation for kindness and liberal leanings as well as competence, and had been appointed Corregidor of Querétaro. His wife, Josefa Ortiz de Domínguez, whose likeness is featured today on the money of Mexico, was a spirited lady known in Mexican history as "La Corregidora." She not only took an active part in the planning of the conspiracy, but risked her life (and her husband's) to warn Hidalgo when the plot was discovered. There were dozens of others, and together they represented something of a cross section of Mexico's middle-class *criollos*. They were neither very wealthy nor very poor. Many were of the Church, some were merchants, Domínguez was a public official, a number were members of the militia. From the beginning the leader was Hidalgo, for a number of reasons. They must, if the revolution was to succeed, have the support of the Indians and the *mestizos* and have it in overwhelming numbers to compensate for the lack of military training and weapons. Hidalgo was an experienced administrator and a natural leader. He was popular at every level and his achievements at Dolores had won him great respect from the Indians and the *mestizos*. Allende was a natural choice for second place. If Hidalgo was the prototype of the Mexican padre, Allende was the prototype of Mexican *machismo* or manliness—strongly built, proud, an accomplished fighter of the bulls, a skilled horseman, fond of gambling and of the ladies, all with a quality of command and military training.

The conspirators chose the annual fair at San Juan de los Lagos, a town west of Guanajuato, held annually from December 1 to December 15, as the time and place to launch the rebellion. The fair was popular and on December 8 the day was dedicated to the Virgin of Candelaria, a popular saint; there would be some 35,000 people attending. The fair featured sales of horses, mules, and burros. It was the intention that Hidalgo, at the height of the celebration on December 8, would ascend a rostrum, sound a battle call, and exhort the throng to join him in a freedom march on the capital. The Virgin of Candelaria would be appropriated as the patroness of the rebellion and there would be plenty of horses and mules for transportation. In preparation, Hidalgo turned his artisans in Dolores to the manufacture of implements of warfare.

By August too many people knew of the conspiracy, and what had been a secret was a secret no longer. The first leak was an anonymous letter to the government in Mexico City, so vaguely worded that little attention was paid to it. Then came another, and then a flood, as conspirators learned of the betrayal and sought to save their own skins by turning informer. The raft of accusations coincided with the arrival of a new Viceroy, Francisco Xavier de Venegas, a distinguished career soldier whose ability to make quick, hard decisions and take rapid action was well known; certainly it was well known to Captain Allende and other military conspirators. Viceroy Venegas arrived in New Spain on September 13. By September 14 he had started the machinery to suppress the plot and round up the conspirators.

The action began with a message to Intendente Juan Antonio Riaño of Guanajuato to arrest Miguel Hidalgo and a number of other conspirators. Loath to take action against a group, most of whom he knew as friends, and especially reluctant in the case of Hidalgo, Riaño hesitated. Meantime a similar message went to Corregidor Domínguez.

At this point La Corregidora, the Señora Domínguez, made herself a legendary figure in Mexican history. Listening either at the door or from a floor overhead (the accounts vary) La Corregidora overheard the orders given to her husband, who was at the moment protesting that the very thought of Hidalgo plotting a revolution was preposterous. She knew, of course, that he was guilty indeed of such plotting, because both she and her husband were co-conspirators. But La Corregidora remained not to protest but hastily got word to Ignacio Pérez, chief magistrate of the province—and another conspirator. Pérez, too, could cope in a crisis. He saddled a horse and rode to the home of Juan de Aldama. The two of them then rode the fifty miles to Dolores, where Allende was staying in the home of Padre Hidalgo.

The course which followed was swiftly taken. At a pre-dawn conference of Hidalgo, Allende, and Aldama, and Hidalgo's brother and cousin, they quickly concluded that there were three courses open to them. They could flee; they could stay and be taken and probably executed; they could put the plan for the revolution into operation instantly.

It was Hidalgo who made the decision. Independence and freedom, he said, were what their entire movement had been all about. Starting now was the same as starting later; it was just not quite as convenient. He finished with: "Gentlemen, in action everything is accomplished. We must not lose time if we are to see the oppressor's yoke broken and beaten into the ground." He also declared it was time to "seize the *gachupines.*"

The day just breaking was Sunday, September 16. Hidalgo summoned his workers and others who were privy to the plot, and the arms they had surreptitiously made—mostly machetes—were brought out of hiding and distributed. Some thirty political prisoners were freed from the local jail and invited to join the insurrection, an invitation they happily accepted. A score of *gachupines* were surprised in their beds and given the space newly vacated by the prisoners. As the morning hours moved on, several hundred persons who had come for Mass and for the usual Sunday market day, gathered in front of Hidalgo's house in response to stories they had heard, some true, some rumors. Learning they were there, Hidalgo came out and spoke to them. There are several accounts, probably none exact, of his words to his friends and parishioners. According to one, of reasonable authenticity, he said:

"My friends and countrymen: neither the king nor tributes exist for us any longer. . . . The moment of our freedom has arrived; the hour of our liberty has struck, and if you recognize its great value, you will help me defend it from the ambitious grasp of the tyrants. . . . The cause is holy and God will protect it. . . . Long live, then, Our Lady of Guadalupe! Long live independence!"

It was the cry of the revolution, the *Grito de Dolores*.

There was no point in waiting longer. Through his stirring speech, plus the fact that most of the people who heard it would have followed him practically anywhere anyhow, Hidalgo had acquired an initial force, untrained but very much in being, of from six to eight hundred men, many of them mounted. The little army, with Hidalgo leading on horseback, started off. They reached San Miguel, which was Aldama's home town, at dusk and bivouacked for the night. A council of war was held in one of the friendly homes and it was formally voted that Hidalgo should be the leader of the revolt with the rank of "Captain-General of America." Allende was second-in-command and given the rank of Lieutenant General. Other lesser officers were named.

Passing through Antonilco, on the way to San Miguel, Hidalgo had stopped briefly and taken from the church a banner of the Virgin of Guadalupe, an even more popular saint than the Virgin of Candelaria. Her churches throughout Mexico remain sanctuaries of the accused, and she became a symbol of the revolution and the patron saint of the revolutionists. Hidalgo's freedom crusade had become a holy crusade as well.

Hidalgo remained at San Miguel two days and the ranks of his force swelled by several hundred volunteers. On Septem-

ber 19 the rebels reached the rich mining town of Celaya.
Hidalgo sent the Celaya city fathers an ultimatum to surrender or he would immediately put to death several Spanish
hostages he was holding. Celaya capitulated and Hidalgo did
not or could not restrain his followers from pillaging the city
and looting both shops and homes. Within a week the *Grito
de Dolores* had been heard and heeded in half a dozen provinces and Hidalgo's army had grown to some 25,000. Of
these only a hundred or so militiamen had any sort of military training or discipline.

By September 28 Hidalgo had reached the high grounds
overlooking Guanajuato where his old friend Riaño was the
Intendente. Guanajuato was the third largest city in Mexico
and, from the standpoint of wealth, art, and culture, the second in importance. Its population of more than 60,000 included many wealthy Spanish-born *gachupines* and Mexican-
born Creoles of pure Spanish blood. It was a city Hidalgo
knew very well and as he sat there looking down on the
buildings, the church spires and domes, he must have remembered many of the days and nights he had spent there so
pleasantly in company with friends.

The city lay along a valley, flanked on either side by steeply
rising hills and was not suitable for normal defense. When
the *Grito de Dolores* reached Intendente Riaño after the
rebel army had laid waste Celaya, he had determined his own
strategy. In the center of Guanajuato was the town granary,
the Alhóndiga de Granaditas. It had been built several years
ago to withstand the ages, with a huge oaken door and walls
several feet thick. It was only partly stocked with grain, leaving considerable room for refugees and their possessions. And
there was a deep water well within the granary. Riaño felt
that it could be held for months, if needed, and though the

rebels might loot the city, he and his friends could survive in modest comfort.

So, by the morning of September 28, Riaño and several hundred of the Spanish and well-to-do Creoles were barricaded behind the walls of the Alhóndiga and manning the narrow slits of windows with muskets. The granary was a clutter of wives and children, food, servants, personal belongings, chests of money and jewelry, even of treasured furniture.

Outside the granary walls the lesser *criollos*, the *mestizos*, and the Indians looked upon this blatantly unequal consideration for their well-being, not to mention safety, first with indignation and then mounting anger. Not only had Riaño and his friends left them to the mercy of the rebels, they had left them hungry as well, for the town had been stripped of its food stores to supply the Alhóndiga for its long siege. Some of the thousands outside the walls took to the hills quite literally. Others simply joined Hidalgo's force when it reached the city.

From the gates of the city that morning of September 28, Hidalgo and Allende sent a messenger to Riaño, beseeching him to surrender the city and promising to spare its citizens. (It is somewhat doubtful if they could have complied with this promise.) Riaño sent back his refusal and Hidalgo could only exhort as many of his followers as could hear his voice to spare lives and property. Then he waved his arm in command and the mounted rebels galloped into the city, followed by the horde on foot, most of them armed with machetes, bows and arrows, knives, or simply clubs.

Like a tidal wave, it was an unstoppable force. On the way to the granary, some of the rebels stopped to loot and burn stores and houses, but the main force surged on to the Alhóndiga. Riaño's men were firing from the windows, but the effect was simply to infuriate the mob, by this time half Hidalgo's men and half Guanajuato citizens.

Many of those in the forefront were shot. The fortunate ones were those fatally wounded. The more unfortunate fell and were trampled to death by the following ranks. By sheer weight of numbers the mob broke down the huge oaken doors and the carnage began. The fortress which was to have withstood a long siege fell in half a day. Men, women, and children were slaughtered, including Intendente Riaño and son. The stores were taken or destroyed. The money and jewelry were grabbed by greedy handfuls, pocketed or scattered. Hours after the first attack the rebels left the Alhóndiga a smoking mass of bodies and rubble and turned to the rest of the city. For two days Guanajuato was the scene of drunken looting, killing, and destruction.

Hidalgo finally got his troops under control and they remained in Guanajuato for a week while a command structure was organized (or attempted) before advancing on Valladolid, where the priest had spent the major part of his younger days in school or teaching. The authorities there had received graphic descriptions of the carnage at Guanajuato, and on October 17 surrendered to Hidalgo's army, which had now grown to between sixty and eighty thousand men. Here the city was spared. One of those who joined there was another priest, José María Morelos y Pavón, who was to pick up the banner of revolution after Hidalgo's death, and to carry it through another struggle for independence.

The new Viceroy, Francisco Xavier de Venegas, was much too much a man of action and military experience to have been idle since his first move against the revolutionists had been foiled by La Corregidora. He had delegated the command of three small armies, ranging in force from 1,500 to 3,000 soldiers each, to three of his officers. Manuel de Flon

was given command of forces in the neighborhood of Querétaro; General Félix María Calleja del Rey was ordered to
take his force to the area of Guanajuata; and General Tor-
cuato Trujillo was to guard the approaches to Mexico City.
He also placed a price of 10,000 pesos each on the heads of
Hidalgo, Allende, and Aldama, and abolished the tribute
which had long been levied against the Indians, in a reasonable attempt to woo them away from the warring priest.

The Church and the Inquisition were not to be outdone
by any of the military's campaign. Their printing presses almost immediately started turning out a snowstorm of broad-
sides or handbills, the fastest communication of the day, all
vilifying Hidalgo. The old charges which had lain dormant
these many years were brought out and dusted off to be
added to others which were fresher and somewhat more accurate in basic fact if not in detail. Hidalgo was condemned
for heresy and sacrilege because he had taken the Virgin of
Guadalupe as a symbol of the revolution. He was termed "a
clerical bully, a priest bearing arms, a *cura* commanding
highwaymen, sacking cities, and killing innocent people."
The bogie of French influence was raised—might Napoleon
not indeed be behind this infamous insurrection and waiting
in the wings to take over? This latter, of course, was to ward
off *criollo* support for Hidalgo. As bad as the *gachupín* was,
the *criollos* might well prefer the Spaniard to being turned
over to rule by the French.

Hidalgo left Valladolid on October 20 and by the twenty-
ninth had reached the small town of Toluca. Here he was
separated from Mexico City, the royalist capital, by only a
few miles of road and a low range of mountains—and the
troops of Colonel Trujillo, probably about 2,500. And here,
at the Monte de las Cruces (Mount of the Crossroads) the two
forces met and were locked in battle throughout one whole

day. The Trujillo forces held the high ground and tactical advantages, plus superior weapons and discipline. Hidalgo relied on numbers, and by nightfall the royalist forces were considerably mauled and had to escape.

It was a victory, but an expensive one for Hidalgo. He had lost some 2,000 men killed and about 18,000 more through wounds and desertion. It was the first taste of professional military resistance for the rebels, and grapeshot pouring from the mouth of a cannon can be a terrifying thing. Hidalgo had gone into the battle with about 80,000 men. His victory cost him, at least temporarily, probably a quarter of this force.

The sobering, frightening losses were bad enough, but both Hidalgo and Allende were greatly disappointed at the failure of the *criollos* to join their cause. There were two main reasons for this. One was Hidalgo's inability to publicize his cause and to offset the flood of propaganda emanating from the Inquisition. The other was his inability to control his *mestizos* and Indians, who knew very little difference between the *gachupin* and the *criollo* and massacred each with total indifference. This also troubled Allende greatly and he took no pains to hide his contempt for the undisciplined rabble which followed him into battle. Hidalgo cared also, but was able to rationalize that the long downtrodden Indians and half-castes were simply getting revenge for scores of years of persecution; this, he said, was something which could not be denied them in exchange for their support.

It was probably the lack of this support (coupled with a shortage of ammunition) which led Hidalgo and Allende to decide not to advance on Mexico City at this time, but to consolidate their strength and buildup in the home area instead, and on November 3 they turned the army back toward Querétaro. Four days later, at the town of Aculco, about half the distance to Querétaro, the rebels were intercepted by a royalist army of 7,000 men led by Flon, Conde de la Cadena, and Trujillo. The insurrectionists attempted a withdrawal, but it turned into a rout and they lost their artillery and most of their baggage before the disaster ended.

When they were finally able to regroup their forces, Hidalgo and Allende decided to divide the army. Hidalgo would take half and go to Valladolid where he would try to attract new recruits and build up their strength. Allende would go to Guanajuato where there were facilities to replenish their lost artillery, ammunition, and other military stores.

On November 24 the armies of Flon and Calleja drove Allende out of Guanajuato and he marched his rebels to Guadalajara, where Hidalgo had preceded him shortly before. The history of some of the events of those days is not pretty, nor are they readily understandable. Hidalgo, reportedly, ordered the death of some sixty *gachupines* in Valladolid before leaving his old home town, and of 350 more in Guadalajara. All, of course, had been accused of plotting against his cause—which would have been a quite natural thing for them to have done—but it is difficult to reconcile the accounts of these summary executions without trial with the nature of Hidalgo the man, let alone Hidalgo the priest.

In Guadalajara, Hidalgo became very active. He organized a provisional government which would rule the country, naming ministers and cabinet members, setting forth plans for a Congress, and even naming a diplomatic agent to the United States. He also amassed a considerable treasury through confiscation of both public and private funds, and by December had raised his depleted army back to some 36,000 men. By mid-January, 1811, the force had grown to almost 70,000.

At this time word reached Hidalgo and Allende that 2,000

troops under General José de la Cruz were approaching
Guadalajara from one quarter, while an even more immediate threat was posed by their old enemies Flon and Calleja
with some 6,000 men from another. The two leaders disagreed
violently as to the means of defense. Allende wanted to split
the rebel forces into six groups which would be more manageable, and greet the approaching royalists with both frontal
and flank resistance. Hidalgo was for mass attack and his
view prevailed in a six-hour battle at the Bridge of Calderón,
twenty-five miles east of Guadalajara on January 17. Toward
the end of the battle Flon was killed and the rebels might
have won had not a royalist cannon ball struck an ammunition wagon. The terror and havoc it caused in the immediate
vicinity spread and was accentuated by a resultant grass fire
which an unlucky wind blew down on the insurgents. They
fled and the government forces mopped up at their leisure.
The rebels lost some 1,500 killed, many more wounded and
captured (to be executed later) and thousands through desertion. They also lost all their cannon and other supplies.

It wasn't the end of everything, just very nearly the end.
Hidalgo fled with two aides, riding north throughout the
night and stopping only at mid-morning of January 18 for
rest and food at the little town of Cuquio, where he was still
able to express optimism. Two days later when the leaders
met at an hacienda near Aquascalientes, a hundred or so
miles north of the recent battle site, what had been only a
simmering discontent in the other revolt leaders—principally
Allende—now turned in full fury on the one man they could
hold responsible for their losses. So Hidalgo was stripped of
his authority, although it was done secretly because the others still needed the priest's enormous appeal to the mass
public.

The events of the next weeks were both confused and confusing. Allende, who had promoted himself to the rank of *Generalísimo,* was in charge. The rebel headquarters was established in Saltillo.

At this point Allende determined that the only hope for the cause was to enlist the aid of the United States and to hire a force of mercenaries—perhaps as many as 30,000—to counter the royalist forces. To act for him in both tasks, Allende named his old comrade in arms, Juan de Aldama, as minister plenipotentiary and a monk named Juan de Salazar as his assistant.

He had been influenced to this decision to seek help from the north by an event which made such a possibility seem plausible, or at least seemed to clear the way for such an attempt. In Texas, which was then part of Mexico, rebel sympathizer Juan Bautista Casa had engineered a coup and overthrown the royalist government at San Antonio de Bexar in Texas. The deposed governor, Manuel Salcedo, was imprisoned.

It is necessary now to go back several weeks. Before the battle of Calderón, a retired Creole officer, Captain Francisco Ignacio Elizondo, had been recalled by the royalist forces. Discontented with his minor rank, Captain Elizondo defected to the rebel command of Mariano Jiménez, where he was offered the rank of lieutenant colonel. He approached Allende with a request that he be given an immediate promotion to rank of general. At this point Allende was concerned about many things—money, troops, supplies—but the one thing he did not need was more generals and he gave Elizondo a very short reply to his request and sent him packing back to his post of the moment, which was guarding the deposed Governor Salcedo in Coahuila. Had Allende been wiser he would have considered the dangers of treading on the pride of a vain man, as Elizonda obviously was. The mistake cost his life.

And, a little later, an event occurred of which Allende and Hidalgo did not learn, but of which Elizondo did. Juan Bautista Casa, after a very brief and unpopular reign as Governor of Texas, was overthrown in a coup by a minor church official, Juan Manuel Zambrano.

This then was the murky picture which faced Allende in mid-March. It was even further clouded by some information and many suspicions that his royalist foes were closing in on his rear, as they were.

He had, at this point, already dispatched Aldama and Salazar to San Antonio de Bexar (which he believed safely in rebel hands) with one hundred bars of silver and most of the remaining treasury, and he and Hidalgo planned to follow them to add their strength and acumen in getting aid for the rebel cause. Unfortunately, Aldama and Salazar arrived in San Antonio just after Zambrano's coup and he happily took their silver and cash and clapped them into the local dungeon.

Elizondo in the meantime kept carefully informed on the plans and movements of the rebels. He knew Aldama and Salazar had left with the treasure and had been jailed. He knew Allende and Hidalgo were about to follow. And he knew, as they did not, that they were running directly into royalist territory. Elizondo had switched sides once and now it seemed like a good time to consider switching back. His prisoner Salcedo was not long in perceiving how the wind was blowing. He could, and did, offer Elizondo the rank of general which Allende had scornfully refused.

Elizondo switched. Working together, he and Salcedo organized their own counterrevolution, captured the governor of Coahuila at a dance, and took over command of the state. Now, both Coahuila and the adjoining Texas were in enemy hands, a state of events of which Allende and Hidalgo were totally unaware.

On the night of March 17, Elizondo, still acting in his old capacity as a rebel officer, read dispatches which gave the route Allende and Hidalgo were to take to San Antonio de Bexar and sent word that his force of some 1,500 troups would string themselves out along the road in an honor guard near the town of Nuestra Señora de Guadalupe. Selecting that town, with that name—the symbol of the revolution—was the final Judas touch for Elizondo.

Thus, on March 21, 1811, the little entourage of fourteen coaches, with Hidalgo, who preferred to ride, and an escort of twenty other horsemen bringing up the rear, rolled unsuspectingly through a narrow ravine leading to Guadalupe. For a mile along each side Elizondo had stationed his "honor guard." And at the end and around a curve, two mounted troops of cavalry lay in waiting. As the carriages rounded the bend they were neatly and quietly picked off, one by one.

Allende saw the trap too late. He fired once at the turncoat, Elizondo, and missed. It was the only shot fired in resistance. A return volley killed Allende's son and another companion in the carriage. Allende was clubbed unconscious. Hidalgo drew his pistol, but one of his own guardsmen gently pulled down his arm. It was, he said, hopeless. And thus, on a dusty, desert road in northern Mexico ended the *Grito de Dolores.*

Fearing that an attempt would be made to free the captured Hidalgo, he was taken even farther north to Chihuahua for trial, along with the other leaders of the rebellion. They were imprisoned in improvised cells of a Jesuit college and the trials began two weeks later. Hidalgo, who was fifty-eight years old on that May 8, 1811, was saved for the last, and his hearings were a combination of military and Inquisition excoriation. He was found guilty and condemned to death (a foregone conclusion), and executed by a firing squad. The execution took place in the college courtyard and, due to his priesthood (although the Church had stripped him of that the day before), Hidalgo was granted two courtesies not permitted for his colleagues: to be shot in the chest and not in the back, and to meet death unblindfolded and unbound. Before his execution Hidalgo distributed candies to his embarrassed captors and firing squad.

The Inquisition, though, had the last revenge. After Hidalgo's execution, his head, along with those af Allende, Aldama, and his friend Mariano Jiménez, were placed in iron cages and displayed at the four corners of the Alhóndiga in Guanajuato. They had taken him back to the scene of the first battle in his fight to liberate his country.

LA CORREGIDORA

Doña Josefa Ortiz de Domínguez, the woman known in history as La Corregidora, became the heroine of the Mexican rebellion against Spanish rule by warning Miguel Hidalgo and the other conspirators that their plot had been discovered and that their arrest and probable execution for treason was only hours away. Without her courage, her determination, and her warning, the independence movement would have been thwarted and might have been delayed for several years. She is buried with the other heroes of the rebellion under the Column of Independence on the Paseo de la Reforma in Mexico City.

Doña Josefa was born in Valladolid—which today has been renamed Morelia and is the capital of the state of Michoacán —of well-to-do parents, Juan José Ortiz and Manuela Giron. Both her father and mother were of pure Spanish blood, though born in Mexico, and were thus *criollos* or Creoles, as was Doña Josefa, of course. Her mother died a few years after Josefa's birth and the girl was reared by an older married sister.

Josefa was educated at the Colegio de las Vizcainas in Mexico City. The Colegio was a well-established school for the daughters of the upper middle-class families and enjoyed an excellent reputation. "Education" for Mexican girls at the turn of the eighteenth century bore little resemblance to the present-day concept. Such courses as science, mathematics, and higher humanities were regarded as eminently unnecessary for a young girl; most males of that era probably would not have believed a girl could even comprehend such things. The girls were taught to read and write, sometimes a foreign language (usually French) and a little history. But the emphasis was on things deemed proper for a young lady—music (girls were started at the piano by the age of five), embroidery and other ornamental sewing, riding and dancing, plus a great deal of religious instruction.

In 1781, when she was only thirteen, Josefa married Don Miguel Domínguez, who was already Corregidor or chief administrator, of the Province of Querétaro, a position of considerable political importance. Josefa's affectionately given designation of La Corregidora came, of course, from her husband's title.

During much of the year of 1810 when Hidalgo and Captains Allende and Aldama, along with many others, were laying the groundwork for their rebellion, many of the meetings were held in Querétaro, where Captain Allende lived. Moreover, they were held in the home of Corregidor Domínguez and his wife.

There is ample evidence that Don Domínguez, as well as his strong-willed *señora,* were actively engaged in the conspiracy, although he later denied it. There is also considerable evidence that La Corregidora influenced her husband to be at least a passive participant, and probably more. To cover the secret meetings held in her home, which was on the second floor of a rather large building that also contained the territorial offices and jail, La Corregidora organized social gatherings. They were innocent in appearance and much in keeping with the customs of the times. There was almost always music, both from the piano and stringed instruments, and guests frequently danced the quadrille. There were parlor games and poetry readings. Wine flowed freely, keeping pace with the gay conversation and occasional flirtations. And while the other guests danced, encouraged by Doña Josefa, the plotters laid their plans in an adjoining room.

Doña Josefa, who was a strong, handsome woman of forty-two at this time, had other motives besides her patriotism. Her eldest daughter would have been a perfect match for the dashing Captain Allende, who commanded royal troops when not engaged in plotting against them. (Doña Josefa herself, incidentally, was pregnant at the start of the Hidalgo rebellion later that year.)

On September 12, 1810, word reached Querétaro that traitors among the conspirators had denounced the plot to the authorities. Captain Allende left immediately with the news, to confer with Hidalgo in Dolores. He was there on September 14 when orders arrived from the new Viceroy for the arrest of Padre Hidalgo and the other plotters. The orders were sent several places simultaneously, evidently to insure Hidalgo's seizure.

Domínguez learned of the news in Querétaro when a city official arrived with a contingent of soldiers. The official had been fully informed of the plot and related the details to Don Domínguez, mentioning sadly that Doña Josefa, Domínguez' own wife, might be involved. The Corregidor knew exactly how far his wife was involved and wished it weren't true, but had to be satisfied with the fact that he himself was clear, at least for the moment.

So, when the official requested the Corregidor to accompany the party of soldiers to the home of one Epigmenio González, where powder and arms had supposedly been hidden, the Corregidor thought it best to play along. Before leaving, however, he went to the door of the family quarters at the head of the stairs, locked it, and put the key in his pocket.

He reckoned without the determination of his lady. La Corregidora had been listening at a vent in the floor and had heard the entire conversation. She watched the squad of soldiers leave, checked and found the door locked, and put into effect her emergency plan.

Perhaps her husband had threatened or perhaps La Corregidora had foreseen just such a contingency. In any event, she was prepared. Ignacio Pérez, magistrate, jailer, and one of the conspirators, lived beneath the Domínguez chambers. Doña Josefa, according to a prearranged plan between herself and Pérez, rapped sharply three times on the floor with the broom handle. Pérez raced up the stairs. They carried on a whispered conversation through the keyhole.

Don Ignacio must immediately saddle his horse and ride to San Miguel, the nearby small town in which Captain Aldama lived, Doña Josefa told him. He must waste no time. The fate of many people, perhaps of the nation, depended on his strength and courage. Aldama must be warned and then he and Aldama must get word to Father Hidalgo and Captain Allende in Dolores.

Don Ignacio was equal to the task. He reached San Miguel about two in the morning and awakened Aldama. Together the two of them rode the almost fifty miles to Dolores, arriving as the town was awakening for early Mass. Hidalgo made the immediate decision to start the rebellion there and then. Calling the villagers from Mass, he enlisted them into the revolt to a man, sounding the historical *Grito de Dolores*.

La Corregidora's bravery and determination brought her several bad years. When the home of Epigmenío González was searched, both Don Miguel and Doña Josefa Domínguez were discovered to be clearly incriminated in the Querétaro plot. Don Miguel was suspended from his position as Corregidor and, to save his life, denounced his wife (quite probably at her urging), giving full details of her role in the plotting and the warning to Hidalgo.

La Corregidora was first imprisoned in the Convent of Santa Clara in Querétaro, but as both the rebellion and her pregnancy progressed, she was transferred to the Convent of Santa Teresa in Mexico City. From there, after the birth of her child, she was moved to the Convent of Santa Cataline de Sena, also in Mexico City, where she remained three years. She never regretted nor recanted her part in the rebellion, but did condemn the cruelty and excesses of Hidalgo's plundering forces. With the lull in hostilities, she was released from the convent in 1814 and rejoined her husband.

In 1821, when Mexico finally won independence from Spain, La Corregidora was honored throughout the country as the principal living precursor of independence. When Iturbide became Emperor, he invited her to become lady-in-waiting to the Empress, an honor she declined. Years later, after the restoration of the republic, La Corregidora was offered a special stipend from the government, but this too she refused.

When Doña Josefa died in 1829, Mexico went into national mourning for their heroine of the rebellion, with special services held in Mexico City and many of the state capitals. Today, streets and plazas throughout the country have been named for her and Querétaro has an heroic statue of La Corregidora. Her likeness is on both the five and twenty peso notes of Mexico. They show a woman of strong, plain features in a portrait probably painted about 1820 when she would have been fifty years old. Her hair is parted in the middle and falls in sloping lines over her forehead and ears, end-

ing in a coil at the back of her head in which a Spanish comb
is set. She wears ear pendants, and the cowl collar of her
dress, ornamented with embroidered clusters of pearls, re-
veals her throat rising in a firm column to the stern, chiseled
face.

JOSÉ MARÍA MORELOS

HIDALGO DIED, but the insurrection, the *Grito de Dolores,* did not. The horde he had led to disaster scattered and was never united again, but throughout Mexico a dozen other insurgent forces fought on under a dozen other leaders. Some were little better than bandits; others were great idealists and great leaders; foremost among the latter was José María Morelos.

Like Hidalgo, Morelos was a priest. He had joined the Hidalgo movement in October of 1810 and was commissioned to carry the rebellion into the south of Mexico. Unlike Hidalgo, however, Morelos proved to be a brilliant general. Napoleon studied his campaigns and said: "Give me three generals like him and I can conquer the world." But Morelos failed, too, in the end, and suffered the same fate as the priest of Dolores—death before a firing squad.

José María Teclo Morelos y Pavón was born on September 30, 1765, in Valladolid, a town of wide tree-lined streets and open plazas. The town looks much the same today, but the name of it was changed to Morelia in his memory. A house on the southwest corner where La Corregidora and García Obesa streets come together bears a plaque stating that José María Morelos was born there. Mexican history relates that his mother was passing the house on that late September day when she was overcome by labor pains and retreated into the doorway where her first son was born.

The mother was Juana Pavón, the *criolla* daughter of a schoolmaster, and his father was Manuel Morelos, a *mestizo* of mixed Spanish and Indian blood, and a carpenter by trade. Two other children were born subsequently, a boy Nicolás, and a girl María Antonia.

Due to her schoolmaster father, Juana Pavón had received a better education than most girls of that period in Mexico, and this she passed along to José. He was learning the carpenter trade as an apprentice to his father, but Juana Pavón, as she taught him to read and write, spell and cipher, had higher aims for her elder son—the priesthood, although that was an uncertain aspiration in those days. Spanish-born *gachupines* held the high offices of the Church and the Mexican-born *criollos* of pure Spanish blood filled the lower posts; any trace of Indian blood usually acted as a barrier to Church positions.

When José was fourteen his father died and he was sent to live with his uncle, Felipe Morelos, who owned and lived in an hacienda near the town of Apatzingán in Mexico's *tierra caliente* or hot country above the Pacific coastal city of Acapulco. In addition to the hacienda, Uncle Felipe also operated a mule train between Acapulco and Mexico City. José worked first as a *labrador* or farm hand for his uncle and then, as he grew older and proved his reliability, as a better paid *arriero*—a mule driver on the pack train.

The operation of pack trains was a thriving industry in Mexico in those days (and was later brought by the Mexicans to the southwestern part of the United States), and the route which the Morelos trains took was the only practical way of moving material from the important port of Acapulco to the capital. The coastal city at that time was the off-loading point for the galleons from Manila which carried the rich cargoes of silks and spices from China and other lands of the Far East. From the ships in the Acapulco harbor these cargoes were loaded on the backs of mules and started on the three-hundred-mile journey to Mexico City. It took them northward over the Sierra Colorado, through the *tierra caliente* and Iguala to Cuernavaca on the high plateau and thence into the valley of Mexico City.

In the 1930s a road was built between Mexico City and the booming resort town of Acapulco, which permitted an automobile to make the journey in hours. Today the jet flight between the two cities takes minutes. In those days of the "China Road," as it was called, it took weeks to shepherd the laden mules along the trails. It was rough and a difficult life, but it did two things for young José Morelos: it provided a regular job and money he could save and send to his mother; and it gave him an intimate knowledge of that part of Mexico and its people. He learned the local Indian dialects and how to live and survive there. These things helped make him a superb military tactician in the same area years later.

When José Morelos was almost twenty-five years old and had spent nearly a dozen years with his uncle, he returned to Valladolid to visit his mother. Partly as a result of a promised inheritance and partly as the fulfillment of an early dream, Juana Pavón persuaded José to apply at the College of San Nicolás Obispo. He did, and became a student there in 1790.

Miguel Hidalgo was rector of San Nicolás when Morelos was a student there. Some twelve years his senior, he was already enjoying a reputation for brilliance in both teaching and debate. San Nicolás was comparatively a small institution and the two men undoubtedly knew each other. There is no record that their association was intimate or important, but whatever relationship did exist almost certainly was responsible for the fact that Morelos chose to join the Hidalgo revolt fifteen years later.

Morelos did well at the college, so well that one of his teachers wrote: "José María Morelos has . . . conducted himself with such prudence and irreproachable conduct that he has never done anything to deserve any kind of punishment; he has performed his duties . . . with such application that he has elevated himself above all the other students."

In October of 1792 Morelos transferred to the Seminario Tridentino, also in Valladolid, so that he could take certain courses not available at San Nicolás, and in 1795 went to Mexico City where he took and passed the exams for a Bachelor of Arts degree which he was awarded on April 28. Due to his age (he was now thirty) and to his excellent scholastic record, Morelos was permitted to shorten some of the steps toward the priesthood. In 1796 he was granted a license to teach in the town of Uruapan, near Valladolid, where he remained two years. On December 20, 1797, he was ordained as a priest. A few months later he was named *cura* or parish priest of Tamacuaro de la Aguacana, described by one writer as the "hottest, most miserable town in the state of Michoacán."

Morelos was familiar with the region; it was not too distant from the hacienda of his Uncle Felipe, but even he found the heat, drouth, poverty, and monotony of the life difficult after the cool greenness of Valladolid and Uruapan. His mother, who had accompanied him to Tamacuaro, gave into it entirely and after a year fell ill and died on her way back to Valladolid. Soon thereafter Morelos was transferred to the parish of Caracuaro, some thirty miles to the east, an equally unprepossessing assignment. There he remained for eleven years, until he joined Hidalgo and the insurrection.

Morelos was, at this time, a dark, stocky man with a shock of black hair, immensely strong, at home on horseback and in the open. He was a kind man who carried out his unexciting parish duties conscientiously and with a minimum of complaints to his superiors; he was frequently unpaid and almost certainly unappreciated. He rarely drank, and smoked only an occasional cigar, but did succumb to other worldly temptations. He was the father of three children whom he recognized and there may have been a fourth child he did not. But this was no different than a considerable number of other parish priests of his day.

Word of the *Grito de Dolores* reached Morelos in October, 1810, Hidalgo, with an army of nearly 60,000 had occupied Morelos' home town of Valladolid and at about the same time Morelos received instructions from the Bishop of Michoacán to publish throughout his curacy word of the ban of excommunication against Hidalgo which had been issued by the Church. Morelos said later that he "felt compelled" to go and talk to his former rector, friend, and fellow priest. Their talk in Valladolid lasted several hours. Morelos had come prepared to offer his services as a chaplain if he found himself in agreement with Hidalgo's goals. He was in agreement; he too was frustrated and discontented with the life of the people. But the Dolores priest recognized in Morelos two qualities he liked—leadership and trustworthiness—and he had greater needs than religious solace for his troops. He offered Morelos an immediate officer's commission and, when Morelos accepted, wrote out the following order: "I commission in due form Señor Don José Morelos, *cura* of Caracuaro, as my *lugarteniente* [junior grade lieutenant] and order him to proceed to the south coast, raise troops, and carry out the verbal instructions which I have given him."

The verbal orders were extensive. When he left Valladolid on October 25, 1810, Morelos had been instructed to reorganize the government of southern Mexico, capture and imprison the *gachupines,* deport their families and confiscate their property—and to capture the highly fortified port of Acapulco. It was quite an assignment for a junior officer whose starting force numbered less than twenty-five men who had to make up in enthusiasm for their lack of military equipment.

The first year of the Morelos campaign is remarkable as a military achievement. Within three weeks of receiving his commission, moving over ground completely familiar to him from his farming and mule train days, his little band which started out a scant two dozen had grown to nearly 2,000. His growing force had swept through his old parish of Caracuaro, collecting both men and a considerable store of arms and ammunition. Reaching the Pacific coast, he captured the towns of Petatlán, Tecpan, El Zanjon, and Coyuca, ending up in what today are the suburbs of Acapulco.

Morelos understood, as Hidalgo had not, the finer points of guerrilla warfare. He wanted and had a comparatively small and manageable force of 2,000 drilled, trained, and disciplined men, able to strike swiftly and move on, nip at the enemy's flanks, harass lines of communication and supply. Morelos picked his officers on the basis of their abilities, and sent them home for the lack of it. He was rigid in his prohibition of looting; he needed the support of the people. He ruthlessly executed any of the soldiers found guilty of insubordination or cowardice—or of theft or plundering.

During the first year of the Morelos insurrection, his military skill, his obvious qualities of leadership, and the force of his personality attracted to his ranks a number of patriots who served the cause of independence with distinction. There were the five Bravo men—brothers Leonardo, Miguel, Victor, and Maximo, and Leonardo's son Nicolás—who had fled their hacienda of Chichihualco to hide out in a cave for months when the royalists sought to force them to fight for the government. At least two of them died in battle for Morelos. Among the earlier to join was Hermenegildo Galeana, grandson of an English privateer who had been shipwrecked on the Pacific coast and had married into a *hacendado* family of Tecpan. Both he and different Bravos, at various times, proved able generals. Others who joined were Mariano Matamoros, another priest; Vicente Guerrero, who became the heir to the Morelos cause; and Manuel Félix Fernández, better known by his political pseudonym of Guadalupe Victoria, who under that name was to become the first President of Mexico.

The port of Acapulco, although still notable for its magnificent harbor, is better known today for bikinis than battles. In the early nineteenth century, however, it was a major stronghold of New Spain and heavily fortified for both land and sea defense. Five outlying towns had facilities for garrisons—La Sabana, Las Cruces, El Veladero, Llano Largo, and Marques—and constituted the first line of defense in case of attack by land. The inner fortification was built around a fortress which reputedly had stone walls twelve feet thick and an armament of nearly a hundred long-range guns.

From his headquarters in Aguacatillo, Morelos was able to convey cordial invitations to members of the royalist forces defending Acapulco to desert and join the insurrection. So many of them did that Viceroy Xavier Venegas was forced to send reinforcements, an indication of the aura of popularity that was beginning to surround the Morelos name.

After some backing and filling, his forces captured the towns of El Veladero and La Sabana, and on January 4, 1811, achieved a notable victory with the capture of a great royalist military storehouse at Tres Palos. He laid siege to Acapulco itself for nine days but finally decided that his forces were not strong enough for this type of warfare and withdrew, marching northward through the passes and along the mountain trails he had followed as an *arriero* with his uncle's mule train. It must have been a triumphant homecoming.

Toward the last of May, 1811, he defeated a moderate royalist force at the Bravo hacienda of Chichihualco. This victory opened the path to Chilpancingo and a little later to Tixtla, where he captured both muskets and cannon. He promptly employed the cannon in fortifying the town as a strong point on the "China Road" to Mexico City. Two months later his preparations paid off in the defeat of an attacking royalist force, after which he moved a few miles up the road to Chilapa. It was August and he remained in Chilapa until November.

History has always been so intrigued by the Morelos military activities that it often neglects Morelos the statesman and civil administrator. In Aguacatillo on November 17, 1810—it was less than a month after Hidalgo had commissioned him to "capture" south Mexico—Morelos proclaimed "a new government, by which all inhabitants except *gachupines* would no longer be designated as Indians, mulattoes, or castes, but all would be known as Americans." At the same time he proclaimed the abolition of slavery (this was almost half a century before the United States got around to it) and the custom of tribute, declaring that the Indians were to keep the income they were able to wring from the land on which they worked and lived. Morelos justified the revolution of which he was to become the vortex because the *gachupines* for three centuries had enslaved and subjugated the native Indian population, choked the natural development of the country, and usurped its wealth and resources. Morelos appealed to the *criollos* and they responded as they had not to Hidalgo—and there was a reason. Morelos maintained discipline and shepherded no hordes across country to kill, burn, and pillage. He took an interesting attitude toward Spain and Mexico's relation thereto: since Spain was in the hands of the French, he said, and since a puppet of the infamous Napoleon was on the Spanish throne, the residents of New Spain were justified in setting up their own rule for themselves. He concluded that "when kings are absent, sovereignty resides in the nation, which is free to form the type of government which it desires. No nation is obligated to remain a slave of another."

When Miguel Hidalgo left his last headquarters at Saltillo and rode into the trap laid by Francisco Ignacio Elizondo along a dusty desert trail at Nuestra Señora de la Guadalupe, he left Ignacio López Rayón as commander-in-chief of the remnants of his army. (Rayón, a young and enthusiastic follower, had previously borne the title of Secretary of State in the Hidalgo entourage.) After Hidalgo's execution, Rayón moved the somewhat tenuous headquarters from Saltillo to Zacatecas. In midsummer of 1811, he received word that the Viceroy's favorite general, the ubiquitous Félix María Calleja, was approaching. He retreated to Zitácuaro, a mountain stronghold about halfway between Valladolid and Mexico City.

In the meantime Morelos had been in rather loose touch with Rayón and had constantly preached that the different insurgent groups operating independently in various parts of the country should maintain communications with each other and attempt, in some degree, to coordinate their activities. Morelos had set up a courier service throughout his own units and enlarged it to include Rayón. The latter now used it to write Morelos, urging his cooperation in the formation of a national *junta* which would actually achieve a coordinated insurgent effort. Morelos concurred, but being far too wise to expose himself to treachery from any direction, declared he was unable to leave his own command and named José Sixto Verduzco, *cura* of Tuzantla, as his representative. He also suggested that too many members would make the *junta* unwieldy and wondered if it might not be held to three.

A meeting, composed of nearby landowners and officers in the Rayón command, was held with Rayón as chairman. He was named head of the *junta,* with Verduzco and a Rayón subordinate, José María Liceaga, as the other two. Rayón took to himself the title of President of the Supreme Junta and Universal Minister of the Nation.

Not surprisingly, a number of insurrection leaders either laughed at the *junta* or ignored it. Morelos laughed at Rayón's title and objected strongly to the fact that the *junta* had declared allegiance to the crown, but supported it as a matter of principle. He felt it must be preserved if the insurrection was to achieve any aim whatsoever. It was a conviction which later was to cost him his life.

Morelos resumed his military operations in November, 1811, moving up the "China Road" toward Puebla and Mexico City. He took Tlapa and Chiutla. The commander at the latter town hated the priest-turned-general so intensely that he had cast a special cannon on which he inscribed the words "Mata Morelos" ("Kill Morelos"), but it didn't. Morelos took the town and the commander, Mateo Muzitu, was duly executed according to custom. In the guerrilla warfare of the day, neither side gave or expected quarter. It was kill or be killed.

After Chiutla, Morelos divided his forces, sending Miguel Bravo south and Galeana west against Taxco. Morelos himself took the center, intent on clearing the path to the capital. His first target was Cuautla de las Amilpas, which he took on Christmas Day and then turned to join Galeana who had taken Taxco. Later he consolidated his army and returned to Cuautla in February to complete plans for the drive into Mexico City.

Meantime, the old nemesis of the insurgents, General Calleja, had not been idle. At the orders of the Viceroy he had attacked Rayón's forces at Zitácuaro and virtually annihilated them. The three members of the *junta* escaped by the skin of their teeth, as did a few officers and soldiers of the command. This success, however, did little to relieve the pressure on the capital and the fears of the Viceroy for its safety, and his own. When his spies brought word of the impending drive by Morelos, he sent a hurried dispatch to Calleja, as follows:

"The capital of Mexico has been encircled by gangs of bandits, who have interrupted communications, mail facilities, and supply lines from all directions. . . . The danger of our commerce with Acapulco being interrupted, the impossibility of carrying on overseas trade, the difficulty of shipping goods to the interior, the deprivation of a million pesos which the treasury should have received from a certain shipment, the imminence of the collapse of the port of Veracruz to the insurgent forces—all of these factors are caused by the person of Morelos, the chief leader of the insurrection, of which he is the guiding genius."

There was more in this vein and then, a little later in the message, the Viceroy continued: "It is essential to conceive a plan to strike Morelos and his band a smashing blow that will terrorize his followers to such a degree that they will at least desert him, even if they do not seize him."

Thus, Calleja, with the army which had successfully stormed the Rayón stronghold and was now reinforced by a division from Puebla, moved to attack Cuautla. And Morelos, his own intelligence advising him of the impending attack, called in his troops from outlying posts. He sent word to Sultepec, where the remnants of the *junta* forces had regrouped, and both sides prepared for the showdown at Cuautla. Word of the battle spread over all of Mexico, and there were hopes and fears and prayers for the outcome. Calleja wrote the Viceroy: "The fate of Cuautla will decide the fate of the kingdom."

Cuautla had been selected by Morelos with a practiced military eye for defense. Its buildings clustered together on a gently rolling plain and it was protected on the west by a sturdy wall and on the east by a river both broad and swift enough to discourage casual crossing. The insurgents further fortified the town with trench and breastworks, using the two dozen-odd cannon in their possession to sweep the ground over which any attack must come. Morelos had, at this time, just over 4,000 men, most of them armed with muskets. They were well trained and in good fettle. His chief handicap in the historic battle which followed, as he was to find, were the hundreds of civilians who did not trouble to leave and whom he did not have the foresight to evacuate.

Morelos at this time was forty-seven years old. He was a short man, barely over five feet, with a dark, swarthy skin marked by moles and blemishes. A long scar ran across his nose, the result of a childhood accident. Although strong and capable of great endurance, he suffered from frequent bouts of malaria and equally frequent wracking headaches. Morelos is always pictured with a white cloth bound around his forehead and it is not unlikely he wore it to contain the pain of his migraines as well as to keep the hair and sweat out of his eyes. Despite the long days in the saddle, his arduous life, and the price on his head, Morelos was a cheerful man with a sense of humor. He was constantly being warned of plots against his life and threats to his safety. In one instance (so the story is told) a visiting insurgent officer warned him that a "fat man" was on the way to assassinate him. Morelos looked ruefully at his own expanding belly and said: "If he's any fatter than I am, he won't be much of a menace."

Calleja's attack on Cuautla began on the morning of February 19, 1812, with the royalists putting into the field a force which about doubled that of Morelos, although their heavy armament was about the same. When the insurgent cannon raked the field over which the royalists approached, the casualties quickly became so great and so constant that Calleja had to withdraw and formulate a new plan. The decision was to besiege the town, and on March 10, after accumulating vast stores of ammunition from the north, a bombardment of Cuautla began. The resultant rain of lead on the town at first terrified the villagers but they soon learned to take cover and during lulls in the shelling the children ran out and collected cannon balls which they sold to the insurgents for a few centavos—and which were quickly fired back at the royalists.

When, after four days, the bombardment brought no signs of capitulation, Calleja tried unsuccessfully to divert the river; this too failed, so he settled down to a long siege. Through March the insurgents fared reasonably well but by mid-April the food stores in Cuautla were all but exhausted. The soldiers and townspeople were eating beetles, soap, and bark from the trees. There were hundreds of cases of malnutrition. A British historian relates that during the siege "a cat sold for six pesos, a lizard for two, and rats for a peso apiece." Even Calleja, who was able to keep informed of the situation within the city, was moved to admiration of the rebels' "fanaticism and devotion." He remarked that "The

priest is a second Mohammed." On April 17, Calleja sent to
the defenders a proclamation from his government offering
amnesty to all rebels who would renounce the revolution and
lay down their arms. Morelos sent it back, offering the same
terms to Calleja and his men.

By May 1, 1812, Morelos had reached the end of a long
road. The town had been under siege for seventy-two days
and the deaths from starvation had mounted to thirty or more
a day and the number was growing. If death must come, better that it come in action.

Just before midnight the soldiers and townspeople—elderly
men, women, and children—were assembled in the square
and the exodus began. Galeana led an advance guard of a
thousand men. Morelos followed with 250 cavalry men, a
body of foot soldiers, and the townspeople. A rear guard accompanied the artillery. Cat-footed insurgent scouts had silenced the royalist sentries posted near the city walls. The
hooves of the horses were muffled, and the entire body of people maintained such an incredible silence that it was not for
two hours, and after they had crossed the river well below
the town, that the flight was detected.

With the discovery, however, came havoc and slaughter.
Handicapped by the civilians and their own weakened condition, Morelos quite reasonably decided that the two-to-one
odds against him were too great and ordered his men to scat-
ter and reassemble in Izúcar. With the end of resistance, the
royalists simply rode down and slaughtered anyone they
caught up with in the darkness—soldiers, civilians, women,
children, and frequently their own men. The road of retreat
became so clogged with bodies it was impossible to ride a
horse over it. The insurgent losses were estimated at some
3,000, but most of these were the noncombatant women and
children. The major rebel loss was the capture of Leonardo

Bravo, who was duly executed by Calleja. Morelos broke two ribs when his horse fell into a ditch, but escaped safely as did most of his army.

As a major battle in world history, Cuautla has very little prestige, but in Mexican history and indeed in the annals of hardship, bravery, and human suffering, the siege of Cuautla does have a place in all history. The Viceroy, who had spent two million pesos on the siege, claimed a great victory, but Calleja's reception on his return to the capital was notably apathetic and all of the accounts of the day mention a play which was produced in Mexico City at the time. A soldier returning from battle hands the general a turban and cries, "Here is the turban of the Moor which I took prisoner."

"And the Moor himself?" inquires the general.

"Oh, he escaped." And the audience collapses with laughter.

Within a few weeks Morelos had reassembled his forces. He immediately reoccupied Cuautla and established a new headquarters at Tehuacán, which commanded the "China Road" from Acapulco to Mexico City. He stormed and took the town of Orizaba, capturing and burning a great store of tobacco which supplied the *gachupín* government with a fair share of its revenues. Though he might better have marched on Puebla and Mexico City then, he was content to turn southward, taking Oaxaca and regaining control over the whole of southern Mexico. The big and important Pacific port of Acapulco fell before his assault in the spring of 1813.

At this time Morelos turned his attention to setting up a formal and legal government. Rayón and his *junta* had been discredited by defeats and intrigues, and it was apparent to royalist and revolutionist alike that Morelos was the strongest force in Mexico aside from the Viceroy himself. At this time, Morelos summoned eight delegates from the areas under control of the insurrectionists to what has since been known as the Congress of Chilpancingo.

The first order of business taken by the delegates was to elect Morelos as *Generalísimo* of the Revolutionary Army, a title which he at first declined in preference to his own selection, "Servant of the People." Having accepted the honor, Morelos then propounded his ideas for a constitution and a government.

As a first step, he abandoned any pretense of loyalty to the crown of Spain. Mexico, he said, should be an independent republic. Other principles included:

1. Racial equality for all, and the stripping away of the special privileges of military officers and the clergy.

2. Breaking up the great holdings of the *hacendados* and turning them into small farms for the peasants.

3. The property of the ultra-rich to be confiscated with half being used to support the government.

4. The practice of compulsory tithing was to be abandoned, and the vast lands of the Church put to common usage.

5. Universal suffrage, with a Congress, a Supreme Court, and an Executive Branch of three persons appointed by Congress.

Morelos did not live to see any of these reforms put into effect; in fact, his anxiety to rid himself of his own dictatorial powers and to turn authority over to the Congress brought about his own capture and death. They did, however, guide the battles for a constitutional Mexican government for the next century.

In February of 1913, Viceroy Venegas was recalled to Spain and General Calleja, the old nemesis of the rebels, was named to replace him and immediately took the measures which led to two eventualities: the defeat of the insurrectionists and the independence of Mexico. Calleja armed the *criollo* population of Mexico which, after defeating Morelos, then moved successfully to free themselves from Spanish rule.

Calleja's initial step was to drive the rebels from the northern provinces of Zacatecas and San Luis Potosí, which Moreles' preoccupation with Acapulco permitted. Then the Viceroy turned his attention to the south.

It was in December of 1813 that Morelos marched on his birthplace of Valladolid, which was to be the capital of the independent government he was forming. Defending the town were two officers, one of them a young colonel named Agustín de Iturbide, also a native of Valladolid and also an acquaintance, at least, of the late Hidalgo. Iturbide, who played a major part in the events which followed Morelos' death, was from a wealthy family which claimed to be *criollo* but probably was *mestizo*. He was in sympathy with the idea of independence from Spain, but not with the socialist theories of Hidalgo, Morelos, and the other revolutionaries.

The night before his intended assault on Valladolid, Morelos camped his men on a rocky hill outside the city. The attack was to be at dawn and, in order that they might easily distinguish each other in the early light, Morelos ordered his men to blacken their faces with burned cork. It was a good idea—so good that when Iturbide learned of it from an informer, he ordered the defenders to also blacken their faces and attack first. His attack took the army of Morelos by surprise. In the darkness defenders shot at each other and then dropped their arms and fled. The result was a rout; the army simply disintegrated. His friend and faithful general, Matamoros, was captured and shot. Morelos barely escaped with a few of his followers.

The new Viceroy followed up this victory with a campaign

to the south which in a few weeks recaptured the towns and territory that Morelos had battled months for. Oaxaca fell back into royalist hands, as did Taxco, Chilpancingo, and historic Cuautla. Hermenegildo Galeana was captured and with him went the defense of Acapulco; it rejoined the government without a shot being fired.

Morelos doubled back into Michoacán (the state in which Valladolid is located), only to find that Iturbide was capturing and executing rebels at a furious rate, and so decided to relocate his headquarters at Tehuacán, south of Puebla. With him was the Congress to which, unfortunately, Morelos had turned over the conduct of the war. The Congress had neither Morelos' personal magnetism which drew and held followers, nor his military skill. Proceeding southward, they crossed the Mescala River safely, avoided one government force, and then fell virtually into the arms of another at the town of Termalaca, on November 5, 1813.

Morelos could have, and for the sake of the revolution should have, escaped. But instead, confronted by the superior force of the royalists, he directed Nicolás Bravo, one of his veteran followers, to lead the Congress to safety while he diverted the ambuscade. He was captured and taken to Mexico City where, the first night in prison, he refused an offer from his jailer to let him escape. It would have meant the probable execution of the jailer, and he would not live at the expense of another man's death.

The capture of Morelos and his return to the capital immediately gave rise to an argument as to the conduct of his trial, with three different authorities competing—the Church, the Inquisition, and the military. It was decided, rather confusingly, that all three should do it jointly, with the result that Morelos actually endured three cross-examinations designed for maximum humiliation. He had arrived in Mexico

City early in the morning of November 22 and the trial began later that same day.

The Church decreed that he should be deprived of all offices and benefits—stripped of his priesthood. The Inquisition, which had been pretty thoroughly discredited by this time in most of Europe, decreed that Morelos should be condemned to the *auto de fe,* an "act of faith," a public degradation that was a relic of the Dark Ages. It took the form of a procession through the streets to the church where a sermon was preached on the true faith, after which the condemned were turned over to the secular power. Witnesses or advocates (defenders) of the accused before the Inquisition shared the guilt of the accused. In other words, if you felt inclined to testify for or defend a friend and he was still found guilty and condemned—so might you be.

After the *auto de fe,* Morelos was turned over to the military or secular authorities where he was questioned for days about military matters of his own forces and those of other rebel leaders. Calleja delayed his approval of the Inquisition death sentence for three weeks and then, on December 22, 1813, Morelos was taken in a coach with two officers and the prison chaplain, Father Salazar, to San Cristóbal Ecatepec, a little way past Guadalupe, north of the city.

The local garrison commander had had no warning of the part he was to play in history. While preparations were made, Morelos had time for a bowl of soup and prayers with Father Salazar. Then his eyes were covered and his arms bound behind his back and he was carried (because of heavy shackles) into a courtyard. Here he knelt on order and uttered his last words: "Lord, thou knowest if I have done well; if ill, I implore Thy infinite mercy."

There were only four men in the firing squad and it took two volleys to still the body of one of Mexico's greatest heroes. He was covered by Father Salazar's cape and then buried in the cemetery of the parish church. By congressional decree on July 23, 1823, the body was removed to the Cathedral in Mexico City. Later, with the remains of other independence leaders, it was moved again to a crypt at the base of a column dedicated to them on the Paseo de la Reforma.

AGUSTÍN DE ITURBIDE AND
GUADALUPE VICTORIA

In that portion of Mexican history which covers the revolt from Spain in the first quarter of the nineteenth century, the lives of Agustín de Iturbide and Guadalupe Victoria were entangled at a dozen points. In a way the two men complemented each other; perhaps, compensated for, would be more accurate. Iturbide was the first native-born ruler of Mexico, its first emperor; Guadalupe Victoria was the first President of Mexico, elected after the rule of Iturbide was overthrown and Iturbide himself was exiled.

When Morelos was captured and executed, the revolution did not die with him. Splinter bands under regional leaders were operating in virtually every section of the country. A year after the death of Morelos, his old enemy, General Calleja, was replaced by Juan Ruíz de Apodaca, who arrived in Veracruz about the end of August, 1816. Applying more restraint and good sense than his predecessor, Apodaca mixed the judicious use of pardons with his far superior military strength to clean up the rebel bands, one by one, until by 1819 there were only two dissident forces remaining. The largest, a rebel army of some 2,500, was operating south of Mexico City and was led by Vicente Guerrero. The other, a smaller group marauding freely around the swampy, malarial lands of Veracruz, was led by two former lieutenants of José María Morelos—Guadalupe Victoria and Nicolás Bravo.

Due partly to some behind-the-scenes intrigue and partly because it must have seemed like a good idea, Viceroy Apodaca at this time decided to remain in his capital and send an agent after Guerrero who, reportedly, had plans of attacking Mexico City. For this military errand, Apodaca chose Agustín de Iturbide.

Iturbide was born in Valladolid on September 27, 1783, to José Joaquín de Iturbide and María Josefa Abramburu. The father was Spanish and the owner of a modest hacienda, but the mother was of mixed blood. This made Agustín a *mestizo,* although he always claimed to be a *criollo,* an important distinction of the class system of that day and time. Although exposed to the same schools where Hidalgo and Morelos had been educated, Iturbide had no liking for things scholastic and was satisfied with the bare rudiments of formal learning. At the age of sixteen he joined the provincial militia where he served without pay (as was customary with the sons of the better-off families) and where he acquired a solid basic military training and emerged a lieutenant. In 1805, at the age of twenty-two, he married the daughter of a well-to-do Valladolid family and settled into the provincial life of those days.

In 1810, Iturbide received an offer from Hidalgo to join his insurrectionist forces but turned it down because, as he later wrote: "I was of the opinion that the curate's plans were badly conceived and could not fail to produce disorders, blood, and destruction, without ever attaining the real object in view. Time proved the truth of my predictions."

Iturbide joined the royalists instead, particularly distinguishing himself in the famous battle of Valladolid in which he wrecked the rebel forces of Morelos in December of 1813.

As a reward for this and other services, he was given the command of a large military district and charged with maintaining law and order therein.

The assignment was not a success. In an age when cruelty was common and self-interest accepted as normal, Iturbide exceeded the permissible limits of both. His arrogance and high-handed dealings with the people of the area brought complaints from the Church, and his habit of charging safe-conduct fees from the mine owners for guarding their silver shipments—which fees he pocketed—caught up with him after some months. He was never actually tried on charges which had been placed, but did permit his name to go in the army's inactive list while he retired to private life.

Iturbide's recall to active duty in 1820 was probably engineered by the high officials of the Church who had become alarmed at liberal moves in both Old and New Spain. These posed a threat to their privilege and power, and in Iturbide they saw a reactionary who would be useful if properly guided to power. So, the appointment was maneuvered and on November 20, 1820, he set out from Mexico City at the head of a military force of 2,500 with orders to subdue the insurrectionist army and bring its leader, Guerrero, to the capital in chains.

Iturbide, however, had other ideas. After a few minor skirmishes with the rebels, he invited Guerrero to a parley and there proposed a plan whereby the two would join forces to emancipate Mexico from Spain completely. Guerrero was both skeptical and distrusting, and it took Iturbide many weeks of argument, but in the end they drew up an agreement which came to be known as the Plan de Iguala. It was proclaimed to the nation on February 24, 1821—a plan whereby all ranks and classes of the country would unite in establishing independence.

The Plan of Iguala was not the liberal document of independence of which both Hidalgo and Morelos had dreamed— but then, Iturbide was neither Hidalgo nor Morelos. The Plan did, however, offer a setup to which both revolutionists and conservatives could adhere, based on the "Three Guarantees." These were:

1. Maintenance of the Catholic religion and clerical privileges
2. Absolute independence from Spain
3. Racial equality

Both Guerrero and Iturbide favored a monarchy, in the beginning at least, neither feeling that the country was ready for a republican form of government. Iturbide, of course, had plans of eventually taking over total power in any event. So the Plan of Iguala provided that the throne should be offered to a member of the reigning house of Spain who would be designated by a Mexican Congress. Pending election of the Congress, the country would be ruled by a *junta*. The members of this *junta* were named by the original document prepared by Iturbide and Guerrero and included Viceroy Apodaca as president of it.

Apodaca vehemently opposed the Plan and declared Iturbide an outlaw, but delayed so long in seeking to bring him to justice that Iturbide and Guerrero were able to group their forces and plan a campaign with Guerrero fighting in the south and Iturbide in the north, both returning to their old stamping grounds. At this point, one of the royalist leaders, for reasons of his own, took his army of several thousand over to the cause of independence, joining the Iturbide forces. The other royalists fell into line like dominoes.

Apodaca resigned and was succeeded by the last Viceroy of Mexico, Juan O'Donojú, who landed in Veracruz but was

unable to go inland to the capital, due to rebel forces. Iturbide permitted him to move to the higher and healthier
ground of Córdoba where the two met and signed the Treaty
of Córdoba on August 24, 1821. The treaty incorporated the
provisions of the Plan of Iguala, but provided that the Mexican throne might be given to anyone designated by the Mexican Congress (and not just Spanish royalty). It guaranteed the
speedy return to their homeland of all Spanish troops and
placed the safekeeping of Mexican independence in the
hands of the Army of the Three Guarantees, which was to
march immediately into the capital. The commander, of
course, was Iturbide, who lost no time making a triumphant
entry into the capital city where he was hailed as "El Libertador." There he formed a regency to hold the crown, naming
himself President and granting O'Donojú a member's spot.
The others were the old guard, mostly the high Church reactionaries who had nursed Iturbide's career to this point and
were now reaping their rewards.

Iturbide was approaching the apex of his career. He was
thirty-eight years old, above average height, and slender. His
dark hair came to a widow's peak rather high on his forehead
and his full sideburns were reddish in color. He was vain,
ambitious, with no scruples against sacrificing honor for personal gain, a competent field commander, and a blundering
politician. He commanded an army of some 80,000 which
was both his source of power and of worry, for its personnel—
the Indians and *mestizos* who made up the ranks and the
criollos of the officer class—all expected to be paid. And Mexico was broke; the royal exchequer was empty.

In spite of this, Iturbide gave himself the titles of Generalísimo and High Admiral with an annual salary of 120,000
pesos. This the other insurrectionist generals around the
country could forgive, for most of them would have done the

same, given the opportunity. What they did not forgive, however, was the fact that they and the other liberal thinkers were completely ignored in the formation of the new government. All places on the *junta* and all high appointments went to the reactionaries, while the old insurgents—men like Victoria, Guerrero, and Bravo—who had been fighting for independence for more than a decade, were ignored. Even the Congress, when it was elected and met in February, 1822, was composed mostly of wealthy *criollos*. These were major mistakes on the part of Iturbide, and they eventually proved fatal to his ambitions and to him personally.

With the convening of the Congress on February 4, 1822, it had been expected that Iturbide would step down, indeed that the entire *junta* would be dissolved, while the Congress would find a ruler from the Spanish royal family. Spain, however, rejected completely any invitation to participate in the newly created Mexican independence and disavowed both the Treaty of Córdoba and Viceroy O'Donojú's signing of it.

O'Donojú died shortly thereafter, increasing Iturbide's power and authority in the *junta,* and instead of stepping down, he immediately showed signs of intending to dominate the Congress instead. An historic and bitter feud followed, until on May 18, 1822, he put into effect the beautifully planned and enacted scheme which placed him on the throne of Mexico as its first Emperor.

In spite of his quarrels with the Congress and his mistreatment of old friends and allies, Iturbide was still immensely popular in Mexico City and with the people of the country as a whole. He also commanded the army (which the Congress was trying to reduce, greatly against the army's will), and the Church adhered stoutly to his protection of its privileges and prerogatives. With this atmosphere prevailing, Iturbide made his move.

Late in the evening on May 18, 1822, a well-schooled sergeant named Pio Marcha ran out into the street in front of his barracks at the San Hipolito garrison and shouted to his comrades to join him in a march to the home of their leader. His cry, "Viva Agustín I," was picked up by the others and the crowd gathered strength as it moved through the streets. Agustín Iturbide appeared on a balcony of his home and, after a becoming show of reluctance, bowed to the will of the multitude. He would, he said, consent to be the nation's first Emperor.

Congress was hastily summoned to make it all legal. Convened into a session that lacked some twenty-odd members of constituting a quorum—a number of delegates who could not be expected to vote yes were not notified—the legislators acquiesced and on July 25, Iturbide took the oath of office and the throne. Many of the onlookers were members of his family and friends who had been given royal titles.

With this matter over, the Congress settled down to the business of framing a new constitution for the country and the quarrel between the law-making and executive branches of the government was resumed. The Emperor, among other things, demanded the right to veto individual items in the constitution, a demand which the Congress indignantly rejected. So Iturbide, in a complete rage, dissolved the Congress and named in its place a small constitution-framing body which would be responsive to his will.

This was too much. These acts had no semblance of legality. They went blatantly against the will of the people. Iturbide began to lose friends and allies; even the Church retreated from its support.

And in Veracruz, where Guadalupe Victoria and his insurrectionists still held a sizable area, a new force in Mexican politics was rising—Antonio López de Santa Anna. Nominally in command of the government troops in Veracruz, Santa Anna defected and formed a loose alliance with Guadalupe Victoria, who was by far the most popular of the rebel leaders, and they gathered in with them a number of the old rebel leaders. Together the generals formulated the Plan de Casa Mata, which proclaimed abolition of the empire and the establishment of a republic. The plan found immediate acceptance and momentum. The *criollos* who made up the officer corps of Iturbide's army and who had supported the Plan de Iguala were either disappointed with their own roles or disillusioned with Iturbide's; they left his sinking ship. When the old Congress he had dissolved reassembled, Iturbide abdicated. The date was February 19, 1823. The members of the Congress, still mindful of his role as Libertador, voted Iturbide an annual pension of 25,000 pesos and directed him into exile. On May 11 he and his family left Veracruz on an English merchant vessel bound for Italy.

A year later he learned of a European plot to take over the Spanish colonies and sailed for Mexico. His motivation? Probably partly patriotism and partly personal ambition. What he did not know, however, was that after his departure the Congress had declared him an outlaw and an enemy of the people of Mexico. When Iturbide landed at Soto la Marina on the Gulf of Mexico in July of 1824 he was arrested, tried, and summarily shot on orders of the legislature of the state of Tamaulipas.

Iturbide is probably the most controversial figure in Mexican history. He was both loved and hated during his lifetime and his memory is accorded the same distinction. Historian John Anthony Caruso says of him: "Even today the mention of his name in a group of his countrymen provokes heated debate. One side will praise him as a wise and unselfish hero who sacrificed wealth and military position in order to lead his people to freedom. The other will denounce him as a wily opportunist who, after serving the royalist cause for ten years, sensed that Mexican independence was inevitable and put himself at the head of the revolution for the same personal aggrandizement."

That his countrymen in the main do not think too badly of him is the fact that in 1838 his body was moved from Padilla to Mexico City and placed in a sarcophagus in the National Cathedral. The two words on his tomb read: "El Libertador."

José Miguel Ramón Audaucto Fernández y Félix, who adopted the highly patriotic pseudonym of Guadalupe Victoria during the insurrection from Spain, and who became Mexico's first President, was born in 1786 in Tamazula, the province of New Vizcaya, now the state of Durango. Today, Tamazula is a town of some 25,000 persons lying near the larger town of Culiacán, slightly to the east. Then, Tamazula was a village of a few hundred souls nestled in the foothills of the Sierra Madres.

His father was Don Manuel Fernández and his mother Doña Alexandra Félix, both of whom had been born in Spain, and who were cultured, educated people. Don Manuel was a well-to-do mine owner and operator. The boy's education was entrusted to an uncle who was the prior of the Convento del San Francisco where Victoria first studied. Later he was sent to the Colegio de San Ildefonso, part of the "Real y Pontiface" University of Mexico, and from 1807 to 1811 he studied law at the same institution.

Compared to other Mexican revolutionary figures, Guadalupe Victoria has been singularly neglected by historians— Mexican, American, serious, or romantic. Most histories published in English accord him a page or two at most. Mexican school textbooks slide over his story briefly and there are few serious accounts in the Spanish language.

His pseudonym was taken, of course, from two fairly obvious sources: Guadalupe, for the Virgin of Guadalupe, selected by Hidalgo to be the symbol of the revolution, and Victoria for victory. But its selection was quite in keeping with the personality of the bearer. He is pictured as tall, slender, clean-shaven, and almost fair in coloring, quite handsome. By nature he was a romantic—brave, daring, and inspired—and a leader whose followers adored and died for him. His military training was learned on the scene.

The battle of Oaxaca was almost his first taste of combat after joining the Morelos forces in 1811. He had been entrusted with the leadership of a small unit in the siege of the city. At the height of the battle his soldiers were temporarily halted by a deep and well-defended ditch. As they paused there, Victoria heard the church bells ringing in the town, a clear message that others of the Morelos forces had breached defenses and were within Oaxaca.

Brandishing his sword over his head, he threw it across the ditch, crying: "Here is my sword. Now I am coming after it." Followed by his men, he stormed over and they won their way into Oaxaca. Later, almost single-handed, he captured a full supply train. Within a few months he had become third in command, behind Nicolás Bravo, of the Morelos forces.

When Morelos was captured and executed late in 1813, Victoria refused a pardon from the Viceroy and spent most of the next decade in guerrilla warfare against the government forces, much of it in the state of Veracruz. At one point he set up his own customs service and collected duty from incoming vessels.

In 1816, when Juan Ruíz de Apodaca arrived from Cuba, where he had been governor, to be the new Viceroy of Mexico, the story is told that Victoria met him in Veracruz, "forgave" him for having to take the position, and gave him safe escort out of the steaming town. If true, the incident may explain why Apodaca adopted a kinder attitude toward the revolutionists than his predecessor, mixing pardons with executions occasionally. Later, of course, Apodaca sent many expeditions after Victoria, who alternated his hiding places between the swamplands of Veracruz and the mountains farther inland. Although Victoria was enormously popular in the area which covered his many hiding places, the native Indians and *mestizos* must have dreaded his appearances; they were so frequently followed by searching government bands that killed and burned in reprisal because the townspeople gave him shelter. On several occasions Apodaca offered to pardon Victoria, referring to him in exasperation as a "stubborn day-dreamer." The same term had been used by Iturbide.

In addition to his other worries, Victoria was frequently troubled at this time—in fact, for the rest of his life—by ill health. He suffered from both malaria and epilepsy, a nervous disease which caused frequent seizures.

By 1816, Antonio López de Santa Anna had been appointed a captain of the royalist forces and assigned to make life miserable for Victoria, which he did until the two joined forces some years later. Santa Anna drove Victoria out of the port of Veracruz and destroyed his customs collection business. He subverted one of Victoria's lieutenants, who revealed the insurgent leader's hiding place and Victoria narrowly escaped Santa Anna's men. It was at this point that a thirty-month "retirement" or hiding out period began for Victoria—an endurance contest which only ended when government troops became so weary of it they falsely announced they had found Victoria's corpse.

By the time Iturbide formulated his plot against Apodaca and had drawn up the Plan de Iguala in February of 1821, Victoria had come out of hiding and regrouped his forces. He supported the Iturbide cause at first, along with other rebel leaders. Then all of the old freedom fighters discovered, to their disappointment, that Iturbide had simply overthrown one reactionary government to impose another on the people of Mexico. At the conclusion of the first one hundred days of Iturbide dominance, Victoria and Bravo, along with other insurrection leaders, met in Querétaro at the home of an old friend and conspirator, Corregidor Don Miguel Domínguez, whose wife, La Corregidora, had warned Hidalgo. Their objective was to draw up plans for a republic, but they had included among the conspirators one Don Pedro Celestino Negrete who permitted, willingly or otherwise, the plans to fall into the hands of Iturbide.

They were all clapped into jail but were freed within a few days, except Victoria, who remained incarcerated several months until he could escape. He returned to his old stamping ground in Veracruz and was promptly elected to Congress, an honor he declined (probably as the better part of valor) and instead took to the hills again as a guerrilla fighter against Iturbide who by this time had proclaimed himself Emperor.

At this point Iturbide sent orders to Santa Anna to capture Victoria, but Santa Anna was much too wise and conscious of his own ambitions to move against anyone as popular as Victoria. Instead, after some maneuvering of his own against the Emperor, he joined forces with Victoria and together with royalist General Echávarri, who had switched sides, they promulgated the Plan de Casa Mata, proclaiming for a republic. In the first battle the "liberating army" was soundly trounced by Iturbide's forces, and Santa Anna supposedly suggested they flee to the United States and safety. Victoria restrained him, saying that there would be time for that when his own head was presented to him. Santa Anna bucked up and returned to his command at Veracruz. Victoria was given command of the other rebel forces.

Within a few days of the Plan of Casa Mata, Iturbide found himself deserted by all of his supporters, including his personal troops in Mexico City, who marched out in broad daylight with banners streaming and their band playing. Iturbide then abdicated and was exiled. Victoria was the only one of the rebel generals who went to bid Iturbide farewell, and during their conversation he asked Iturbide to accept a memento from a man who never had anything to give except his patriotism. Victoria gave him his neckerchief.

Iturbide had abdicated on February 19, 1823, and Congress immediately set up a governing *junta* composed of Guadalupe Victoria, Nicolás Bravo, and Pedro Celestino Negrete. Then, in 1824, Victoria was elected President and Bravo Vice President. Both were sworn in on October 10.

Guadalupe Victoria, as pointed out earlier, has not been greatly appreciated by historians. Two of his contemporaries, Lucas Alamán and Carlos Maria Bustamante, thoroughly deprecated the first President. Both of them, however, are careful at the same time to note that with Mexico in the condition it was after the fall of the crown, almost no one could have guided it successfully—and no one did, for the next several decades. Actually, Victoria's accomplishments were considerable and he was, above all things, completely honest. In addition, he was the only President in almost the next half century who completed a legal term in office.

Among the major obstacles to success for any President at this time were the following: The national treasury was empty. The old Indian tribute had been abolished but no attempt to tax Church lands was made to compensate. Virtually the only revenue came from the customs. And Mexico, with a voting mass of several million illiterate peasants, was totally unready for a republic. Local leaders simply bought votes or got the Indians drunk on pulque and told them how to mark their ballots.

Taxing Church property and reducing the army rosters would have been the logical step toward balancing the budget; it also was a logical step toward bringing down the government, so Victoria chose instead to borrow. Most of the loans came from Great Britain, but unfortunately the interest rates were ruinously high and the money was not too wisely spent. Mexico's financial plight was never really lessened greatly during Victoria's time in office.

In other ways, however, Guadalupe accomplished a great deal for Mexico. He was strongly conscious of the need for his country to assume her place in the world of international affairs and advocated this need constantly to the Congress, which he kept in session eight and nine months a year. During his term treaties were signed with other nations and Victoria's government was recognized as legitimate. The United States sent their first Minister, Joel Roberts Poinsett, in 1825, and Britain followed with George Ward. Germany and the Low Countries of Europe were the next to accord recognition and exchange representatives. Victoria made it possible for young men of good families to study the art of diplomacy and encouraged them in this.

Slavery had been abolished, of course, along with the establishment of universal suffrage. A National Museum was built and the first plans for the federal system of education were drawn up. He sent the Minister from the United States packing for meddling in Mexico's political affairs.

By the end of his first term in office, Guadalupe Victoria

was weary of the political life of the capital, his health was deteriorating, and he was content to retire to his home, the Hacienda El Jobo in the state of Veracruz. It was the spring of 1829. At this time, according to the Academy of American Franciscan History, he borrowed some 16,000 pesos from the Church to carry out work on his lands in Veracruz. The debt was eventually written off.

His health continued to worsen and he was taken to the Castle of Peroté, in the mountains near Puebla, for treatment of his epileptic seizures. He died there, on March 21, 1842, and was buried in the castle fortress.

A few months after his death, on August 25, 1843, the Congress declared him an Illustrious Son of the Republic and a Benefactor of the Nation. His body was removed to Puebla in 1863 and a little later placed under the Column of Independence in Mexico City, where he lies with the other heroes of Mexico's struggle for independence.

ANTONIO LÓPEZ DE SANTA ANNA

❋

ANTONIO LÓPEZ DE SANTA ANNA PERÉZ DE LABRÓN lived for eighty-two years, all but six of them in the nineteenth century. Thirty-five of those years are known in the history of Mexico as the Age of Santa Anna. Alive, he was a contradiction to those who knew him. Dead, he is a contradiction to historians. Santa Anna was cruel and kind, selfish and generous, brilliant and stupid, arrogant and humble, lion brave and mouse timid. He was possessed of an intense personal magnetism and ability to inspire the men he led, sometimes gloriously, sometimes unwisely.

Santa Anna was five times President of his country, five times deposed and twice exiled. He led the armies of Mexico against forces from Spain, France, the United States, and a dozen insurgent leaders. He was cool under fire and casual to danger. He had a leg shot off by the ball from a French cannon (but he died quietly in bed forty years later). He was nearly a perfect example of the *caudillo*—the military-political boss—of the nineteenth century. No other man had such a lasting effect on Mexico, for during the Age of Santa Anna, Mexico lost by treaty, sale, or conquest what is now just about one-third of the United States: the states of Texas, New Mexico, Arizona, California, Nevada, Utah, and part of Colorado. Neither Mexican history nor Mexican textbooks is kind to Santa Anna.

Santa Anna was born in Jalapa, Veracruz, on February 21, 1794. The father was Antonio Lafey de Santa Anna and his mother was Manuela Peréz de Labrón, both of pure Spanish blood, so the boy was a *criollo,* that is, a Spaniard born in Mexico. Very little is known of his parents. His father, probably a merchant, participated in the state government of Veracruz as a subdelegate, and the family was relatively well-off. Young Santa Anna grew up in the city of Veracruz, where the family maintained their home and, after futile tries toward higher education and merchandising, he entered the military, which was what he had always wanted.

In June, 1810, he became a cadet in the Veracruz militia, falsifying his age to get in. Cadets participated in the action in those days and Santa Anna was precipitated into his first engagement early in 1811 when he was barely seventeen. All of the fighting in the state of Veracruz was against the various insurrectionist leaders and the young *soldado* spent the next five years battling various insurgent bands and acquitting himself so well that he was promoted to second and then first lieutenant. He also escaped from the infantry into the cavalry, his true love.

In 1817 young Santa Anna had his first taste of the more sophisticated life of the country when Viceroy Apodaca ordered him to Mexico City as one of his aides-de-camp. Although he apparently didn't care for the life and social whirl there and asked to be returned to field duty, there is some evidence that the young lieutenant's good looks and pleasant manners found favor with the ladies. And certainly he was well accepted by Apodaca, for after his return he was brevetted (given a temporary promotion) to captain and put in charge of "all forces in Veracruz outside the city itself." Dur-

Miguel Hidalgo

Josefa Ortiz de Domínguez
(La Corregidora)

Excelsior

José María Morelos

Agustín de Iturbide

Guadalupe Victoria

Excelsior

Antonio López de Santa Anna

Benito Juárez

Porfirio Díaz

Francisco I. Madero

Emiliano Zapata

Excelsior

Pancho Villa

Lázaro Cárdenas

Both photos: Excelsior

Alvaro Obregón

José Vasconcelos

Excelsior

Diego Rivera

Excelsior

Carlos Chávez

Cantinflas

Pedro Ramírez Vasquez

Martín Luis Guzmán

Amalia Ledón

Both photos: Excelsior

Jorge Pasquel

Antonio Ortiz Mena

Luis Echeverría

ing the next four years he continued to acquit himself with apparent bravery and daring, and by 1821 had been awarded half a dozen medals and held the temporary rank of lieutenant colonel. And at this time Agustín Iturbide, with his Plan de Iguala, took charge of Mexico as its first Emperor.

Santa Anna demonstrated, at this point and for the first time, his absolute genius for recognizing an opportunity and seizing it firmly. Sent by Apodaca to quell a rebel force operating around Jalapa and Orizaba, he deserted Spain for Mexico, in effect, and joined forces with the rebel leaders, Guadalupe Victoria and José Joaquín de Herrera. Part of his motivation lay in the fact that Herrera had offered him a full colonel's rank and command of Veracruz, including the city itself, which Santa Anna would have to wrest from his old commander. After taking time out to effectively subdue the other towns in the area, and to escort the new Viceroy O'Donojú from Veracruz to Córdoba during a temporary truce, Santa Anna won control of the city on October 26, 1821. It was not so much a military victory as a compromise. Santa Anna's former commander, José Davila, surrendered the city itself but moved, with his defenders, into the harbor fortress of San Juan de Ulúa, from where he collected customs and proved a sharp thorn in the side of both Santa Anna and various governments for some time.

At this point Iturbide, who had become Emperor, committed one of many errors in judgment. He refused to promote Santa Anna to brigadier general and in so doing created for himself a very dangerous and wily enemy. Santa Anna devised a plan to take the harbor fortress and presented it to Iturbide, who dispatched his top general, José Antonio Echávarri, to carry it out. The plan involved luring the Spanish from San Juan de Ulúa into the streets of Veracruz where the Mexican forces would fall upon them. The lure worked but Santa Anna was so casual about springing his trap that Echávarri narrowly escaped capture and the Spaniards retreated safely to the fort.

Understandably incensed, Echávarri complained bitterly to Iturbide, who went in person to meet Santa Anna at Jalapa and invited him to Mexico City where, said Iturbide, he would be honored and promoted. Santa Anna was not a fool and he felt reasonably sure that if he went to Mexico City he would never leave it alive. He pleaded private affairs, pressing duties, a sick wife—anything—and promised to follow Iturbide back in a few days. Instead, he got on his horse and rode all night back to Veracruz where he proclaimed a republic. Later he wrote of his meeting with Iturbide and his subsequent actions:

"Such a blow wounded my military pride and tore the bandage from my eyes. I beheld absolutism in all its power and I felt encouraged to enter into a struggle with Agustín I. After he had left I proceeded rapidly to the city of Veracruz where I addressed the people. At four o'clock in the afternoon of December 2, at the head of my soldiers, I proclaimed the republic."

Santa Anna was the leader in a long list of Iturbide generals and followers to desert the monarchy. Those who followed, including Vicente Guerrero and Nicolás Bravo, Guadalupe Victoria, who had been in "retirement," and Echávarri, both former enemies, joined Santa Anna. Together they drew up the Plan of Casa Mata, which proclaimed the abolition of the empire and establishment of a republic, the framing of a constitution and a representative Congress, and led to Iturbide's abdication. The old Congress, still in session after a desperation recall from Iturbide, placed the executive power in the hands of a new *junta* composed of Guadalupe Victoria, Nicolás Bravo, and a third general, Pedro Celestino

Negrete. A constitution was drawn up modelled after that of the United States. Guadalupe Victoria was elected the first President. Nicolás Bravo was named Vice President. The two assumed office in the first Republic of Mexico on October 10, 1824.

Aside from his first proclamation and his later participation in the Plan of Casa Mata, Santa Anna took no part in the establishment of the new government or its functioning. In fact, for the decade following the overthrow of Iturbide he played no real part in the national politics of his country. He did, however, devote his considerable talents to keeping his name before the people of Mexico, always being sure that his personal publicity concerned his devotion to duty, his love of Mexico, and his success as a military leader. When a revolt over office-holding broke out in Mexico City, Santa Anna offered his "sword and his life for the preservation of the public tranquility." His service was accepted and with some help from Vicente Guerrero, the revolt was stiffled in three days. His popularity led cautious government leaders to send him to distant Yucatán in May of 1824, as Governor and Commandante General, with instructions that he was not to leave the province "without written permission."

One of his assignments in Yucatán was to find a solution to a bitter trade war between the cities of Mérida, capital of Yucatán, and Campeche, in the neighboring state of the same name. This he managed, by applying military pressure, but he also managed to ignore or disobey instructions from the federal government in Mexico City, and tried to mount a rather foolish project to invade Cuba. President Victoria denounced the project and accepted Santa Anna's resignation on April 25, 1825.

The next seven years Santa Anna chose to dedicate to a young wife and his extensive estate, both newly acquired.

The road from Veracruz to Piedras Negras and Tierra Blan-
cas where it forked ran, in those days, for miles through a
tropical jungle. There were a thousand flowering trees and
shrubs and plants, the flamboyan and mimosa and orchids
in profusion, and the vine-wrapped branches took added
color from the plumage of the macaws and parrots, the bright
flash of the mockingbird, and the contrasting black of the
chacalaca. Oxen pulled the high-wheeled carts and the infre-
quent plows of the residents of the bamboo huts which lined
the road and dotted the clearings between banana groves.
Much of this trail ran through Manga de Clavo (Spike of the
Clove), the hacienda property of Santa Anna. He had purchased the estate for a recorded 25,000 pesos on his return
from Yucatán.

Santa Anna at the time was just thirty. Henry M. Bamford
Parkes, in his graceful and accurate *History of Mexico,* de-
scribes him thus: "Visitors to the hacienda found a man of
medium height, with black hair and eyes, pale and melancholy features, an air of dignified resignation and manners
so courteous and tactful that even his bitterest enemies occasionally succumbed to their charm." However, Parkes also
calls Santa Anna "the curse of his country" and writes of his
"taste for pageantry and personal display, his love for fine
appearances and his blindness to realities, his frivolity and
his dishonesty, his overweening pretensions and his amazing
ignorance."

A revealing factor of Santa Anna's character might be the
fact that his idol was Napoleon, whose campaigns Santa Anna
followed in detail. His most trusted military advisor was one
of Napoleon's old campaigners.

Lorenzo de Zavala, later to be one of the leaders of the
Texas revolt, has left a description of Santa Anna from his
personal acquaintance with him: "The soul of Santa Anna

does not fit his body. It lives in perpetual motion. It permits him to be dragged along by the insatiable desire to acquire glory. . . . He gets angry with the boldness that denies him immortal fame. From his childhood he has distinguished himself by a courage that never has deserted him . . . a courage that touches the summits of recklessness."

Santa Anna's first wife was Doña Inés García, a lovely Creole girl just fourteen, who lived for nineteen years after her marriage to Santa Anna and bore him four children. Two were daughters, María Guadalupe and María del Carmen, and two were sons, Manuel and Antonio. Antonio died at the age of five.

Doña Inés was content to remain always at the hacienda where she managed its affairs efficiently. Santa Anna used Manga de Clavo as a base of operations between forays into national affairs for nearly two decades, entertaining foreign visitors, staging a continual round of cock fights, a sport he loved, riding, which came second nature to him, and occasionally hunting the predatory cats of the neighborhood. It was also a retreat, a place he could retire to when the affairs of the nation were going so badly that he had to wait until they got worse—so much worse that he could then emerge once more as Mexico's savior.

Santa Anna's old comrade in arms, Vicente Guerrero, was elected President in 1828 and Santa Anna helped him with various military chores during the next two years. In return Guerrero promoted him to General of Division, the highest rank in the Mexican Army, and named him governor of Veracruz. He really came to the surface, however, in 1829 when the Spanish staged an ill-advised invasion of Mexico.

Although the Spanish had abandoned San Juan de Ulúa in the harbor of Veracruz some two years before, and held no other Mexican territory, Spain's King Ferdinand had never ceased to consider the nation as simply a rebellious colony. Listening to accounts of Mexico's constant strife, he decided the people might welcome a return to the old order and thus dispatched a fleet to cajole, if possible, and conquer if not.

Unfortunately for the expedition, the general in charge of the troops and the admiral in charge of the ships quarreled on the way from Cuba to the Gulf Coast, and after landing the army of 2,700 men at Tampico, the admiral departed. The Spaniards took the Tampico fortress and the yellow fever in just about the same length of time; they had reached a spot that was safe, but safe only to die in.

Meanwhile, word of the Spanish landing had reached Santa Anna at the hacienda and, without waiting for authorization from Mexico City, he raised and equipped a force of 2,000 men and hastened to Tampico where he took command of the few Mexican forces there from the awed junior officer. Thus, when the Spanish surrendered, as they were compelled to do in a few days, they surrendered to Santa Anna. As the word spread throughout Mexico, he became the Hero of Tampico and basked in the light of this triumph some weeks before retiring to Manga de Clavo again.

In 1830 Guerrero was overthrown and eventually executed by his Vice President, Anastasio Bustamante. Bustamante, as reactionary as Guerrero had been liberal, formed an efficient government, checking banditry and collecting taxes to the point where the government actually had a surplus. He also, however, shot or exiled most of the liberal leaders in the country, shut down liberal newspapers, and replaced the provincial governors with his own men.

There were mutterings of revolt and they reached Santa Anna. Early in 1832, with presidential elections coming up, he took over the customs office in Veracruz, appropriating the proceeds, and when government troops were sent to bring him to heel, Santa Anna permitted them to sit in the swamps outside the city long enough to contract yellow fever. (Like his troops, Santa Anna was native to Veracruz and immune from the disease.) After some weeks the survivors pulled out.

This was on May 13, 1832, and Santa Anna immediately marched toward Mexico City, taking Jalapa, Orizaba, and finally Puebla on October 22. He then laid siege to Mexico City and President Bustamante finally agreed, on December 21, to abdicate. Santa Anna made a triumphant entry into the capital, but quickly retired to Manga de Clavo to await the outcome of an election of a new President by the state legislatures. To the surprise of no one, Santa Anna was the choice of sixteen of the eighteen voting. Gómez Farías was named Vice President. Santa Anna did not appear for the inauguration on April 1, 1833, but instead asked Farías to take the oath for him, which Farías did. Having achieved the presidency, Santa Anna had won the goal he had set for him-self—the highest honor Mexico could bestow. But he had no desire to participate in the day-to-day chores of the office, preferring to leave these to his Vice President while he remained at his hacienda. This led inevitably to some very confusing situations, for the two men held widely different views on many things. Farías was a dedicated liberal. He believed in state rights and opposed privilege for the Church and the military; he also was sincerely dedicated to Mexico and her welfare. Santa Anna was an opportunist who wanted always to be his country's hero and greatest military leader.

While Santa Anna was relaxing at Manga de Clavo, his Vice President was active indeed. The new Congress, under his urging, passed a series of reform measures which trod heavily on some very sensitive toes, for they struck equally at two powerful institutions—the army and the Church. One law took away from the army its right of immunity to civil regulation and, even worse, the size of the military force was drastically reduced. Striking at similar Church privileges and prerogatives, the payment of tithes was made voluntary and no longer compulsory, monks and nuns were free to retract their vows, the clerical University of Mexico was strictly limited in scope, and appointment to ecclesiastical offices was taken from the Church and given to the state.

About this same time an epidemic of Asiatic cholera struck the nation and Mexico City in particular, and raged virulently from June to September of 1833, killing thousands of people. On one August day alone burials in Mexico City numbered more than 1,200. The city was hung with the black and yellow banners of the plague. The churches remained open day and night for prayer and the main sound of the city was the rattle of the wheels of the burial wagons.

With this situation Santa Anna played a cat-and-mouse game. In twelve months he came to the capital twice in the course of subduing minor insurrections, and he never actually repudiated his Vice President—until April of 1834 when he judged the time to be right.

Then, with the predicatable support of both the Church and the military, Santa Anna moved swiftly. He removed Gómez Farías from office, dismissed Congress, exiled liberal leaders, and assumed dictatorial powers, at the same time repealing the antimilitary and anticlerical legislation with one stroke of the pen.

Santa Anna remained in Mexico City this time for a full year, consolidating his position. With the aid of a new and conservative Congress, he removed the governors of the states and ruled them from the capital as "departments." Most accounts of the times accuse him of accumulating a personal fortune—which was to provide security almost to the time of his death—at the expense of the national treasury. In 1835 the state or "department" of Zacatecas, under Governor Francisco García, refused to abide by the decrees Santa Anna had issued and announced itself in open rebellion.

Congress duly requested Santa Anna to subdue the insurrection and he found himself again in the position he preferred over all others: astride a horse and at the head of his own army. On May 11, 1835, he encountered Governor García and his force at the town of Guadalupe, near the city of Zacatecas. Santa Anna soundly trounced the rebel forces, sacking the city as an object lesson to other possible rebels, and returned to Mexico City in a triumphal march through Aguascalientes, Guadalajara, Querétaro, and Valladolid. The capital welcomed him back and Congress conferred on him the title of El Benemerito (Savior). His name was added to the list of Heroes of Independence and the name of Tampico was changed to Santa Anna de las Tamaulipas.

Somewhere during the following months, however, the Congress whose election Santa Anna had supervised, came to feel that while they wanted a conservative chief they really didn't need another Napoleon. Relations began to cool. Santa Anna took his usual evasive action. He pleaded ill health, named General of Division Miguel Barragan interim President to act in his absence, and retired to Manga de Clavo to await a deterioration of affairs and another public clamor for his return. It was a long wait—seven years—during which the surge of land-hungry settlers into Texas occupied him much of the time and robbed him of both honor and laurels.

Some months after the formation of the Republic of Mexico in 1824, Stephen F. Austin (probably with his father Moses Austin) visited Mexico City and laid the groundwork for land grants to himself and other settlers. These pioneers were to be under the nominal control of the state of Coahuila and, to encourage them, the central government agreed to virtually donate the land and to forego taxes and any other fees for a period of seven years. Mexico's first President, Guadalupe Victoria, saw the settlers as creating a buffer state against the land encroachments of the United States, which had already acquired Florida and Louisiana.

The agreement opened a Pandora's box for Mexico. Not only did the legal settlers take up Texas land but so did hundreds of others whose only right of title were the rifles they carried. In 1823 there had been less than 3,000 Anglo-Saxons in Texas. Within ten years that number had grown to some 25,000 whites, plus uncounted black slaves imported to work in the cotton fields. Slavery had been abolished in Mexico; the new Texans paid scant attention to that. And, instead of a buffer colony, Mexico began to fear they had simply invited a viper into the bosom of the family of states.

The uprising of the Texans ultimately stemmed, really, from a dozen reasons: its vigorous promotion by the exhortations of Lorenzo de Zavala, a liberal politician who was in virtual rebellion against the reactionary government in Mexico; the hostility arising from the Mexican decree halting all immigration and establishing custom collection points on the Louisiana border; the Anglo-Saxon impatience with Mexican rule and the refusal of the central government to permit Texas to become a separate state and rule itself; scores of individual irritations inherent in the constant rubbing of white race against brown race.

On November 3, 1835, Texas formally proclaimed its independence. The authors of the declaration were Zavala, who had been president of the Mexican constitutional Congress in 1824 and, after the reactionaries took over, a settler in Texas; and Sam Houston. Houston, one of the band of Tennessee woodsmen who fought in the Texas War of Independence, was a large man in all dimensions—physical size, capacity for leadership, and consumption of whiskey. He had been governor of Tennessee but had resigned after a marriage which quickly and unexplainedly disintegrated. The newly-formed Texas government named David G. Burnet, another early settler, as President and Zavala as Vice President.

Santa Anna was in seclusion at Manga de Clavo, but he was still President of Mexico. The move of the Texans came as a personal affront, he said; it also was an opportunity to do what Santa Anna liked to do most—lead an army. He immediately requested and received permission to subdue the "Texicans," and set out for San Luis Potosí, which he reached on December 5, 1835. The Mexican government had not included financing in their acquiescence, and Santa Anna once more showed his genius at the business of raising and equipping an army single-handedly. He mortgaged some of his own property for 10,000 pesos and laid levies on the states of Guanajuato, Jalisco, and Zacatecas as security for another 4,000. By January 2, 1836, he was able to put 6,000 poorly trained and not too well-equipped soldiers on the march, leading them with four subordinate generals, José Andrade, Antonio Gaona, José Urrea, and Vicente Filisola, and his aide and his secretary, Juan Nepomuceno Almonte and Ramón Martínez Caro. The trek to Texas was hampered by cold weather, for which no one was prepared, and by some 2,500 women and children with whom Santa Anna proposed to "populate" Texas after he had chastened it.

Santa Anna reached San Antonio de Bexar late in February and the next several days were occupied in letting his exhausted troops rest and thaw out. The Texans defending the town had taken refuge in an old Franciscan mission, the Alamo. Their roster of 180-odd included names well-known in Texas history—William B. Travis, the commander; Davy Crockett, the talkative woodsman-politician; James Bowie, designer of the famous Bowie knife; and a score of others.

Santa Anna attacked on the Sunday morning of March 6 and after the siege had been joined for nearly an hour and after the Texans refused to surrender, he ordered the bugler to sound the famous *deguello* or "no quarter" call of the Spanish-Moorish wars. The Mexicans stormed the mission and killed the Texans to the last man. Santa Anna placed his losses at seventy dead and three hundred wounded. Other estimates run much higher.

After the Battle of the Alamo, Santa Anna divided his army into four units in order to better seek out the main Texas force under Sam Houston. One remained at San Antonio under General Andrade. General Urrea took another force southward to cover the coastal area. General Filisola was dispatched west, and General Gaona north. Santa Anna led the main force up the center. All were to reassemble farther inland. Andrade, Filisola, and Gaona saw no action. Urrea ran into a Texas force commanded by James W. Fannin near Goliad. Faced with a much larger force and believing he was surrendering under amnesty terms, Fannin capitulated. Instead, some three hundred Texans were taken out and massacred.

Shocked and angered by the Alamo and Goliad, the Texans gathered under Houston, who fell back before Santa Anna, scorching the earth as he went, until he reached a juncture of the San Jacinto River and Buffalo Bayou, somewhat east of the present-day city of Houston. There Sam Houston waited, with about 800 men, until Santa Anna's army, now reinforced to about 1,200 men, arrived on April 20.

The actual Battle of San Jacinto by which the Texans won

their independence from Mexico, took place the following day, April 21, 1821. The Mexican forces had marched throughout most of the day before, maintained a watchful vigil during the night, and had been engaged in minor skirmishes during the forenoon. They paused for a midday meal and Houston was waiting. He struck during the siesta hour.

The battle lasted less than twenty minutes. Santa Anna himself was awakened from a deep sleep and found the Texans occupying the middle of his encampment. He shouted out in despair, which didn't help the morale of his forces, managed to saddle a horse, and escaped through the battle lines. His army was destroyed—killed, wounded, or captured. The Texans lost six dead, about thirty wounded. The fleeing Santa Anna found peasant clothes in an abandoned house and might have made his way back to safety had his horse not died. Two days after the battle he was taken prisoner by a young Texan who had no idea of his captive's identity. Back in camp, however, Santa Anna was recognized and there formally surrendered to Houston. On May 14, 1836, he signed armistice agreements, which have become known as the Treaties of Velasco. After several weeks of total confusion, during which Mexico refused to recognize the new republic but did nothing about recapturing it, Santa Anna persuaded Houston to let him go personally to Washington to confer with President Jackson. He had been imprisoned, shackled in chains, threatened with death innumerable times, but had never, according to all accounts, lost the quiet imperturability and resigned courage which was usually characteristic.

Much has been written about Santa Anna and his war with Texas, and much of it by Texans or Texas sympathizers who tend to get hysterical at the mention of his name. The simple truth about Santa Anna is bad enough and need not be embellished.

Yet Santa Anna was a product of his times and his country, even of a special class of his country, the Creole politico-generalísimo, to whom greed and graft and even incompetence were a way of life—and the bullet was a way of death. The Texans were no angels either. Some were fleeing the law, some were adventurers, and most all were quite willing to grab anything not nailed down.

There were four major events in Santa Anna's Texas foray: the Alamo, Goliad, San Jacinto, and Santa Anna's actions after his defeat. All of them have been documented in detail by at least two of the generals who accompanied him on the campaign, Urrea and Filisola. Partly from them and partly from Santa Anna's own writings come at least a degree of explanation.

At the Alamo, Santa Anna was facing a force which had been branded as rebels by his government and the rule of "no quarter" was well understood by both sides in those days. Santa Anna also wrote that he would have preferred not to take his own losses here but dared not bypass this small Texas force and leave it to harass his rear.

The massacre at Goliad was carried out by General Urrea and not Santa Anna, although Urrea later claimed that he was acting under orders of Santa Anna to "execute at once all prisoners taken by force of arms agreeable to the general orders on the subject." The "general orders" are supposedly the same Santa Anna was acting under at the Alamo.

Santa Anna has been greatly ridiculed for being caught asleep at San Jacinto. His sin there was not sleeping, but in trusting subordinates. He had given orders for the posting of guards and a vigilant watch. The orders were not carried out.

After his defeat, Santa Anna displayed both high courage

and qualities not so estimable. When captured, his calm attitude won the admiration of Houston and his associates. His transparent willingness to trade off Texas in return for his own safety, however, can be admired by no one.

After pleasant but inconsequential conversations with President Jackson, Santa Anna returned to Veracruz in the corvette *Pioneer* which the United States President had provided for the purpose. Word of his willingness to deal for his freedom had reached Mexico before him and Santa Anna found his reception cool. He told General Antonio Castro, the Commandant of Veracruz (who was almost the only one to meet him), that the hardships of the Texas campaign had embittered and wearied him; all he wanted was to retire to Manga de Clavo and never emerge. That good resolution lasted some eighteen months.

Almost a decade before—in 1828—the Parian Market in Mexico City had suffered a series of riots with considerable resultant damage, much of it to a French pastry shop. The owner had submitted claims to the government for damage which had been both ignored and increased over the years until in 1838 they had swollen to 600,000 pesos. At this point the French government, with what concealed motives it is difficult to know, intervened and when payment wasn't forthcoming, sent a blockading naval force to Veracruz, thus depriving Mexico of the customs revenue, about the only income she had. Mexico promptly took formal action and the affair developed into what became known world-wide as "La guerra de los pasteles" or the Pastry War.

President Bustamante sent General Manuel Rincón to defend Veracruz. He arrived to find the French bombarding San Juan de Ulúa and the city itself, and at this point—enter Santa Anna. He had suspected the French of the very worst intentions, which they may have had, and hurried to Veracruz. Rincón asked his advice regarding the defendability of the fort. When Santa Anna told him it could stand the artillery bombardments of a hundred years ago but not of that day, Rincón started negotiations for surrender.

Bustamante was enraged. He immediately fired Rincón and unsuspectingly named Santa Anna to defend the fort and the city. When announcement of his appointment was made in the Mexican Congress, the galleries rang with wild applause. Santa Anna took command on December 4, 1838, and notified the French that the surrender had not been ratified and that he was prepared to defend the city.

Prince de Joinville, the son of the French ruler, was a member of the expedition and shortly after daybreak on December 5, he led a raiding party of some 3,000 men into the city. The intent of this nearly successful foray was to spike the guns of the fortress and to capture Santa Anna for a hostage.

The raiding force was well into the city when discovered, but the resultant volley of shots awoke Santa Anna, who leaped out of bed and, half-dressed, reached his horse and the street. There he managed to rally his own men and led an attack which drove the French back to the docks. They had left a cannon there to cover just such a retreat and the first shot from it struck Santa Anna, killing his horse and wounding him seriously in the left leg and less seriously in the right arm.

His forces fell back out of artillery range where Santa Anna's leg was amputated, painfully and inexpertly. Sincerely believing he was going to die, Santa Anna proclaimed a great victory for Mexico and bade farewell to his country in the following message:

"On coming to the conclusion of my life, I cannot but manifest the satisfaction that accompanies me of having seen the beginnings of cohesion among my countrymen. I ask that my body be interred in these same sand dunes, so that all my companions in arms will know that this is the battle line that I leave marked for them. I know that Mexico will not deny me the only title I want to leave my children and history: that of a good Mexican."

It was not, of course, the conclusion of his life.

The Pastry War ended the following spring after Mexico agreed to pay the damages which had been sought and Santa Anna retired again to Manga de Clavo to recuperate. He suffered great pain from his bungled amputation which left, it was said, the bone protruding some two inches beyond the flesh. This fact was well known and may have contributed to the sympathetic popularity he enjoyed throughout Mexico at this time. Even military observers from other nations had nothing but praise for his high courage in repulsing the French attack. A Spanish minister and his wife, who visited Manga de Clavo in 1839, found Santa Anna gentlemanly, quietly dressed, rather melancholy and inclined to become bitter when he looked down at his foreshortened leg.

He had, the minister's wife noted, "a sallow complexion, fine dark eyes, soft and penetrating, and an interesting expression of face." She doubted, and quite correctly, that Santa Anna would be content to desert completely the political and military affairs of his country. They found him well looked-after by his tall, slender wife and a retinue of military aides and other offices, and his home was "a veritable garden spot."

Bustamante had retained the presidency for four years, largely because no other conservative wanted it, but in 1840 and 1841 the country was again in the throes of revolution and counterrevolution, with Santa Anna always in the role of either peacemaker or restorer of order. He was dictator again briefly in 1841 while a new Congress was being organized. When that was complete and a new constitution written, giving the President virtually dictatorial powers, he permitted himself to be elected to that office, being sworn in, in January, 1844.

During his presidency Santa Anna managed to put down Indian revolts in Sonora and Chihuahua, and settled fresh troubles in Yucatán, but aside from these odd constructive measures, his tenure was hardly illustrious. He temporarily solved the government's financial problems by extracting huge sums from the Church, but then squandered the money by naming thousands of officers to the military rolls. He staged elaborate dinners and, while dressing unostentatiously himself, encouraged brilliant uniforms and gowns in what was practically a royal court. The amputated section of his leg was ceremoniously removed from Manga de Clavo and interred in the National Cathedral. A new national theater was named El Teatro Santa Anna. A bronze statue was erected in the Plaza de Volador with Santa Anna's outstretched hand pointing dramatically toward Texas (and the mint, as someone pointed out). When his wife, Doña Inés, died in the late summer of 1844, a state funeral was held for her burial in Puebla.

In 1842, Santa Anna had acquired new lands, the Hacienda El Encero, near Jalapa in a much better climate. Encero gradually replaced Manga de Clavo in his affections and as a retirement spot. It was to this hacienda that he went after the death of his wife, pleading intense grief as he named General Valentín Canalizo interim President to serve in his absence. His grief, however, did not prevent him from remarrying in the fall of 1844, only a few months after the death of Doña Inés. Though somewhat remote, Doña Inés had been a popular figure and this hasty acquisition of a successor, fifteen-year-old Doña María Dolores de Tosta, on October 3,

1844, turned many of Santa Anna's supporters against him. The marriage was performed by proxy with the bride journeying to El Encero after the ceremony. Actually, she never spent much time at the hacienda, greatly preferring the gayer life of the capital, even when Santa Anna was not with her.

Taking advantage of Santa Anna's absence from the capital and his unpopular marriage, a former ally, Mariano Paredes, staged a successful revolt in November, 1844, accusing Santa Anna of varied crimes, including the misappropriation of some sixty million pesos from the national treasury. Joined by other dissident leaders, Paredes led a sizable army to Mexico City and forced Santa Anna to flee to Querétaro. Mobs in the capital pulled down his statue and disinterred his amputated leg and dragged it through the streets. Trying to escape from Querétaro, he was captured and jailed. In May of 1845 Congress exiled him to Venezuela "for life" with the half pay of a general.

Santa Anna returned to his home town of Veracruz on August 16, 1846, fourteen and a half months after he had been exiled. He had not gone to Venezuela as ordered but, once clear of the mainland, had changed destinations and sailed to Havana where he settled down to the leisurely life of the *hacendado,* much the same as he had enjoyed at Manga de Clavo or Encero. He had the same fighting cocks, the same young wife, the same military entourage, and the never-ending plots to return and pick up the reins of Mexican rule.

The primary cause of his return, of course, was the War with the United States. In 1845 the American Congress had agreed to the annexation of Texas and was taking long looks at California, as Mexico well knew. After a series of diplomatic skirmishes, President Polk dispatched Zachary Taylor across the disputed territory between the Nueces and the Rio

Grande Rivers to establish himself on the banks of the latter. Mexico regarded this as an act of war and resisted the American action, capturing a troop of American dragoons. Polk responded with a war message to Congress and war fever swept the nation. Mexico had a romantic sound in a humdrum and unexciting era. Someone coined the phrase "the halls of Montezuma" (which didn't exist) and half the young men in the States suddenly wanted to fight their way to them.

In May of 1846, Taylor took Matamoros, moved on through Monterrey and established headquarters at Saltillo. And, as if an external war wasn't enough, Mexico created an internal one as well. After an insurrection which threw President Paredes out of power, an old-line liberal political plotter, Gómez Farías, emerged as the country's new strong man. Protesting that Mexico should not let the Americans win by default, he proposed bringing Santa Anna, the ablest of all Mexican generals, back to be President again and to lead the Mexican forces. To finance the war Farías proposed a plan no more original than the idea of bringing back Santa Anna; he would confiscate the property of the Church.

Word was sent to Santa Anna but there was one major difficulty; the American fleet lay between Havana and Mexico and any ship with Santa Anna aboard would have a slim chance of getting through under normal circumstances. There are two versions of his return.

The first is that Santa Anna had been in touch with President Polk for months, suggesting certain steps on the part of the United States military which would pave the way for his return to Mexican power. In payment for this he would negotiate a peace which would give Texas to the United States —it was already lost—and other parts of the Southwest, including most of California, in exchange for $30 million to clear up Mexico's debts.

The second version is that Santa Anna entered into similar negotiations with President Polk *after* his invitation to return to Mexico and only as a means of returning to fight the invaders. In both cases the negotiations included safe passage through the blockade for Santa Anna. Polk didn't trust Santa Anna for a minute but he felt that where money was involved, he could be induced to come to terms, and so he ordered the safe passage.

Santa Anna went directly from Veracruz to Mexico City where he paused only long enough to permit the Congress to elect him President and then proceeded to San Luis Potosí to raise an army to fight General Zachary Taylor, who was still encamped with half his army at Saltillo. The other half had been turned over to another American general, Winfield Scott, who set sail for Veracruz.

By January of 1847 Santa Anna had again exercised his genius for raising armies and was approaching Saltillo with a force of nearly 20,000 men (and almost an equal number of *soldaderas*, women camp followers). Of the men, some thirteen or fourteen thousand were infantry and six thousand cavalry. His artillery consisted of forty pieces, with five hundred artillerymen. As usual, Santa Anna had been far too busy raising and equipping the army to train it. He attacked Taylor some ten miles south of Saltillo at a pass and hacienda known as La Angostura, and though he had a numerical advantage and was a far superior tactician to Taylor, the latter's men were better marksmen; and they stood their ground, which Mexican soldiers always found surprising. After fighting all one day both sides withdrew and Santa Anna, having captured three United States regimental standards or flags, and several cannon, headed back toward the capital proclaiming a great victory—while Taylor headed the other way proclaiming the same thing.

In Mexico City, Santa Anna found himself in the midst of another revolt and paused there long enough to have his election and position endorsed. Then he sent ex-Vice President Gómez Farías into exile and appointed Pedro María Anaya as provisional President.

The succeeding phase of the War with the United States was undoubtedly Santa Anna's finest hour, the high point of his long career as a military leader. For once he forgot his own aims and ambitions and fought like a great patriot—for Mexico; and in so doing he inspired others to equal sincerity and valor.

On March 7, 1847, General Scott landed south of Veracruz and immediately bombarded that city into submission. Heading inland toward the capital, he found Santa Anna waiting for him with a new army at Cerro Gordo, some twenty miles east of Jalapa and not far from Santa Anna's own hacienda, El Encero. Again, it was a matter of men, training, and equipment. Scott's engineers found a way to drag guns across a ravine which Santa Anna had thought impassable, and Santa Anna found his army flanked and his entire position untenable. His men broke ranks and fled. Santa Anna retired to Mexico City and Scott followed at a more leisurely pace.

At this point the United States government would have made peace but Santa Anna, for once demonstrating a talent for cohesive political leadership, had united all the quarrelling Mexican factions under a banner of patriotism. He raised another army—his third in a matter of months—and this one was not composed of impressed Indians but of Creoles and *mestizos* who were ready to fight in defense of their country and to die for it if need be. Scott marched his men to the Mexican plateau and through the pass below Popocatepetl, as Cortés had done three centuries earlier. Skirting the foothills, he struck the Mexico-Puebla road where he found Santa Anna waiting.

Again it was a matter of superior skills and weaponry. Scott defeated the Mexican forces at Contreras and at Churubusco on August 20. Stalling for time, Santa Anna requested and got a truce which lasted until September 7, ending with a third American victory at Milino del Rey. Scott's forces then advanced on the heights of Chapultepec, which was defended by cadets of the military academy there. Legendary now, Mexican history relates that in the "Battle of Niños Heroes" the cadets defended their position until they ran out of ammunition and then leaped to their death from the heights of Chapultepec fortress rather than surrender to the *gringos.*

Scott entered Mexico City and Santa Anna left, naming Manuel Peña y Peña, a Supreme Court justice, as interim President. Nicholas Trist, a United States State Department official, and General Scott negotiated a treaty with Peña y Peña and the Mexican Congress, under the threat of resuming hostilities. The Treaty of Guadalupe Hidalgo was signed on March 10, 1848. Under it Mexico ceded Texas and California to the United States, along with the vast, empty space between; the present states of New Mexico, Arizona, Nevada, Utah, and part of Colorado. Mexico was to be paid $15 million and given a clean bill on all United States claims for any damages.

Hiding in the mountains, Santa Anna had several brushes with American troops and once narrowly missed capture by a force of Texas Rangers out to avenge the Alamo. He finally requested and was given permission by the Americans to go into exile in Jamaica, departing from Mexico on the Spanish brig *Pepita* on April 5, 1848. This exile lasted five years.

Santa Anna, his family and usual retinue of military aides, other officers, and servants lived in Jamaica two years but the Mexican general found life with the British uncomfortable and he never was able to master remotely the English language. In the spring of 1850, he purchased an hacienda near Turbaco, on the northwest coast of Colombia (then New Granada), where he moved with his entourage and where he became, apparently, a much beloved local *patrón*.

During his absence Mexico had five Presidents—Peña y Peña, who had been named by Santa Anna, and José Joaquín de Herrera, Mariano Arista, Juan Ceballos, and General Manuel María Lombardini. Although the nation was exhausted from the War with the United States and had no shooting revolutions during this time, neither did it have political peace. And, although it seems incredible, the clamor for Santa Anna's return began as early as 1851 and continued until March 17, 1853, when a newly assembled Congress voted overwhelmingly to return him to the presidency with the powers of rule even more strongly controlled by the central government. Emissaries were dispatched to Colombia and Santa Anna accepted, arriving back in Veracruz on April 1, 1853. Inhabitants of that city must have grown weary just remembering the number of times they had welcomed and bade farewell to their most illustrious native son. En route to Mexico City, Santa Anna spent ten days at Encero and three at the Shrine of Guadalupe, finally entering the capital to take the oath of office on April 20.

Santa Anna immediately embarked on a fresh career as a dictator. By decree he abolished all state legislatures, making the governors responsible to him. He put the press under censorship, named military *jefes* for all towns of more than 10,000 population, increased the military by thousands, including hundreds of Creole officers, thus insuring their loyalty. He restored the military Order of Iturbide, established by the late Emperor, with a gaudy accompanying certificate showing Iturbide as "Founder" and Santa Anna as "Restorer" of the nation. He chose the title of His Most Serene Highness, which Congress conferred on him, although he also occasionally signed himself "Savior of the Fatherland" along with his military titles. He imprisoned the liberal governor of Oaxaca, Benito Juárez, sending his son Manuel Santa Anna to accomplish this task. Facing insurmountable financial difficulties, he sold the Mesilla Valley, now part of southern Arizona, for $10 million to the United States in the Gadsden Treaty, and tried—although a little half-heartedly— to sell two or three entire states in the northernmost part of Mexico as well.

With all of these things, quite predictably, trouble was brewing. Juan Alvarez, a former follower of Morelos, and Ignacio Comonfort, whom Santa Anna had dismissed from his post of customs collector at Acapulco, gathered followers in the state of Guerrero and published the Plan of Ayutla. It called for a new government and a convention to draft a new constitution. By the spring of 1855 the revolt was in full flower and after two unsuccessful attempts to crush it by military force, Santa Anna abdicated and sailed on the steamer *Iturbide* back to his hacienda in Colombia.

Santa Anna lived for twenty years after this last abdication and never ceased plotting another return, another triumph, another military campaign. They all failed, virtually before they started.

He remained in Colombia some thirty months and then moved to the island of St. Thomas in the West Indies when a revolution threatened his property and safety. In the early 1860s he entered into the French intrigue which placed

Maximilian on the Mexican throne as Emperor, and even returned once more to Veracruz in February, 1864, believing he had a place in the new royal government. The French, however, had a reasonable distrust of the former dictator and found an excuse to escort him back to his ship and see it on its way. Two years later he was convinced by swindlers that the United States was willing to spend three million dollars to finance an expedition led by Santa Anna to revolt against the French. He journeyed to New York, only to find that he had been stripped of almost all he owned by the confidence men. A year later, at the age of seventy-three, he left New York and sailed ostensibly for St. Thomas but diverted the trip to his old home port of Veracruz.

From there, for obscure reasons, he went to Yucatán where he was arrested and returned to Veracruz and imprisoned in the old fortress of San Juan de Ulúa. He was ultimately tried for treason and ordered back into exile again, this time on November 1, 1867. The next seven years were spent in Havana, the Dominican Republic, and Nassau. During this time Santa Anna devoted himself largely to completing his memoirs.

In 1870, when Juárez had become President, he issued a general amnesty for all political prisoners and exiles, specifically, however, excluding Santa Anna as a traitor. Santa Anna protested but it was not until two years after the death of Juárez that he was permitted to return. He arrived at Veracruz for the last time on February 27, 1874, just six days after his eightieth birthday. He spent the next two years living quietly in Mexico City with his wife and brother-in-law, on whose bounty he was practically dependent. Virtually blind and deaf, he died early in the morning of June 21, 1876. He was buried at Tepeyac Cemetery, which is located near Guadalupe Hidalgo, on the outskirts of Mexico City.

BENITO JUÁREZ

THE TEN YEARS or so between the last debacle of Santa Anna and the historically famous French Intervention in Mexico (which placed an Austrian prince on a resurrected throne in 1864) are known as the Age of Reform, not so much for what was accomplished but for what was tried. The reform paved the way for social and economic changes which saved the country from being sold to or absorbed by the United States. It transferred the power of government from the rich Creole politicians, generals, churchmen, and *hacendados* to the common people of the country—the *mestizos* and the Indians. The Age of Reform might easily also be called the Age of Juárez, for he was the man whose ideals, conduct, and leadership inspired Mexico to take the course it did.

Pablo Benito Juárez is probably the most revered of all of Mexico's great men. The full-blooded Zapotec Indian who had struggled his way out of the most abject of rural poverty in the *tierra caliente* of Oaxaca and achieved national leadership without ever personally firing a gun (or riding a horse) has often been compared to Abraham Lincoln of the United States.

In the summer of 1972, the Centennial of Juárez' death, President Luis Echevarría of Mexico and Galo Plaza, Director General of the Organization of American States, unveiled a life-sized oil painting of Juárez before an assembly of Latin-American dignitaries in Washington. It will hang in the great vaulted hall of the OAS, along with similar pictures and busts of the other heroes and liberators of Latin America. Said President Echevarría: "Juárez symbolizes our country. To Mexicans, Juárez is Mexico."

Pablo Benito Juárez was born on March 21, 1806, in San Pablo Guelatao, near the city of Oaxaca in the state of Oaxaca. Today the range of mountains to which the tiny mountain village of Guelatao clings are known as the Sierra Juárez. His parents were Marcelino Juárez and Brigida García Juárez, both Indians of the Zapotec nation. They died when Benito was three, and he and his two sisters, María Josefa and Rosa, were taken by his paternal grandparents, Pedro Juárez and Justa López Juárez. By the time the grandparents died his sisters had married and Benito went to live with his uncle, who owned a small piece of land and a flock of sheep. Benito was subjected to some minor schooling, between chores of sheepherding, but never really learned much, including the Spanish language, either to write or speak it. Like other residents of the mountains, he spoke the native Indian dialect.

When he was twelve a maliciously conceived evil deed turned out to be a blessing, if disguised. He was tending his tiny flock when a group of mule drivers from Oaxaca stopped to rest their animals and Benito fell into conversation with them. His curiosity about Oaxaca was endless and they held him spellbound in wonder over their tales of the city until they finally betook themselves down the road.

Returning to his flock, Benito counted his charges and found one of them missing. Writing of the incident in later years, Juárez remembered: "Another boy, a much older boy, approached me and seeing my grief told me that he had seen one of the mule drivers make away with the sheep while the others held my attention."

Rather than face his uncle, and perhaps because he felt driven toward the opportunities Oaxaca might hold, the Indian boy fled tearfully down the mountainside with nothing but the clothes in which he walked. It was December 17, 1818.

In Oaxaca he found temporary shelter in the home of the Antonio Mazza family (who were to figure much more importantly in his life a dozen or so years later) where one of his sisters worked as a cook. After three weeks there, he was more or less indentured to Don Antonio Salanueva, a book-binder. In return for small services around the house, Don Antonio added greatly to the boy's rudimentary education, cared for him, and eventually became his godfather. Don Antonio read, and he was a staunch admirer of Hidalgo and Morelos, and of Guadalupe Victoria, who had by 1821 just become President of Mexico, and it is quite probable that he instilled in Benito some of the liberal ideals which were to guide him in later life. Certainly he taught the boy to be unswervingly honest and trustworthy.

With Victoria and independence came a liberalization of the Mexican educational system also and Oaxaca found itself enriched with a new school which was controlled neither by the Church nor by the city's wealthy. Juárez was permitted to enroll in the Institute of Arts and Sciences where he studied science and law and where he learned, finally, to speak and write the Spanish language. He had attended, briefly, the local seminary before going to the Institute and had been thoroughly bored by the curriculum there, which seemed devised to educate priests to think as little as possible. At this new school he found a new approach to education in the subjects which caught and held his attention. He was able to study philosophy, political economy, and modern languages, and he had a limited access to foreign writings, ideas, and thought. Even his law courses were broadened in dimension over the traditional seminary subjects.

Juárez was a good student and by the time he was twenty-five, in 1831, he had been elected to serve in local offices and was able to take up the practice of law. While Juárez was still in school, in 1829, Santa Anna came through Oaxaca and was tendered a dinner by officials of the Institute. He recalled later with some bitterness—because the two men became mortal enemies—that waiting his table that night was a bare-footed young man in linen breeches whose name he discovered by chance to be Benito Juárez. Santa Anna always preferred to believe that it was this incident—emphasizing the difference in their stations of life—that turned Juárez against him. It probably didn't occur to him that it was his morals and not his money which Juárez despised.

At twenty-five Juárez was short, stocky, and very strong physically, stolid and reserved in temperament. His features were heavy and his skin dark from his Indian ancestry. His dress was unchanging and virtually a uniform—a black suit, high stiff collar, white shirt, and black bow tie. He frequently carried a cane but, contrary to the styles of the times, never a blade nor a gun. His manner was unfailingly courteous. His defense of Indian clients, frequently without money, had earned him a reputation as a champion of the poor and the underprivileged, and his well-grounded knowledge of the law had enlarged that reputation to include the respect of his peers and the better-to-do citizens of Oaxaca. Demonstrable evidence of this was the acceptance of his courtship of Margarita Mazza (of the family which had given him shelter when he fled down the mountains from the wrath of his uncle) and of their marriage. She is known to have told friends that Benito was "homely but a very good man." Reportedly she personally made his white shirts for the rest of his life.

Juárez entered politics seriously in 1844 when he was named secretary of state by the governor of Oaxaca. He served simultaneously as a substitute delegate in the state assembly. After a few months in the office of the secretary, the state government was reorganized and Juárez became assistant state's attorney. It was at this stage of Mexican history that the War with the United States broke out. Juárez was named to the national Congress and served throughout the rule of various Presidents, including Santa Anna, but found little heart for the work, which largely concerned squabbling over ways to raise money and more money. A colleague wrote that Juárez sat in his seat day after day, casting his vote when voting was in order, but never participating in the normal, acrid debate of the assembly. In 1847 he returned to Oaxaca where he joined two friends in a junior-sized revolution which established a new state government. He was named provisional governor at that time and the following year elected to a full four-year term.

If there was one central theme to the accomplishments of his regime in the Oaxaca governorship, it was such social reform as was possible in those days and time. Much of the legislation he fostered during the five years he served was directed toward the needs of his own people. This was a partiality he never denied. At his inaugural his Zapotec kinsmen came down from the mountains, bringing their small gifts of a bright serape, a hand-carved necklace, a kiln-glazed piece of pottery. Juárez welcomed them with sincere reassurances. And for five years the Indian men and women of the Sierra had the run of the halls and state rooms of the governor's mansion, often sleeping the night in the nooks and crannies of its corridor floors.

He added fifty new schools to those already in existence in the state and encouraged the education of women. He built roads, including one through the mountains to Tehuacán, on the way to Puebla and the capital, and opened a port on the Pacific coast which had been closed for almost three hundred years. He also put the state treasury to rights, paying off the deficit he inherited and leaving the state government in reasonably solvent condition when he departed.

During the earliest part of Juárez' tenure as governor, Santa Anna, fleeing after the loss of the War with the United States, came to Oaxaca where he applied for refuge. With some prudence and reason, Juárez closed the state borders and gently informed the old troublemaker that he would doubtless find a warmer welcome elsewhere. Santa Anna never forgot nor forgave this insult. In 1853, when he was recalled from exile once again, this time to be elected dictator, one of his first acts was to send his son to arrest Juárez, who by this time had completed his term as governor and was practicing law in Oaxaca. It was on May 27, 1853. Juárez was forty-seven years old.

He was taken first to Jalapa, near Santa Anna's old hacienda, Manga de Clavo, where he was held in complete isolation for seventy-five days. At the end of this period he was taken in a coach to Veracruz and there imprisoned in the old fortress of San Juan de Ulúa. After twelve days he was put aboard a packet bound for England which, since he had no money, deposited him at the first port of call, Havana. From there he made his way back to New Orleans where he joined a small band of other exiles from the wrath of Santa Anna. This arrest and deportation of the Oaxaca Indian was a gratuitous error on the part of Santa Anna. Juárez was no threat to the dictator at that time; in fact, he had no thoughts of involving himself in national politics in any way. Santa Anna's act turned him into a revolutionary—and into an implacable enemy.

For the next year and a half Juárez remained in exile, spending most of his time in New Orleans, some in Brownsville, Texas, always working with the other plotters to overthrow the rule of Santa Anna. They were all desperately poor, living on occasional remittance from Mexico—Juárez from his wife, who had opened a shop after his disappearance —and what they could make in odd jobs. Juárez worked as a cigar maker, usually. They linked their fortunes to those of Juan Alvarez, who was already in open rebellion in the state of Guerrero. Alvarez, an accomplished guerrilla fighter, welcomed their aid, for Juárez and his companions supplied him with political expertise, and with weapons and ammunition they had begged from the United States, whose government didn't like Santa Anna much either.

In March of 1854 one of the plotters, Ignacio Comonfort, went to Acapulco where he and Alvarez published the Plan of Ayutla. It called for a new government to replace Santa Anna and for the election of a convention which would draft a new constitution. Santa Anna marched out to crush the Alvarez forces, but they scattered to the hills and declined to fight. Santa Anna returned to the capital claiming victory but, in the words of one historian, he "saw the handwriting on the wall and began to bank money abroad in preparation for yet another exile." The Gadsden Treaty, through which the dictator sold part of what is now Arizona to the United States, gave him ten million dollars and temporary respite. But by the spring of 1855 most of northern Mexico had declared for the Plan of Ayutla. Juárez was on his way from New Orleans and landed in Acapulco late in July. Santa

Anna abdicated in August and sailed back to his hacienda in Colombia.

On November 14, 1855, with a bodyguard of Indian warriors in attendance, Alvarez, Comonfort, and Juárez rode into Mexico City where they were confronted with the impossible task of setting to rights a bankrupt nation in turmoil.

A *junta* of rebel generals named Alvarez to head the first provisional government, Juárez was named Minister of Justice and his first official act was to issue the Ley Juárez, the Law of Juárez, which abolished the old and hated *fueros* of the military and the Church. These *fueros,* or privileges, exempted army officers and high Church officials from civilian law to the extent that they could only be tried by their own organizations, that is, by army court martial or Church law.

Alvarez, who preferred life in the field to life in the capital, gave up the presidency after a few months and it was transferred to Comonfort. Juárez was named president of the Supreme Court, a position which automatically carried with it the vice presidency of the nation. Like Juárez, the black-bearded Comonfort was completely honest and was a strong, fearless leader, perhaps too strong for those times. One of the first moves on assuming the presidency was to issue the Ley Lerdo in June of 1856. The Law of Lerdo was devised by the Minister of the Treasury, Miguel Lerdo de Tejada, and was well-intended but proved disastrous. The provisions of the Ley Lerdo were: the Church was forbidden to own land and the great estates belonging to the Church were to be sold, with a heavy tax on the proceeds going to the government. All corporations and organizations of any kind were similarly forbidden to own land, with the same provisions for sale.

The purpose of the law was, of course, to place the ownership of the nation's acres in the hands of individuals and to provide increased revenues for the government, but neither Lerdo, Comonfort, nor Juárez foresaw what would happen.

In the case of the Church estates, few Mexicans had enough money to purchase them and pay the high sales tax. The result was that most of the property went to wealthy foreigners eager to obtain a foothold in the country. And the Church officials, despite their wealth and power, had been, in the main, good and normally considerate landlords, providing schools and care for their tenants. The new owners usually were not.

The second provision of the Ley Lerdo struck hardest at the communal lands owned by towns and villages, and which were farmed by Indians. The towns were corporations, of a sort. When these had to be sold to private owners the result was a series of Indian riots which swept the country.

A new constitution was completed in 1857 which went much farther in guaranteeing civil liberties than Comonfort (and probably Juárez) believed was wise at the time, and the result was a bitter conflict between the combined Church-military faction and the government. After a series of moves and countermoves, Comonfort was forced to flee into exile in the United States and a conservative general, Félix Zuloaga, was declared President. Juárez was placed under arrest but escaped to Querétaro where he set up a rival (and legal) government and named a cabinet. He eventually ended up in Veracruz with the cabinet. There for the next two or more years he collected customs, bought arms, raised forces, and waged a sporadic warfare against the Zuloaga government in Mexico City.

In December, 1859, his forces achieved a decisive victory at the Battle of San Miguel Calpulálpan (near Mexico City) and in January of 1860, Juárez, dressed in his white shirt, bow tie, and black suit, and traveling in his dusty carriage, rode into Mexico City. Again, the country was in turmoil, the government disorganized, and the treasury deeply in debt.

The next few years must have been the ultimate nightmare to Juárez. New elections were held in March and he was elected President, but this did not mean he was supported by his country. The newly elected Congress criticized, badgered, and plagued him. Guerrilla forces were active in Michoacán on the west coast. His conservative enemies, the Church and the army, gave him no peace. Secretaries of the Treasury came, took one look at the nation's fiscal situation, and departed in horror. And this latter fact, too, was tied in with yet another and even greater problem.

Santa Anna and other preceding rulers of Mexico had contracted huge debts from France, England, and Spain, some of them legitimate and others fantastically usurious. These countries had individually sought to collect their money. Juárez freely acknowledged the debts, but also saw no possibility of paying them and said so. And at this point Mexico became the scene of a charade that was romantic, preposterous, ridiculous—and terribly tragic.

Napoleon III was on the throne of France, married to the Empress Eugenie, a slightly dubious countess who had been banished from the court of her native Spain. Although Napoleon and his Empress were not particularly fond of each other at this stage of their marriage, the Emperor permitted himself to be persuaded by Eugenie that Mexico was there for the taking and that it could be used as a base for building a great empire in the Catholic nations of the Americas.

At this point in time the United States was on the verge of its Civil War and had neither the time nor the military means available to enforce the Monroe Doctrine, which said that the Americas were no longer open to colonization by foreign powers under any pretext.

Also, at this time, the Archduke Maximilian, younger brother of Emperor Franz Joseph of Austria, and his wife, the Belgian Princess Carlotta, were living uneventfully in Trieste, on the shores of the Adriatic Sea. Archduke Maximilian was very high in the rank of European royalty. He was handsome, imposing, and charming. Carlotta was pretty and clever. The two adored each other. But Maximilian was unemployed, with neither crown nor kingdom. They were restless.

And living in France (also at this time) were a number of exiles from Mexico who contrived to reach the ear of the Empress Eugenie in her native language and convince her that Mexico was so weary of rapacious dictatorships and ineffectual attempts at republics that the people there would welcome a return to the rule of a royal monarch.

Presented with this picture—people eager to welcome him to a vacant throne, and a romantic and picturesque country— the Archduke found the offer tempting and his princess found it irresistible. Emperor Franz Joseph would hardly object. Maximilian was his successor and far better that a logical way should be found to keep him out of mischief. So it was agreed.

When the large French army arrived at Veracruz it immediately prepared for a march to Mexico City. Napoleon, his court, and his generals had been told that Juárez and his government were a group of cutthroats and thieves who were looting the treasury, that his troops would quickly defect to the French, and that the invaders would be hailed as conquering heroes by the Mexican people. Based on this information and on the French commander's quick glance at a few Mexican guerrillas who had straggled into Veracruz half-starved and half-naked, the French army headed straight for Mexico City.

At Puebla the French commander, General Laurencez, found himself confronting the Juárez forces headed by General Ignacio Zaragoza. Scorning normal precautions, Laurencez threw his men at the Mexican fortifications head-on and, as historian Harry Bamford Parkes notes, "succeeded in adding a new national holiday to the Mexican calendar." It was May 5, 1862, and on this *Cinco de Mayo* the French were thrown back with a loss of more than a thousand men. Napoleon at this point realized he had been tricked but was too far committed to back down; furthermore, he saw no reason to let Maximilian and Carlotta in on the disillusionment. Instead, he sent 30,000 additional troops under the command of General Foray, who laid siege to Puebla and starved the Mexican army out. On June 10, 1863, General Foray marched triumphantly into Mexico City. Juárez, with his cabinet and the battered survivors of the Mexican army, retired to San Luis Potosí.

In Mexico City a group of conservatives and former exiles, gently prodded by General Marshal Bazaine, who had replaced Foray, issued a proclamation inviting Maximilian to become the nation's Emperor, and word of this was duly presented to the Archduke at Miramar, his castle on the Adriatic. When he insisted on a more popular call from the Mexican people, Bazaine obligingly arranged a plebicite which had only one possible outcome, and Maxmilian was informed that he had been elected Emperor by "an overwhelming majority."

Maximilian and Carlotta were honorable and well-intentioned people, sophisticated in the manners of the royal courts of Europe but naive in their political intrigues. The

Hapsburgs had been prominent and numerous among the rulers of the continent for many years and Maximilian never forgot, or wanted to, that he was a Hapsburg and must comport himself as one. And Carlotta—Carlotta's major aim in life was that her husband should never have need to forget it. Both quite naturally believed in the divine right of kings and knew themselves to be gentle and kind; it was not really difficult to persuade themselves that the Mexican people would welcome them with open arms when they came to rule the nation.

They were rudely shocked on arrival in Veracruz on May 26, 1884, when there was no welcoming reception, in fact, no reception of any kind. The vultures which crouched on every roof and limb were foreboding and the trip to Mexico City by carriage was a seventeen-day nightmare of incredibly rocky roads, swirling streams, and overturned vehicles. In Mexico City, Maximilian and Carlotta were taken to the royal palace, by then a rundown gigantic structure of eleven hundred windows. On the first night there they were routed from the suite assigned them by bedbugs, and a day or so later moved to the infinitely more attractive summer palace of Chapultepec on the outskirts of the city.

Maximilian's rule of Mexico was a tragedy of errors. Combined were his betrayal by the Mexican Church leaders, for whom he was too liberal; his parallel betrayal by Napoleon III, who stripped him of authority over the military and treasury; and by his own ineptness. He was impractical in the laws he proposed, the reforms he advocated, and the huge sums of nonexistent money he spent on gifts and royal parties. The failure of his reign was becoming self-evident by 1865 when the civil conflict in the United States had ended and Secretary of State Seward sharply inquired of the French why they were maintaining a huge army and a puppet Emperor in Mexico. American troops were massed on the Mexican border.

During these months and years, Juárez had kept up a sporadic attempt at guerrilla warfare against the forces of Marshal Bazaine while he, himself, maintained what was virtually a one-man government in the dust-stained carriage in which he rode with his state papers. He remained mostly in the north of Mexico, which the French had not been able to capture from the loyal Juárez troops, limited as they were. Neither had the French prevailed in the mountains of Guerrero (where Alvarez, now in his seventies, still held out) or Michoacán.

In October, 1865, Marshal Bazaine told Maximilian that Juárez had given up his struggle and gone into exile, and persuaded him to issue a proclamation declaring anyone fighting against the royalist troops a traitor to be shot. Maximilian admired Juárez and had at least once expressed a wish that a peaceful accommodation could be reached between the two, never understanding that to Juárez, such a thing would be traitorous. The decree, which was swiftly applied against any of the Juaristas captured, only served to make Juárez and his followers more bitter and determined.

Whether by a decision of Napoleon or through the prevalence of the Juárez guerrilla operations is difficult to determine, but by mid-1866, Bazaine was retreating in the north of Mexico and the French had committed themselves to withdraw all of their forces from the country by the end of 1867. With these events, Maximilian was faced with the bitter prospect of abdication, an eventuality which cut sharply against the grain of his Hapsburg honor and which Carlotta looked upon as rank cowardice. In spite of strong objections from Maximilian, she decided to go to France to see Napoleon, in the hope that she might be able to change his mind about withdrawing the French troops. After a terrifying trip back down the mountains to Veracruz during the monsoon rains, she sailed for France.

There, emotionally and physically exhausted, she found herself snubbed by the Emperor in Paris. She finally virtually forced her way in to see him. Napoleon told her that war was threatening in Europe and he needed the troops now committed to Mexico. Furthermore, his subjects were very unsympathetic to the Mexican venture and the idea of committing France to even the possibility of a war with the United States was unthinkable to them and to him.

At this point the frustrations and her own exhaustion became too much for the agonizing Empress of Mexico and she began to have illusions that Napoleon was attempting to poison her. She obtained an audience with the Pope but could talk of nothing but her fears. She refused to leave the Vatican and finally a place was made for her to sleep on a cot. The following day she was moved to a hotel from which her brother eventually retrieved her. She was gently but hopelessly insane and never recovered, spending the rest of her life in Belgium where she died in 1927.

When Maximilian learned that Carlotta was insane, his first thought was to go to her and he actually got as far as Orizaba where he remained for six weeks in a dither of indecision. Eventually the Hapsburg training prevailed; abdication would be dishonorable and cowardly. In February of 1867, Bazaine and the last of the French troops departed, after the Marshal had tried in vain to get Maximilian to change his mind. That same month Maximilian went to Querétaro to take personal command of the royalist army which waited there for an attack by the Juarista forces. The Emperor exposed himself recklessly in minor skirmishes, hoping for the stray bullet which would let him die honorably.

It never came, and in mid-May, after a betrayal by one of his own officers, Maximilian was forced to surrender his army and himself. A court-martial of seven officers tried the Emperor and returned a verdict that he must suffer the same fate he had decreed for others. He was executed by firing squad on June 19, 1887, after Juárez had refused the pleas of clemency from half the royal leaders of Europe. Juárez needed to make it clear, he said, that Mexico wanted no more foreign intervention. Whatever Mexico's destiny, it must be of her own doing.

When Juárez returned to Mexico City on July 17, 1867, in that now famous black carriage, he was sixty-one years old, but except for the graying of his thick black hair, the Zapotec Indian from the mountains of Oaxaca had changed little in the past thirty years. The swarthy, dark face with its strong features, the short, stocky figure, the quiet courtesy, and the unbending determination were all there. And to the people he was "Mexico." His popularity was enormous. Emilio Castelar, Spanish writer and Juárez admirer, had written before the French adventure: "Be sure that if Prince Maximilian goes to Mexico the memory of Juárez will trouble his sleep a thousand times and he will understand (eventually) that while there is a man so firm there, democracy cannot die in America."

The first act which Juárez set for himself was a general election, which would regularize his leadership (since his term as President had expired). He announced plans for this one month after his return, and coupled the election with a program of constitutional reforms. These included the creation of an upper house in Congress (similar to the United States Senate) to complement the lower House of Representatives, veto power for the President, suffrage for the clergy, and permission for federal employees to run for elective office.

The reforms created an outcry from other politicians. Juárez was planning to make himself dictator and to pack federal offices with federal employees, they said.

He had two opponents in the election, one of them being General Porfirio Díaz, a popular hero of the long war against the French. Díaz had led the Juárez forces in a number of important battles, especially distinguishing himself in the sieges of Oaxaca and Puebla during the final struggles against Marshal Bazaine. Partly, perhaps, because of his own distaste for the military, and more because of the drain on the empty treasury, Juárez had summarily dismissed 60,000 soldiers as one of his first acts after re-entering Mexico City, and he virtually snubbed Díaz.

The general, who had retired to his hacienda in Oaxaca in a monumental huff, was a popular hero but he was overwhelmed by the strong sentiment for Juárez, who won the election conclusively.

During the next four years Juárez struggled with his bankrupt nation, the opposition of the military, the suspicion of the hostile Congress, and the ill will of the European powers. The last factor was, of course, due to the still outstanding debts which had been the origin of Napoleon's ill-fated venture. France, England, and Spain, which held Mexico's notes and bonds, might have been willing to work out a compromise, as was Mexico, but pride on both sides restrained either from making the first approach. The result was that Mexico turned to just about the only alternative, and started a thriving trade with the United States. Relations here improved vastly. Late in 1869, Secretary of State Seward visited Mexico and, surprised by the suspicion with which Mexican officialdom regarded "Big Brother" to the north, took occasion to publicly disavow any further annexation ambitions. The United States, he said, wanted commerce and friendship with Mexico, not territory. It was a conciliatory gesture and dispelled some of the old fears.

Juárez continued his efforts toward the liberal reforms which were constantly uppermost in his mind—more and better schools, education and medical facilities for the Indians, better roads. He saw the completion of one of his greatest ambitions—the rail line from Veracruz to Mexico City. Traversing the valleys and rivers, clinging tenuously to the mountain precipices, giving the rider some of the world's greatest views, the railroad was a feat of engineering that has rarely been duplicated. In 1870 he pronounced a general amnesty for all political prisoners (specifically excepting the exiled Santa Anna). This was a bit of statesmanship which brought him the plaudits of the world and turned loose a horde of political enemies.

During the entire four years of this term, Juárez was never free of the threat and actuality of rebel opposition. His act of reducing the military to a bare minimum had thrown 60,000 men out of work, so to speak, and they were men who really had no taste for much of anything except soldiering— for just about any cause which would accept them.

And, in 1871, when his term expired and Juárez announced that he would run again (against the advice of most of his friends), the cry of "dictator" went up. There were three candidates again, including Díaz. None of them received 50 per cent of the votes and the election was thus thrown into Congress. An otherwise undistinguished citizen named Aureliano Rivera chose this time to organize and lead a revolt, which swept through the streets of Mexico City. With the Minister of War absent, Juárez took personal charge and, in probably his first actual military command, ordered the shelling of the citadel where the rebels had gone to ground. The fortress was overwhelmed and the leaders shot. The government set the executions at seventy. Other reports ran as high as a thousand.

The re-election of Juárez as President was ratified by Congress on October 12, 1871. Díaz immediately rose in revolt, but the Mexican people, though they might grumble mightily about the stern regime of the Indian, wanted no more of war (and perhaps no more of generals; Juárez was Mexico's first civilian elected President). Finding his followers deserting in droves, Díaz disbanded the remnants and fled into hiding.

But another, more implacable, enemy chose to intervene. In 1870, shortly after his sixty-fourth birthday, Juárez had been stricken with a cerebral congestion from which he quickly recovered. Then in early 1871 his wife of twenty-eight years died. She had been greatly loved and respected by the nation as well as by her husband and her death was a heartfelt loss for the now lonely Juárez.

Then on the morning of July 18, 1872, Juárez suffered a series of heart attacks. They came in waves of pain which Juárez chose to accept standing, refusing to acknowledge that his always strong body could not throw them off. During the hours of pain he gave at least two audiences, talking calmly to the callers, who were horrified at his appearance. Eventually forced off his feet, he lay on the floor and there submitted to the barbaric treatment of the day—having boiling water poured over his chest. The involuntary shock kept him alive until about midnight, when the physician finally announced his death.

He was buried in the Pantheon, the cemetery for heroes, three days later after a procession from the presidential palace through the throngs of thousands who stood silently with bowed heads as the funeral cortege passed.

PORFIRIO DÍAZ

AFTER THE DEATH of Benito Juárez in 1872, the mantle of the presidency of Mexico fell on the shoulders of Sebastián Lerdo de Tejada, who had been president of the Supreme Court. This Lerdo (brother of the better known Miguel Lerdo, who had died) was a well-educated Creole of considerable intellectual gifts, and that autumn was elected to a full term by a large majority. By the end of his term, however, he had alienated most of his supporters by a combination of arrogance and indolence, and his announcement, in 1876, that he was seeking a second term was a signal for rebellion. Quite aware that any President could manipulate an election, General Porfirio Díaz and his Porfiristas issued the Plan of Tuxtepec, which called for legitimate suffrage and no reelection. After several months of political and military maneuvering, the Porfiristas inflicted a decisive defeat on the Lerdistas and the road to Mexico City was open to a new popular hero, General Díaz.

With the exception of one four-year span, Díaz was to rule Mexico for the next thirty-four years. During the years of the reform and during his own presidency, Juárez had kept alive a principle; Díaz created a nation. Juárez wanted freedom and progress for his country. Díaz wanted progress, and believed that a certain amount of freedom had to be sacrificed to obtain it. During his rule, the last twenty-six years as absolute dictator, he established national credit, brought in millions of pesos in foreign capital, added schools, built roads, constructed seaports, crisscrossed Mexico with a network of railroads, and checked banditry effectively. Of him, President Theodore Roosevelt wrote, on March 7, 1908: "President Díaz is the greatest statesman now living, and he has done for his country what no living man has done for any other country—which is the supreme test of the value of statesmanship."

Díaz was ruthless in exterminating enemies when they really threatened him, but preferred letting them spend their animosities on each other. He provoked rivalries and competition between the power groups around him to prevent them from ever uniting against him. To certain foes, when it was more convenient, he offered opportunities for prestige and riches, doing so with the remark that a dog with a bone in its mouth doesn't bite. He was more than ordinarily honest. He, himself, was loved, revered, and respected. While keeping his own hands reasonably clean, he permitted others to enslave, plunder, and murder.

Porfirio Díaz was born in Oaxaca on September 15, 1830, the anniversary of Padre Hidalgo's famous *Grito de Dolores* made twenty years before. His father, José de la Cruz Díaz, was descended from the Andalusian settlers of the area. His mother was the daughter of Mariano Mori, also of pure Spanish blood, and of María Tecla Cortés, a Mixtec Indian from the ancient mountain village of Yodocomo, legendary home of fearsome warriors who returned from battle bearing the heads of their enemies across the pommels of their saddles; and of an equally legendary Mixtec princess whose blood-stained body was returned and left on the outskirts of the village after she had refused to reveal tribal secrets. Her return, so that she could be buried with her people, was a mark of respect for her bravery.

The elder Díaz was something of a Jack-of-all-trades; he was a miner, he was a *cargador* on the pack trains carrying silver ore from the mines to Oaxaca, and later he became variously a sugar cane farmer, a tanner, a blacksmith, a store-keeper and an innkeeper.

Once, before Porfirio was born, José Díaz had hidden the famous guerrilla leader Vicente Guerrero from royalist pursuers. In gratitude for this service of saving his life, General Guerrero commissioned Díaz a captain. Until his death, his wife and Porfirio's mother never addressed him by any other name than *Mi Capitan.*

The elder Díaz died when Porfirio was three, and his mother soon wearied of trying to keep up the inn and moved into a small house where she, with the help of Porfirio's two elder sisters, eked out a living spinning out wool on the distaff and weaving it into *rebozos,* the Mexican shawls, for sale. The inn, where Porfirio had been born and near which he still lived, was across the street from the large convent and church of La Soledad, which was immensely wealthy. There on feast days the boy would be taken by his mother to kneel before the great image of the Virgin, wrapped in gold leaf and adorned with precious stones, according to one biographer, who wonders if this contrast of poverty and wealth might not have been at the root of certain Porfiristian anticlerical acts in later years. His mother, who had learned to read and write and passed this bare knowledge along to her children, decided that Porfirio should be educated for the Church. He was an altar boy at seven and was turned over to his cousin, Ramon Pardo, a priest, for further education at the age of twelve. Even at this age, Porfirio had inherited the appearance and many of the traits of his father. He was of medium height, slender but immensely strong, reticent and given to brooding. By the time he was prepared to enter the Oaxaca Seminary at the age of fifteen, he was pretty well supporting himself by his skill as a gunsmith, carpenter, and cobbler. He also knew Latin well enough to tutor other less learned students.

At this point, the life and education of Díaz showed a remarkable parallel to that of Benito Juárez. Both had gone to the Seminary where they had studied theology, philosophy, logic, Latin, and literature. Both had found the educational process there dull and uninteresting, and neither could get very enthused about the prospect of life as a priest. Díaz actually first met Juárez when the latter was teaching at the Institute of Oaxaca, from which he had graduated. And it was partly due to conversations with the Zapotec Indian that made Díaz convince his mother that the priesthood was not for him.

He entered the Institute at the age of nineteen (virtually breaking relations with his outraged cousin, the priest) where he undertook the study of law in all phases available, along with French and some of the humanities. He was there five years, seventeen months of which he had Juárez as one of his teachers. Díaz passed his law examinations on January 2, 1854, and went to work in the law offices of one Marcos Peréz. After some months there, he was appointed village attorney in the town of Valle Nacional and while here was instrumental in probably saving the life of his former employer.

Peréz had got himself involved in a plot against the ubiquitous Santa Anna and was jailed in a highly impregnable monastery while awaiting trial. During the course of his duties as village attorney, Díaz by lucky accident saw and read the prosecution brief of evidence against Peréz, including the names of co-conspirators. Realizing how valuable this information would be to his friend, Díaz had his brother lower him by rope to the window of the cell where Peréz was kept. The night was pitch black but there was imminent danger of the guard at the cell door hearing any conversation, so Díaz labored back to the roof where he wrote out the information and then passed it through the bars. With this (and perhaps additional help) Peréz was able to fashion a defense that was good enough to win clemency at the trial. That same year Díaz demonstrated his courage in another way. He was one of only a few persons in the nation who dared the wrath of Santa Anna by voting "No" on a national plebicite of confidence rigged by Santa Anna.

In 1855, when Díaz was twenty-five, he became sub-prefect of the Zapotec mountain village of Ixtlán. It must have been at about this time that he decided he was really cut out to be a soldier; he liked the military life and the idea of being a military leader. Although he had had only a few weeks of training in the militia, he undertook in Ixtlán to recruit and train the local males into a unit of foot soldiers. It was at this time, too, in 1855, that he decided to cast his lot with Juárez. He, of course, committed his troops to the same destiny.

Late that summer Santa Anna went into what turned out to be his last exile. In the unrest which followed, Díaz was wounded in a skirmish in support of Juárez at the village of Ixcapa on August 13, 1856, an injury which probably would have killed a man of lesser physique. After recovering, he continued fighting for Juárez, serving under other leaders (including his old friend Marcos Peréz, who had taken to the field also), and rising to the rank of colonel.

The three-year War of the Reform began in January, 1858, with Juárez in Veracruz collecting the customs revenues and waging unremitting guerrilla warfare against the reactionary President Félix Zuloaga in Mexico City. A dozen local liberal leaders supported the cause of Juárez and word was beginning to get around that Porfirio Díaz, who led a band of guerrillas in Oaxaca, centering his operations in the valley of Tehuantepec, was a man to watch. By the end of 1860 the liberal Juárez forces had successfully outfought the conservatives on every front and Juárez himself resumed the leadership of his country. When he entered Mexico City in January, Díaz was one of the officers of the liberal troops stationed there. In June of that year, impressed by a Díaz victory over rebelling guerrillas, Juárez promoted him to the rank of brigadier general.

Porfirio Díaz was thirty-one years old at the time. A portrait shows him with short black hair combed forward over his forehead in Roman fashion. His mustaches were long, but not drooping, and militarily tidy. His chin sported a small goatee, trimmed in Southern colonel style. His head was square in shape, like his father's had been, and his features were strong. When he spoke, his words were measured; he had a reputation as a considerate man, reserved and still inclined toward moodiness. In his talk or mannerisms there was little trace of his poverty-stricken childhood and upbringing.

The year 1862 saw the invasion of Mexico in support of placing Maximilian on the throne. The French troops under command of General Laurencez landed in Veracruz, but were opposed at Puebla by forces of General Ignacio Zaragoza and a subordinate, General Díaz. The Mexican defenders were armed with ancient equipment which the British had captured at Waterloo and kindly sold to the Mexican government, but Díaz had been in charge of fortifying the city and it was virtually impregnable. In the battle which followed, Laurencez lost more than a thousand men while the Zaragoza men went virtually unscathed.

Early in 1863, however, General Foray, who had replaced Laurencez, marched again on the city of Puebla where the bulk of the Mexican army, some 30,000 men, were in readiness. The defenders had made a successful assault on the city impossible, but were not able to supply it for an indefinite period. Foray simply laid down a siege and after two months the army and the civilian population of Puebla were starving. On March 16 the city was surrendered. Díaz, along with a number of other officers, escaped. He went back to Oaxaca where he raised an army and soon was in control of the state.

With the arrival of Archduke Maximilian and Carlotta in Mexico came also Marshal Bazaine as French commander to replace General Foray. Fighting against the scattered Mexican troops, in most cases small guerrilla bands, Bazaine was gradually able to subdue for a time most of the opposition. Having conquered much of the area to the north of Mexico City, he turned in February of 1865 to Oaxaca where he launched a four-pronged attack on the city and captured Díaz and his small army.

Díaz was imprisoned in the Convent of Santa Catarina on February 10 and immediately began digging a tunnel in his cell. He was coming along nicely on the project when, at the end of five months, he was transferred to another jail, this time in the Convent of La Compañia.

Díaz had no stomach for further digging—it was too slow— but he was still determined to escape. Through judicious bribery he was able to obtain three small coils of rope and a short, heavy dagger. The latter almost proved his undoing.

Choosing a dark night illuminated only by occasional lightning flashes, Díaz timed the steps of the sentry in the courtyard below his window and then climbed on the window sill. Using the rope coil as a lariat, he cast it repeatedly until it went over a chimney and pulled himself up and over the roof. Creeping along slippery clay tiles, he made his way to a statue of the Virgin which had been placed there in a niche to guide travelers. He was able to get the rope around that and then started down into what he thought was an empty lot outside the wall. The lot, however, wasn't empty. It was a pigpen and in the descent the dagger slipped from Díaz' belt and dropped, blade end first, on one of the pigs. The resultant squeal startled the sentry inside and Díaz clung helplessly to his rope in the darkness while the man investigated and then returned to his post. Díaz slipped on down, crouched for a few minutes in the mud and then ran swiftly to a rendezvous point where a horse had been placed for him. He forded a river and escaped to the friendly mountains he knew so well.

After riding across half of two states, Díaz found refuge with Juan Alvarez in the state of Guerrero and then continued on to his own ground—Oaxaca. Here he quickly reorganized his own guerrilla army and continued the endless battle against the French forces.

By the spring of 1866, Marshal Bazaine began a withdrawal movement, partly due, perhaps, to his own weariness in fighting a hopeless war, and partly because Napoleon III was secretly advising him that he intended to pull out all of the French forces. The Americans were insistent on this and the war clouds were gathering in Europe again; Napoleon needed his armies there.

In February, Marshal Bazaine left Veracruz with the last of the French soldiers and Maximilian was left with a force of reasonably loyal Mexicans led by two conservative generals, Miguel Miramón and Leonardo Márquez. They left Mexico City for Querétaro to meet the Juárez forces.

In the meantime Díaz, by now in full control of his state of Oaxaca, was marching north toward the capital, pausing en route to lay siege to Puebla, which must have been a very familiar battle scene to him by this time. In April, Maximilian sent General Márquez back to Mexico City for men, money, and supplies, supposing he would return immediately. Instead, Márquez decided to march to the relief of Puebla. Hearing of his approach, Díaz stormed the city on April 4 and overwhelmed the defenses. A week later he overtook Márquez returning to Mexico City and routed his force. Maximilian was captured, tried, and executed on June 19 (as was Miramón and Tomás Mejia, the Indian general) and a few days later Díaz defeated the last defenders of Mexico City and marched into the capital. (He had permitted Márquez to escape and the general fled to Panama where he lived for almost forty years, supporting himself by buying and selling old silver, gold, and jewelry.)

In July of 1867, when Juárez rode into Mexico City to become the head of government, the great liberal leader made a serious mistake in his handling of one of his more competent generals, Porfirio Díaz.

Díaz waited loyally for Juárez to resume his presidency, quite ready to continue his allegiance. As the nation's first civilian President, however, Juárez distrusted the military, felt they had been the curse of the country, and was determined to undermine their power. One of his first acts on arriving in the capital was to dismiss 40,000 of the 80,000-man army which had fought for him. And when Díaz rode to the outskirts of Mexico City to meet him, Juárez received him with nothing more than a short nod; nor was Díaz invited to ride into Mexico City with Juárez. There is no way of telling, of course, how long Díaz might have remained trustworthy had Juárez chosen to make a place in the new government for his former student. It is quite certain, however, that the Juárez snub turned Díaz into an angry opponent.

In the meantime the 40,000 troops Juárez had dismissed, and who were now in the ranks of Mexico's unemployed, began minor rebellions here and there. But when Juárez renewed Díaz' commission as a general and proposed to send him out in charge of government forces to subdue these guerrilla bands, Díaz resigned. He would not, he said, fight against his former comrades.

That fall he ran for President against Juárez and Sebastián Lerdo de Tejada, coming in a poor third, and retired to his hacienda in Oaxaca to raise sugar cane for the next four years. In 1871 he, along with Lerdo, ran against Juárez again. This time no one had a majority of the votes and the election was thrown into Congress, which declared for Juárez. At his death, as noted earlier, the presidency went to Lerdo, and he, in the special elections held that fall, was elected almost unanimously.

Díaz waited with some patience in Oaxaca, but when Lerdo announced in 1876 that he would run again, Díaz had tested the flavor of Lerdo's unpopularity and decided to wait no longer. After issuing the Plan of Tuxtepec, he made a trip to Brownsville where he was successful in raising both money and mercenary recruits. In this he had the full support of pertinent United States officials who saw in Díaz "a man with whom they could do business." (The United States was at this time more interested in trade than territory.)

With his forces assembled in the north, Díaz then journeyed to Veracruz in disguise and continued on to Oaxaca, where he gathered up his old guerrilla troops, augumented by other dissidents, and headed for Mexico City. At Tecoac, Díaz was reinforced by General Manuel González who had helped him in Brownsville and had been left in command of the troops there when Díaz went to Veracruz. Here in Tecoac on November 16, 1876, he met the Lerdo forces and won a desperately fought battle which lasted several hours. Lerdo escaped and retired to New York where he died two years later. Díaz marched into Mexico City and proclaimed himself President.

On May 2 a newly elected Congress made everything legal by declaring Díaz the constitutional President for a term which would end on November 30, 1880. Díaz was at this time forty-six years old. He was destined to live thirty-nine more years, thirty of them as President of Mexico.

During his first term Díaz was content to bind the wounds of the liberal party and reshape its leadership. Most of the old guard was gone—dead, exiled, or resigned to taking a back seat. Díaz formed a new cabinet composed almost equally of Porfiristas, Juaristas, and Lerdistas, but things were not peaceable in the beginning. He quelled rebellions in 1877 and 1878, and then in 1879 found a way to make it clear that armed opposition was not looked upon with favor. In June of that year a group of Lerdistas organized a revolt in Veracruz and the crew of a government gunboat there mutinied. Convinced at this point that he faced a serious rebellion, Díaz sent a telegram to Luis Mier y Terán, governor of Veracruz, which read: *"Aprehendidos infraganti, matolos en caliente,"* which can be translated as "When they are caught in the act, kill them while their blood is still hot." Governor Mier arrested nine supposed conspirators and had them executed. There is still argument as to how many were guilty and how many guiltless, but the brutal ruthlessness of the deed served to stop most of the conspiracies for many years.

One of the more famous of Díaz' early presidential acts was the establishments of the *rurales,* a national police force which effectively cut down on banditry and crime on the highways.

He distributed favors to win the support of the more important in the class strata of Mexico—the landowners and clergy,
the merchants and professional people—and ignored the
peasants and Indians because they would never be dangerous
without leadership. He set general against general and politician against politician in their rivalry for power. He put
military commanders he could trust over the troops in the
states of governors he could not trust.

When the end of his term came in 1880, Díaz was careful
not to seek reelection—which would be against the tenets of
his own Plan of Tuxtepec—but he was firmly established
enough to be able to dictate his successor and chose his old
friend, General Manual González, whose reinforcements had
saved his skin at the battle of Tecoac.

González was either one of the worst Presidents Mexico
ever had or just medium bad, depending on which historian
you read. Certainly he stimulated the economic development
of the country, but in so doing he gave great chunks of it
away to both foreign and local capitalists in the process of
enticing money for railroads, mining, and oil development.
Much of the land belonged to the government; even more
had been the property of the Indians which they had clung
to despite the rapacity of the Spanish Dons.

During the four years between 1880 and 1884, Díaz kept
busy and out of mischief. In 1882 he was chosen as a member
of the Supreme Court and elected to the Senate at the same
time. He resigned both to become governor of Oaxaca, and
in 1883 he made a triumphal visit to the United States where
he found renewed assurances of support from the American
version of the Mexican *caudillo,* sometimes known unkindly
as robber barons.

In 1881, on November 7, Díaz had married Carmen Romero Rubio, the daughter of Romero Rubio. The father had

been political manager for Sebastián Lerdo de Tejada and had fled to New York with the former President after the defeat of the Lerdistas at Tecoac by Díaz. With the fine ability of the cat to land on its feet, Rubio deserted Lerdo after a few months and immediately contrived to attach himself to Díaz on his return to Mexico City. Rubio was made Minister of the Interior during the first Díaz term and remained a political ally for years.

It was the second marriage for Díaz, who had been a widower for many years. He was fifty-one and his bride just turned sixteen and, according to all accounts of the times, their marriage was a love match which endured until Díaz died in 1915. In her diary, shortly after the marriage, Carmelita, as Díaz called her, wrote: "He is the beginning and the end of my existence. Life has no other meaning, no other value. I have only my youth to give him."

Díaz had no trouble being reelected in 1884 but, on taking office, found an empty treasury. The Congress started an investigation of the González regime which pretty well discredited him before it was halted by Díaz, who preferred attention to be centered elsewhere; after all, he had put González in office. He labored to put the nation's finances to rights by reducing interest rates on the public debt, reducing salaries, continuing the sale of public and Indian lands, and giving subsidies to foreign investments. He also, for the first time, established a form of censorship over the press and even closed down some newspapers that criticized his programs. His financial plan was a ten-year gamble and was taken with some deliberateness as an excuse for his own perpetuation in office, for Díaz had no intention of giving up the presidency again.

Soon after his reelection in 1884, one of the old revolutionaries still in the cabinet, General Carlos Pacheco, introduced an amendment abolishing the Tuxtepec clause in the constitution which prohibited succession in office. By some political maneuvering, Díaz succeeded in getting an amendment passed by Congress and the states which permitted succession for one term. This came on October 21, 1887. Three years later, after Díaz had been reelected in 1888, another amendment was passed permitting indefinite reelections.

An account of the two decades after the 1888 Díaz triumph is a depressing litany of economic success for which the Mexican nation paid a terrible price in social depression and human misery. The dream of Morelos and later of Juárez and other leaders of the reform had been to divide the vast haciendas and to rescue the Indians from peonage. The Díaz economic system, however, merely imposed an inhumane and immoral capitalism on top of the hacienda system and enlarged it. Instead of dividing the lands and placing them in the hands of small owners, Díaz just accentuated the evil by selling or giving away vast areas of public lands or the Indian lands *(ejidos)* to individuals. There was some slight increase in the number of owners, but the increase in the acreage they owned was enormous. More than twenty-eight million acres in Baja California were handed over to four persons. Ninety-five million acres in the northern states went to five people. One man obtained seventeen million acres in Chihuahua. By 1910, title to almost half of Mexico was held by only three thousand families. Of the ten million Mexicans who were engaged in farming, five million of them lived in the Indian villages. They were now virtually without land of their own. The other five million, with the exception of a few hundred thousand, were reduced to the status of tenant farmers or, in some cases, actual serfdom.

The absentee owners of the haciendas, who usually lived in Mexico City if they were Mexicans, or the United States if they were Americans, cared little for the soil, nor were they concerned about the inefficient farming methods carefully preserved from antiquity by the administrators and overseers. Thus the land went down in quality and the crops in quantity, while the peons who did the backbreaking work from sun to sun existed—and only that—from year to year and lifetime to lifetime. They lived in thatched huts in tiny villages clustered around a grist mill where they brought their corn daily to be ground. They lived on *tortillas,* peppers, and *frijoles,* slept on straw ticks on the floor, and bore stoically their various diseases brought on by impure drinking water and malnutrition.

In the state of Yucatán the "Fifty Henequen Kings" controlled more than a million acres of arid land on which grew the plant known as henequen, or sisal hemp, from which rope is made. They also "owned" more than 100,000 workers, men, women, and children old enough to labor in the fields. While not openly called slaves—although they sometimes virtually were—these workers were occasionally actually bought and sold, and their indenture to the owner was for life if the owner wanted it that way, as he usually did. The workers were Mayan and Yaqui Indians and some Koreans. The Mayas, whose subjugation was completed in 1901 by Díaz' General Victoriano Huerta, were entrapped into their bondage by any one of the scores of small money lenders who operated in the state. A small loan, enough to buy a bottle of medicine (or mescal) was sufficient to bind the borrower to the lender. The Yaquis were lured from their native Sonora on some pretext, usually because they were starving, and the Koreans were simply indentured workers with no possible way of working their way out of the debt they had incurred for passage from their homes to Mexico.

The bondage of these people was complete. Few survived

many years and there was always demand for a fresh supply.
They could be used for work in the fields or drudgery in the
household. The younger girls could be, and frequently were,
used for prostitution; in Mérida, the lovely capital city of
Yucatán, the practice was common. Serfs were frequently
beaten by their owners, or even killed in a moment of anger,
with complete impunity. Slavery had been abolished in
Mexico after the *Grito de Dolores,* but it was partially re-
vived in Yucatán in a virulent form during the Díaz dictatorship. Actually, Díaz did not originate or condone the practice. He simply did not prevent it—a crime which was being
carried out by the governors of Yucatán whose election he
had sanctioned or arranged.

Freedom of the printed word in Mexico virtually disappeared in the latter part of the nineteenth century under the
Díaz regime. The right of trial by jury for persons charged
with any press offense had been abolished by President González during his one term. Thereafter, until the Díaz regime
ended, the poor journalists had no sanctuary whatsoever.
Charged with any crime of the published word, they were
brought before a single magistrate who judged their offense,
the intent behind it, and the damage done—and then pronounced sentence. Since Díaz appointed and removed magis-
trates on whim, the result of any trial could be pretty well
forecast. Those convicted in the capital usually went to the
dungeons in Veracruz to die of yellow fever, (though one,
Filomeno Mata, was jailed thirty-four times and survived).
Some dozen or more were convicted by the governors of the
states and subjected to the *ley fuga,* the law of escape. The
ley fuga was a common practice in those days, that is, being
killed "while trying to escape."

None of these, and other, abuses were exposed to an ex-
terior world which watched Mexico make a place for herself

among the more prosperous and economically progressive nations of the world. Under Díaz and his finance minister, José Ives Limantour, the industry, commerce, and finances of Mexico had taken several giant steps forward.

Limantour was the leader of a new "technocratic" group in Mexico which in time gained the name of the *cientificos,* along with considerable influence, although never any real political power. They believed that all progress was represented by material advancement—more mines, more factories, more industry. They were contemptuous of the workers, the peasants, and even of the middle class, which lacked their education and culture. They were, mainly, young intellectuals—lawyers, bankers, economists, engineers, scientists. Díaz secretly distrusted them but permitted them in the government because they were competent and could carry out programs he wanted. The *cientificos,* who mistrusted and feared Díaz, wanted an honest, open government, but one which would be under the control of the Creole upper class, to which they themselves belonged. While they were capable of political plotting, they were also realistic enough to defer their aims of reform until whatever government would follow Díaz.

The old days of the always bankrupt national treasury had disappeared, at least for the time. By 1900, Mexican revenues had reached 74 million pesos and by 1910 the figure was 110 million. Hundreds of new factories had opened, including cotton and woolen mills, smelters, breweries, chemical works, and textile plants. The peso was so firm that Mexican bonds were considered one of the world's safest investments. By 1910, Mexico, under the guidance of Limantour, had quietly bought up great blocks of Mexican railroad stocks on the American market and was able to nationalize the roads, saving them from consolidation under mergers by American rail tycoons.

Though much of the design tended to be a cross between French and Italian renaissance, the Díaz government carried forward some of the plans of which Maximilian had dreamed. Running westward from the center of the city and bordered by large public buildings and private residences, the Paseo de la Reforma ended at Chapultepec where the dictator lived (as had Maximilian and Carlotta). With this enterprise, and some progress in the theatrical arts, culture pretty well ended, however. Creative writing was impossible in the despotic atmosphere of the time, and Mexico's great painters and sculptors blossomed later, out of the revolution which was coming.

Díaz had no opposition in 1900 and again ran unopposed in 1904 (when the term was lengthened from four years to six). But along about 1908 there came a general rise of criticism throughout the country which would have warned a less complacent man than Díaz that Mexico wanted a change. At this same time the dictator was coming under heavy criticism from the United States because, alarmed at the top-heavy preponderance of United States investment in Mexico (over a billion dollars), he had become less cooperative with Wall Street. Hoping to still this and apparently almost naively unaware of the results in Mexico, Díaz gave an American journalist, James Creelman, an interview in which he said he expected to retire in 1910. The story was printed in *Pearson's Magazine* in February of 1908 and immediately reprinted in Mexico by *El Imparcial,* the *Mexican Herald,* and *El Tiempo.* Filomeno Mata, despite his thirty-four arrests, directed an open letter in his *El Diario del Hogar,* asking the dictator to confirm or deny the story.

Díaz retreated to the politician's refuge of hedging. Retirement was his personal desire, he said, but if the demands from his country were still strong and if he felt that his country still needed him, then he might have to reconsider; and on and on. But the old dictator had no intention of giving up. He was eighty years old and he had had his own way virtually unopposed for thirty-odd years. Why change now?

His only likely opponent was General Bernardo Reyes, the capable, if reactionary, governor of Nueva León, and Díaz promptly sent him on an official mission to Europe when he showed signs of collecting formidable support, and continued preparing for another reelection in November.

But he reckoned without the whims of fate. Francisco Madero, a small, inoffensive, intellectual young man, the eldest son of a wealthy *hacendado* and one-time governor of Coahuila, took a long look at the politics of his day and did not like what he saw. He became, in time, so offended by the Díaz government that he wrote a book, *The Presidential Succession in 1910,* which was pubished and released to the public in January, 1909. In 1903, Madero had been in Monterrey where he had seen Governor Reyes' troops shoot down a handful of political demonstrators, and he had been deeply moved by the sight.

The book was an immediate success, in today's jargon, a best seller. But more, it gave the floundering Díaz opposition a leader around whom to rally. Within a few weeks after the book was published, Madero became that leader.

At first, Díaz refused to take Madero seriously, but then he began to hear of the thousands who attended his rallies. Díaz had Madero jailed at San Luis Potosí on a charge of plotting armed insurrection. (Madero up to that time had advocated only peaceful political opposition.) Early in October, 1910, Díaz announced the results of the election. He, of course, had been reelected with his Vice President, Ramón Corral. He gave a few token votes to Madero and to another candidate, Francisco Vasquez Gómez.

On October 7, Madero, who had been released from prison and placed under house arrest, escaped to San Antonio, Texas, where he published the Plan of San Luis Potosí. It declared the Díaz election fraudulent and revoked, and called for a general insurrection on November 20.

The first weeks of the revolution were absurdly inept and slow. But then a dozen leaders in a dozen parts of the country gradually came to life and found they could raise guerrilla forces—and more, they could win victories. And if the revolutionists found trouble bringing their strength into action, Díaz suddenly discovered he had no strength whatsoever. The long years of political patronage, the soft living, the retention of the old leaders because he knew their weaknesses so well, the refusal to bring in new blood because it might become heated with ambition—all of these had left the Díaz regime with only an illusion of hard cohesion. The majority of the dictator's generals, governors, and cabinet members were past sixty-five, some past seventy, and two past eighty. Like Díaz himself, they were too old for field duty. Díaz suddenly found he had no one he could trust with an army; actually even his army had been allowed to slip from its prescribed strength of 30,000 trained men down to less than 20,000 transcripts led by gaudily dressed officers who were more at home in the ballroom than on the drill grounds.

As the revolution spread, new liberal leaders appeared. In southern Chihuahua a storekeeper named Pascual Orozco raised a body of troops, and his able deputy was a young bandit *cum* guerrilla fighter named Francisco Villa, though everyone called him Pancho. In Morelos a peasant leader, Emiliano Zapata, was raising an army.

Porfirio Díaz suddenly found himself an old man and alone. His brilliant financial assistant Limantour had returned to his father's native France some months before when Díaz refused to put him on the ticket as Vice President because he was dangerously capable and popular. Now Díaz cabled him to return, which Limantour did, but via Coahuila for consultations with the Madero family. The Madero people then brought Francisco Vasquez Gómez, the other unsuccessful candidate, into the picture and negotiations with Díaz began. While these were proceeding, with Vasquez Gómez demanding the resignation of Díaz, and Limantour trying to salvage something for himself, Orozco and Villa stormed the border town of Juárez, which had been under siege, and took it by blasting their way from street to street, blowing out the walls of houses with dynamite to effect a safe route. The capture of Juárez on May 10, 1911, giving the revolutionists an access to the United States and supplies, was a key victory. The next day Zapata took Cuautla, capital of Morelos, and the other state capitals began to fall to the rebel leaders.

Limantour, whose first act on setting foot on Mexican soil was to declare himself head of government and to appoint a new cabinet, took a different view when he faced the carbines and machine guns of the rebel leaders. At a meeting in Juárez on the night of May 21, he signed an agreement which called for his resignation and that of Díaz. Francisco de la Barra, a lawyer and diplomat who had served under Díaz but whom the revolutionists considered a neutral figure, was to fill in as provisional President until elections could be held.

Word of the victory at Cuidad Juárez, and of the treaty, reached Mexico City on May 23. Singing, dancing throngs filled the streets throughout the night. Thousands ringed the palace and demanded that Díaz confirm his resignation. This he did the next day and on the next boarded a train for Veracruz, thence sailing for Europe. The old dictator died in Paris on July 2, 1915, at the age of eighty-five, unshaken in his belief that his had been the best government his country ever had. As he died, rebel chieftains were still fighting in the hills of Mexico over his succession.

FRANCISCO I. MADERO

KIND, GENTLE, intensely patriotic, and absurdly impractical, Francisco Indalecio Madero is known in Mexico as the Apostle of the Revolution. By a political accident he awakened a nation which had been cowed for thirty-five years and caused it to break out of the bonds of absolute tyranny. His reward was scorn, then disgrace, then assassination.

Madero was born in the parlor of the Hacienda of the Rosary in Parras, Coahuila, on October 30, 1873, the first of fifteen children. The Madero family had lived in the north of Mexico since early in the 1800s and were quite wealthy. Francisco's grandfather, Evaristo Madero, as a young man had operated a mule train along the roads which connected San Luis Potosí, Saltillo, Monterrey, and San Antonio, Texas. During the Civil War in the United States, when other foreign markets were closed by the blockade, cotton from Texas and adjoining states offered good trading possibilities, and the profits from the pack and wagon trains were the basis of the Madero fortune. Later it was expanded into the fields of mining, steel rolling mills, wines, farming, and banking. By the time of the revolution in 1910, Evaristo Madero was many times a millionaire, reckoned in either dollars or pesos.

He also served as governor of the state of Coahuila from

1880 to 1884, during the presidency of Manuel González, but was replaced with the reelection of Porfirio Díaz by the latter's good friend, General Bernardo Reyes. Evaristo's two wives presented him with a total of nineteen children, fourteen of whom survived to maturity. At death in 1911 he had thirty-four grandchildren and fifty-six great-grandchildren.

Francisco Indalecio's father, also named Francisco, inherited the family acumen sufficiently to build up a fortune of his own through cattle raising and mining ventures. Francisco's mother was Mercedes González Treviño, the youngest of sixteen children born to the distinguished Treviño family of Monterrey.

As a child Francisco suffered from delicate health and was never robust. He was short, five-feet-three, and seldom took part in the physical contact and competitive sports which interested his brothers and friends, although he was a good swimmer and rider. His early schooling was in Parras and at the age of twelve he attended the Jesuit College of San Juan in Saltillo. The following year, with his younger brother Gustavo, he was sent to St. Mary's College, near Baltimore, Maryland. Though he remained there only one term—and by his own confession learned very little English—the unrestrained atmosphere of the school, as compared to the Mexican schools, remained one of the pleasanter memories of his youth.

In 1887, again with his brother Gustavo, he went to France where he first attended what is now the Lycée Hoche (in Versailles), an elementary school, and then to the School of Advanced Commercial Studies in Paris. There he studied commercial economy, commercial geography, finance, commercial law, shorthand, marketing, cost accounting, and budgetary systems. He remained in Paris until 1892. The French language, unlike English, presented no problem. It was customary in the upper-class families of Mexico of those days to speak in French at all meals; thus, the children grew up speaking it fluently.

The five years Madero spent in France, during which time he traveled a great deal throughout the country and the continent and did not return to Mexico, must have had a great influence on his thinking and his attitudes. When he arrived in Paris in 1887 the country was in the seventeenth year of the Third Republic. Napoleon III and his Empress Eugenie, under whose intrigues Maximilian had ruled briefly and tragically as Emperor of Mexico, had been dethroned by the military calamities of the Franco-Prussian War. France had lost Alsace and Lorraine and incurred a huge indemnity debt to Germany. The country had undergone an internal revolution and civil war, and was, in 1888, just emerging. The last real threat of a coup d'état by a potential dictator had been beaten down. A government that was actually run by the people was becoming stronger month by month.

Madero grew to admire the French and to love the country as a second home, and he watched the emergence of this new democratic nation for five years. He read the great outpouring of modern literature from the French writers—Dumas, Hugo, Balzac, Zola, Daudet, Sardou. Charles Dickens, whose writing so poignantly portrayed the plight of the poor class of that day, was translated and widely read in France.

The people of France and their writers had been conscious of political freedom for a century. Now they were becoming imbued as well with thoughts of social justice, public welfare, and humanity. Some of this, perhaps much of it, must have rubbed off on Francisco Madero, the Mexican student.

After the return from France, Francisco and Gustavo, with two sisters, went to California where the boys enrolled in the University of California at Berkeley and the girls attended a convent school. Francisco had never been good at English and the main purpose of the Berkeley year was to remedy this. His education had always been on the commercial side, intended to fit him for a business career, and when he returned to the Hacienda of the Rosary in 1893 his father had work mapped out for him. He was sent to develop the family property at San Pedro de las Colonias in the southern part of the state, near Torreón and the borders of Durango and Zacatecas.

During the next ten or fifteen years, Francisco must have been a study in contrasts to his family and to the wealthy *hacendado* class to which he belonged, and would always belong. He proved himself a successful businessman by introducing irrigation, improved strains of cotton, and better farming methods to the *mestizo* farmers of San Pedro. He installed modern machinery, and made a study of damming the Nazas River to store water during the frequent droughts. The study was sent to José Ives Limantour, finance minister and leader of the *científicos,* who was well acquainted with the family. (Several members of the extensive Madero clan were associated with the technocratically-inclined *científicos.*) Limantour showed the study to Díaz, who, reportedly, was impressed.

On the other hand, Francisco was several miles (and years) ahead of his time in his ideas of social welfare. He had the notion, far advanced for that day in Mexico, that well-fed, well-housed, and reasonably content workers more than paid for the costs in added production. While making a personal fortune of more than a quarter of a million pesos, he also raised wages, provided decent quarters for his tenants, plus— wonder of wonders—medical care. He established schools and required his workers to send their children. One year, after a drought, he promoted and sold to his neighboring *hacen-*

dados the idea of free soup kitchens for the peons. Madero himself fed fifty or sixty children, most of them orphans, every day at his own home.

The fact that he had proved himself an innovative and successful businessman did not prevent his family from regarding Francisco and his concern with the peons as a little impractical, and more than a little peculiar. He did not sit at the highest levels in the family conferences, or if he did, his voice did not carry the weight an eldest son's should have.

In 1901, Francisco was twenty-eight years old. He was short of figure, barely over five feet, and slim but well proportioned and not unimpressive, as his portraits of the time indicate. His forehead was prominent, accentuated by black hair which was beginning to recede. The lower part of his face was enclosed in beard and mustache which, together, formed an oval. His mouth was wide and his eyes a compelling deep brown. His voice was shrill and tended to become more so when he was excited, but he was an effective speaker. He loved to ride and was almost passionately fond of dancing. He liked beer and wine and was a chain-smoker of cigarettes. (A few years later he decided he was becoming too self-indulgent. He gave up cigarettes and alcohol, and became a vegetarian.)

In 1903 he married Sara Pérez, a friend of his sister with whom he had fallen in love a few years earlier. Since he had done nothing about this emotion (which apparently had been obvious to Sara), he had to persevere for some months in his courtship and to perform all sorts of acts of contrition before she consented. Her father, Marcario Pérez, a wealthy landowner, was definitely not in favor of Francisco as a son-in-law and declined to attend the wedding. It took place in Mexico City on January 26, 1903.

Madero took his bride to San Pedro where they occupied

a pleasant home. Francisco continued his successful development operations and continued also his small social crusade,
with which Sara apparently was in full sympathy. Madero's
dismay at the conditions under which the Mexican peons
lived must have been contagious and imbued his wife with
the same feelings. A recent study of those days by the Educational Systems Corporation, a private, nonprofit organization
in the United States, presents an excellent picture of the
people and the times. It may all seem remote now, but it was
only a little more than half a century ago.

There were two types of peons in the countryside, the resident peon or *peon acasillado,* and the nonresident peon or
peon alquilado. Most workers were resident peons, bound to
the soil and their homes by a system of advanced payments.
A resident peon was usually so poor that he had to borrow
from the landowner before payday to buy what his family
needed. When payday came around, his debts were subtracted
from his wages, leaving him little or nothing.

So the resident peon could never get out of debt. He could
not move in order to find a better job because his wages were
so low he could never repay what he had borrowed. If he
tried to run off, he was jailed. In jail he earned nothing.

When the peons had a little money left over they could
only spend it conveniently at the *tienda de raya* or country
store maintained by the *hacendado.* Therefore, the landowner got not only the worker's debt repayment but also any
money he had left over.

The nonresident peon usually lived in a village or *pueblo*
near a hacienda. The *hacendado* brought him to the hacienda
at certain times of year, usually when the harvest was due.
Once the villages of the nonresident peons had their own
lands, the Indian lands or *ejidos,* which they cultivated, simply adding to their incomes by working extra on the haci-

endas. But these were the lands which Díaz had given away as political favors.

In the cities few men were educated, for the government spent little on building schools or training teachers. A man considered himself lucky if he completed three years of grade school. After that, he had to help support his family.

A young boy often went to work by the time he was ten. If he was lucky he might find work sweeping out a shop and stacking goods on the shelves. Other boys cleaned shoes or ran errands. There were no set wages and the boy was at the mercy of the employer. Often instead of money he was given food or an article of castoff clothing. Mexico badly needed artisans—carpenters, blacksmiths, masons, and the like, but very few boys were able to learn a trade.

The publication continues with many examples of both the rural and urban poverty which was prevalent in the early twentieth century in Mexico. One phase of it, and one which Francisco and Sara Madero must have seen repeated a hundred times is that of the young girl of the average rural peon family.

Her home was a crowded shack with a leaky roof and a dirt floor, her meals a few *tortillas,* beans, or *frijoles.* If she survived infancy the girl would become a full-fledged and full-time field hand or houseworker by the time she was seven years old. She rose before sunrise to start the fire for a sparse breakfast. While the little girl went to draw water from a communal well or stream in a heavy clay jar, her mother prepared the corn meal for *tortillas.* Soon the rest of the family was up and the daughter helped care for her young brothers and sisters while her mother served the simple meal.

How she spent the rest of the day depended on the season. If the planting was going on or the harvest due, she went into the fields. She might be called up to the main house where she would help out in the kitchen, or clean the house or wind wool or run errands for the ladies of the hacienda. Going up to the main house was hard work, but it was better than working in the fields, and if the girl was lucky she would get a good meal and maybe some leftovers to take home.

By fourteen she was married and by fifteen caring for her first child. In most families of the Mexican countryside in the early 1900s, the teen-age girl was looked upon as a grown woman.

Shortly after the elections of 1904, when Díaz was returned to office by the usual "large majority," along with his Vice President, Ramón Corral, Madero began to get interested in politics. (Díaz had selected Corral as a running mate, or so the story goes, because of his unpopularity; Corral was so disliked, so hated, in fact, that Díaz was sure he, himself, would never be assassinated as long as the assassin knew Corral would succeed him in office.) Madero began to organize Anti-reelection clubs and he backed an opposition slate for state offices. It was not elected but it served to get Madero better known in the state of Coahuila.

Then in 1908 came his book, *The Presidential Succession of 1910,* and his sudden catapulting to popularity and prominence. The book, incidentally, was the subject of tremendous controversy within Madero's own family before it was published. He sent it to his grandfather, Evaristo, who didn't believe he had written it himself (nor did a lot of the other people, but there is overwhelming evidence that he did). His parents, too, withheld their sanction for months and Francisco's only support within the Madero clan came from his brother, Gustavo, and his sisters. In justification of the doubts of the elder Madero family members, it must be remembered that they themselves belonged to the strata of Mexican society which kept Díaz in office, that they really believed, along with the *cientificos,* that the lower classes lacked the intelligence to guide their own destinies—and that they knew well that opposing the old dictator was like twisting the lion's tail.

The family finally capitulated, however, and the book appeared. It was outrageously sentimental and frankly political propaganda, as the author admitted. This very admission made the book more appealing. Out of its pages Madero emerged as a kind, liberal, thoughtful man, a believer in social progress and in man's humanity to man. He was a patriot, a man for the people, a man for Mexico. These things were almost forgotten factors in the country, forgotten since Morelos and Juárez. They stirred memories—and hope.

The book's first edition sold out in three months, and the second and third almost as quickly. It lifted Madero from his position of the unknown man into instant prominence and made him the focal point and the beloved leader of the opposition against the dictator Díaz.

The book was in three parts. The first dealt with Mexican history, particularly with the dangers inherent in military domination of government, of which he certainly had plenty of examples. In the second part Madero went back into antiquity to demonstrate the dangers of absolute power. He then listed the accomplishments of the Díaz regime, but he balanced these against the offenses, economic and other, which had been committed against the nation and its people. Finally, in the last section, he concluded that Díaz had no intention of bowing out in 1910, nor would he permit the country to name a Vice President. This latter point, actually, was the main purpose of the book. Madero was not unwilling to see Díaz elected one more time, possibly because he felt that the old man could not live through another term at his age, but he predicated the main thrust of his book on the Vice President. The people should name the man who was on the second spot of the ticket and who would succeed Díaz if he died.

After the book came out, and after Madero began to attract great crowds to his rallies, Díaz sent for him and the two had a long conversation. Madero carefully explained to Díaz that his major purpose was to stimulate the electorate, to get them to take the election seriously. The dictator listened carefully, and told Madero he admired these sentiments, but he still had trouble considering Madero as anything more dangerous than a gadfly, while Madero came away from the interview amazed at the old man's lack of understanding of the times, of Mexico, and even of current events. Díaz was, he said, getting senile.

In April, 1910, a few months before the balloting time, the Anti-reelectionists held a convention. Madero was nominated President and a former Díaz supporter (and family physician) Francisco Vasquez Gómez, was named for the vice presidential spot. In June, Madero was arrested and remained in confinement until after the election results were announced. Díaz and Corral were, of course, reelected and Díaz threw Madero a few votes.

As related earlier, Madero escaped and went to the United States from where, in San Antonio, Texas, he enunciated the Plan of San Luis Potosí, calling the Díaz election null and void. This was followed by the rebellion, the military successes of Pasqual Orozco, Pancho Villa, Emiliano Zapata, and others, and the overthrow of Porfirio Díaz in May of 1911.

Francisco de la Barra, a lawyer and former diplomat in the Díaz government, was named as provisional President to hold the office until, as it was correctly presumed, Madero could be legally elected. De la Barra had agreed to the plan of free elections and had pledged that he would, under no circumstances, run as a candidate.

Madero left Coahuila early in June for the capital. The direct rail line was under repair so he had to take another route, traveling over United States territory to Eagle Pass, Texas, and thence across the border to Cuidad Porfirio Díaz— now Piedras Negras. He was greeted by large, friendly crowds at every stop, both in the United States and Mexico. At San Pedro de las Colonias, his old home, more than five thousand people turned out, including a chorus of little girls who sang the Mexican national anthem, *El Himno Nacional.*

After Torreón, scarcely a mile of the rail line was clear of admirers who had come on foot, on burro, and on horseback to catch a glimpse of the slight figure of Madero. He arrived in Mexico City at midmorning on June 7, 1911. At daylight that morning, a mild earthquake had shaken the city. This did nothing to quiet the enthusiasm of the throngs but did produce a ditty that was soon on the lips of everyone:

> *Cuando Madero llegó*
> *Hasta la tierra tembló*

> When Madero arrived
> Even the earth trembled

It was a good omen and as Madero rode from the station up the Paseo de la Reforma, which had been conceived by the Emperor Maximilian and built by the dictator, Díaz, one of the greatest throngs in Mexican history shouted a tremendous welcome to the "Apostle of the Revolution." Cathedral bells rang, bands played—the Mexican people gave voice to a violent release of long pent-up emotions. At the palace Madero was received by the interim President and both faced the cheering crowd from the balcony.

It was the hour of Madero's greatest triumph, and it would be kind if history could write the end of his life and career at this moment when he was the idol of his nation and quite probably deserved to be.

But triumph did not continue. The arrangement of the interim presidency did not work out. Madero's close supporters, and the people, generally, looked to him for leadership, while de la Barra, somewhat naturally, expected to actually run the country. He had been named to bridge the gap between the old regime and the revolution, but he was still a conservative, still a Porfirista. Only three members of the revolution—one being Madero's brother, Ernesto Madero, and another his cousin, Rafael Hernández—were named to the cabinet and the remainder were holdovers from the Díaz regime. All of the top civil servants had been Porfiristas, naturally, and they were left in their positions because they were most efficient—and because it was the path of least resistance.

Meantime, the Anti-reelection Party, which had evolved itself into the Revolutionary Party, had been reorganized and renamed the Progressive Constitutional Party. It convened at the Hidalgo Theater in Mexico City on August 27, 1911, and duly nominated Madero. He had no opposition. There was, however, serious contention for the second place on the ticket but the convention finally settled on José María Pino Suárez, a confirmed revolutionist from Yucatán, who had been Madero's choice. Pino Suárez was forty years old, Madero was thirty-six. The only candidate against Madero in the campaign was General Bernardo Reyes, the former governor of Coahuila and no friend of the Madero family, though Madero had permitted him to come home from the exile ordered by Díaz. He withdrew after the Madero supporters stoned one of his rallies, but remained in Mexico and caused a great deal of trouble later.

In what was probably the cleanest election in Mexico's history, Madero and Suárez were overwhelmingly elected in October. On November 6, Madero appeared before the Chamber of Deputies and was sworn in as President.

The very qualities which had made the Mexican people love him were the qualities which betrayed Madero in the presidency. He was trustworthy and because he was, he expected other people to be. Because his intentions were inherently good, it never occurred to him that he would have to impose them on others by the strongest of measures. He was kind and honest and sincere. Despite his rather intensive study of historical leaders and their behavior, including those of Mexico, he expected the people around him to be equally motivated. Unfortunately, they were not.

And equally as unfortunate, Madero continued with the policies of his predecessor, de la Barra, after he, himself, assumed the presidency. Hoping to unite the people and the parties and effect a political reform, he balanced the cabinet between his own revolutionaries and the old Porfiristas. He did not realize that these old Díaz hands could not even comprehend political reform, much less carry it out. The words freedom and democracy, which meant so much to Madero, were merely words to them.

Unfortunately also, Madero's goal was freedom for the people, but he did not understand—though he should have—that freedom for the great mass of Mexican people was irrevocably tied to economic reform and that the greatest problem of his country was the redistribution of the millions upon millions of acres of land which Díaz had given away as political favors. For some reason, the euphoric goal of freedom—in itself rather mystical to the Mexican people—obscured the very things which had originally stirred Madero's conscience and that of his wife, Sara. He forgot that he had been first moved by the plight of the virtually enslaved peons *acasillado* and *alquilado,* the jobless boy in the city and the girl on the hacienda whose work-life started at age seven.

When he failed to move toward any kind of land reform, his old revolutionary friends at first deserted him and then turned against him. They were living day to day with the problems Madero had forgotten. The first to turn were Zapata and Orozco, and then Carranza. They were joined by new names—a young rancher, Alvaro Obregón, and a young lieutenant of his, Elías Calles, who, if not in actual opposition, were very suspicious of Madero's policies. One who never turned, who always remained loyal, was Villa.

The old revolutionists, however, were only indirectly involved in the overthrow of the Madero government and the tragedy of his death. The chief villain was Victoriano Huerta. Huerta had been a Díaz general and at his orders had subjugated the Mayas and turned them into slaves for the "henequen kings." De la Barra had sent him to Morelos to pacify the wily Zapata, who both eluded him and laughed at him. Huerta was ruthless and competent as a military man; he was ambitious, cunning, and treacherous, and a monumental drunkard.

The three lesser figures who obligingly and unwittingly paved the way for Huerta's triumph were the old reactionary, Bernardo Reyes; a nephew of the exiled dictator, Félix Díaz; and another Porfirista, Miguel Mondragón, who had grafted his way to a considerable fortune as head of the artillery branch of the Díaz army.

Both General Reyes and Félix Díaz were in prison in Mexico City. General Mondragón was still on active duty. Huerta was in the capital, drinking heavily. President Francisco Madero, along with his brother, Gustavo, had heard reports of an impending coup d'état attempt, but had been unable to trace them into anything solid. Also they had been busy with a round of seasonal official functions, plus trying to cope with the government of the United States, which had grown unsympathetic to Madero's regime.

The rebel action came at dawn on February 8, 1913, and began what is known in Mexican history as "The Ten Tragic Days." Two regiments in the army barracks at the Mexico City suburb of Tacubaya, under command of General Mondragón, marched to Tlatelolco where they released Reyes and thence to the federal prison where they freed Félix Díaz.

Meantime, according to plan, the palace guard had seized command of the National Palace and was expected to hold it for Reyes, Félix Díaz, and Mondragón. However, Gustavo Madero had been warned. He went to the palace where, with a tremendous appeal to the patriotism of the guardsmen, he won them over and placed the palace guard troops under the command of General Lauro Villar, a loyal Maderista.

General Villar was competent. Under orders to defend the palace, he prepared to do that to the best of his military ability. Snipers were placed on the palace roof. Other riflemen were spaced in double ranks across the plaza in front of the building. Mortars were set in the doorways, and machine guns were stationed for effective use.

An advance column of rebels moved into the palace plaza, saw the defenders, and promptly surrendered. A few minutes later the main body, led by General Reyes, followed. General Villar called on Reyes to halt but he continued the advance and Villar gave the order to fire. General Reyes fell, fatally wounded by several bullets. Villar was hit but continued to command and the battle raged on for ten minutes. The most deadly effect was on scores of civilians who had been on their way to Mass and were caught in the cross fire.

When he learned of the plaza battle, Francisco Madero left

Chapultepec and hurried to the palace, surrounded by the cadets of the military school, where he found his forces victorious but leaderless. The bullet Villar took had shattered his collar bone and he was definitely out of consideration for command. Able Felipe Angeles, whom Madero trusted, had been sent to subdue Zapata after Huerta had failed in that mission. The only other general about was Huerta and Madero did not trust him but was forced to place him in command. Huerta pledged undying loyalty and unswerving faithfulness to Madero. He then took command with ultimate treachery in mind.

General Mondragón and Félix Díaz had taken their troops to the Ciudadela, an old fortress which had been converted to a governmental arsenal, and there they were holed up with a considerable force of men, artillery, and ammunition. The Ciudadela is a long, one-story building with walls four feet thick, surrounded by broad streets. Between it and the National Palace, a distance of about one mile, lies the main business district of Mexico City. From these strong points, the two opposing forces shelled each other and launched attack and counterattack. Stanley Ross, in his book on Madero, wrote: ". . . There followed ten days of military sham. It was a ten-day lugubrious farce with terror, suffering, and death for countless noncombants and with extensive property damage. Federal artillery was badly placed and ineffectively employed. Loyal troops were sent to be slaughtered by the entrenched defenders who received supplies from the outside despite federal encirclement. The bloody hoax was played to the last card with a callous disregard for innocent sufferers."

The whole ten-day "sham" was engineered by Huerta, who had planned—and planned well—to permit the revolutionists to win, to overthrow the government of Madero, and to trick both Mondragón and Félix Díaz. During the entire ten days he was in constant touch with Díaz and with the United States Ambassador, Henry Lane Wilson.

While presumably representing his country, Wilson actually was more concerned with the monied interests in the United States. He had tried to maneuver Madero and failed, and Madero distrusted him with a good cause. He sent reports back to President Taft which were misleading, if not completely false, and in the ten-day rebellion of 1913, he was chiefly concerned with getting Madero out and Félix Díaz in. Díaz he could work with.

On February 18 Victoriano Huerta decided the time was right, that the Mexican public was so sick of the constant killing within the city that they would go along with anything. Bodies had piled up by the hundreds and there was no time to bury them; they were stacked in piles, drenched with kerosene, and burned in the streets.

General Huerta, having decided to act, invited Gustavo Madero to lunch to keep him out of the way—a luncheon he stretched out, with one excuse and another, to four hours. During that time a subordinate, acting under Huerta's orders, went with a squad of soldiers to the palace where he placed President Madero and Vice President Pino Suárez under arrest. When word reached Huerta that this had been effected, he had Gustavo Madero arrested also. He then went himself to the National Palace where a beating drum and a few shouts quickly collected a sizable crowd. Huerta told the throng that the cannonading and the street fighting was over; he was in charge, he said, and there would be peace in the capital and in the country.

The ultimate treachery of Huerta now came into play. By promising to send them into exile, he persuaded the arrested Madero and Pino Suárez to resign. The presidency, under

Mexican law, now fell to Pedro Lascurain, Minister of Foreign Affairs. After making Huerta swear that he would spare the lives of Madero and Pino Suárez, Lascurain named Huerta to be Minister of Foreign Affairs and then Lascurain resigned. Congress was dubious and a little bewildered when confronted by this succession of legalities, but finally accepted all three resignations. Huerta thus automatically succeeded to the presidency.

Unbeknownst to Francisco Madero, his brother Gustavo had been turned over to the rebels in the Ciudadela where he was tortured before being shot. It had been arranged with the Cuban Ambassador, Manuel Márquez Sterling, that Francisco Madero and Pino Suárez would be received in exile in Cuba, but after the death of Gustavo became known, the Madero family became concerned for the safety of the two prisoners. They were joined by most of the diplomatic corps of Mexico. The Ambassadors signed petitions which, as a matter of protocol, went to America's Henry Lane Wilson, who was senior in service in the corps. Madero's mother and wife also called upon Wilson, asking that the United States intervene to insure the safety of Madero and Pino Suárez. Wilson made no such move.

Francisco learned of the death of his brother Gustavo on February 22, from his mother, who spent several hours with him in his cell. That same night, still in tears from the sad news, he was aroused, with Pino Suárez, and informed that they were being taken from the National Palace to the penitentiary. Each was placed in a car. Madero's escort was Major Francisco Cárdenas and Pino Suárez' was Lieutenant Rafael Pimienta.

At the gates of the penitentiary they were shot to death. Major Cárdenas and Lieutenant Pimienta reported officially that an angry, armed mob surrounded them and fired into the cars, killing both men. As evidence, they presented the automobiles, both bullet-ridden.

A day passed before the bodies of the two men were turned over to their families, on February 24, for burial. The coffin carrying Francisco Madero was taken to the French cemetery where it was opened briefly while a crucifix was slipped inside at the request of his widow, Sara. That night Sara, Francisco's parents, sisters, and his brother Ernesto, and family went by train to Veracruz and thence by boat to Havana. Brothers Emilio, Alfonso, and Raoul Madero went to the United States.

Both Major Cárdenas and Lieutenant Pimienta received promotions from President Huerta a few weeks later. Generals Mondragón and Félix Díaz received assignments to distant ambassadorial posts.

PANCHO VILLA AND
EMILIANO ZAPATA

FOR NEARLY a decade during and after the Mexican Revolution of 1910, Pancho Villa and Emiliano Zapata controlled most of Mexico's countryside and influenced in one way or another the lives of most of Mexico's ten million people. Villa ruled in the north and Zapata ruled in the south. Their lives were remarkably parallel.

Both came of *mestizo* forebears and were thrust outside the law while still in their teens. Each acquired an idealism rooted in the cause of Mexico's landless peon class. They never were guilty of treachery to any man they served. Neither wanted to be President—though they could and did seat and unseat Presidents. Both died by assassination at about the age of forty.

Doroteo Arango, who became Francisco "Pancho" Villa, was born in July, 1882, in a tiny thatch-roofed hut in Rio Grande, a cluster of similar huts on the Hacienda del Norte which was part of the vast Rancho Santa Catalina owned by one Don Pablo Martínez. His parents, part-Spanish, part-Tarahumare Indian, were Agustín and Carmen Arango. There were two other sons, Hipolito and Antonio, and two girl children, Mariana and Martina.

Agustín Arango died of tuberculosis when Doroteo was

seven. The boy, according to the custom of the times, went to work in the fields of the hacienda, hoeing, weeding, picking bugs off the plants by hand, harvesting. The village land had been given away by President Díaz and the peons worked now for Don Pablo, the *hacendado,* and for wages of a penny or two an hour.

When Doroteo was twelve or thereabouts, he began working part-time for Pascual Orozco, who ran a pack train to Guanacevi and other nearby towns. Doreteo began accompanying Orozco on the trips. He was paid a peso for each, a great sum for him—and for his mother—at that time. More, he learned to handle mules and horses and, most importantly, he learned the trails of the countryside, the hidden canyons and springs of fresh water. Doroteo gave his pesos, one by one, to his mother until they were able to buy a lame burro which they nursed back to health and which gave the boy the nucleus of his own pack train.

At this same time Doroteo succumbed to a malady that was quite common to boys of his age—the urge to become a *charro,* a cowboy. He took jobs herding cattle so that he could ride the horses of the *hacendado,* and he practiced with the lariat until roping became almost reflex action. He spent so many hours in the saddle that horsemanship, too, became second nature.

With his earnings from cattle herding and his frequent pack trips, he outfitted himself with the costume of the *charro:* the tight breeches, with buttons up the sides of the legs, the ruffled shirt and tight leather jacket, the big ornamented sombrero and the star-shaped spurs. Silver was not expensive and it made handsome adornments for his saddle and for the black holster and revolver which completed the outfit. He began competing in rodeos, and within a few months had acquired a reputation and considerable prize money. From here he went to breaking horses, a dangerous job with good pay.

He was, at this time, fifteen years old, and with two hundred pesos he had saved, Doroteo bought a small plot of ground at the nearby Hacienda de Gogojito. He moved his mother and sisters there and undertook to return to farming.

A wiser and older person might have told Doroteo and his mother that they were heading from one form of bondage into another which might be worse. The money they had barely paid for the ground. For the farming tools and seed, as well as their own food, they had to go in debt to the hacienda store and thus they were tied to the land. Legally they literally belonged to the *hacendado* until they had paid off the debt. This form of existence was one of the curses of Mexico.

After a year of trying to wring a living for the Arango family from the Gogojito land, Doroteo determined to escape. (Being in debt to the *hacendado,* it was illegal for him to leave the property). Swearing to his mother that he would return with enough money to buy them out of bondage, the sixteen-year-old took his one horse and, dressed in his working clothes—light cotton pants and shirt—he took to the hills. He planned to join the locally famous bandit, Don Ignacio Parra, who operated in the adjoining state of Chihuahua. In the pursuit which inevitably followed, Doroteo was caught by the *rurales.* He quite easily might have been treated to the *ley fuga,* or law of escape—that is, he might have been shot "while trying to escape" because it would have been simpler than bringing him in. Fortunately for the boy, the lieutenant knew him by sight and also knew his reputation as a horseman. So he permitted him to escape instead, and Doroteo made his way on foot to the "Dove's Nest" where Don Ignacio and his band holed up between cattle raids and other depredations on the countryside.

After convincing Don Ignacio that he was true bandit material and not an informer, and also that he now had a price on his head, Doroteo was given his initiation in stealing a few head of cattle from the Chihuahua barons and then was dispatched to Chihuahua city to serve as a pair of ears for possible silver or gold shipments through the Chihuahua trails from which Don Ignacio extracted largess.

The sister of Doroteo's mother lived in Chihuahua city and he lived with her and her husband while he got a job as a *lechero* delivering milk, and where he decided, since he was a fugitive, it would be wise to change his name. The surname of "Villa" was common in the area and thirty years before, a locally famous bandit by the name of Francisco Villa had enjoyed a brief fame. To the somewhat amusement of his aunt and uncle, Doroteo decided on Francisco Villa—or Pancho Villa, since Pancho is the affectionate diminutive for Francisco—and that became his name thereafter.

There are almost endless stories of Pancho Villa and while those in his later years can usually be checked to sort out fact from legend, the tales of his youth are more difficult. Two or three, however, are fairly well established.

Pancho, who soon became the chief lieutenant of Don Ignacio, was not then the terror of the Chihuahua hills that reports have made him. He and the handful of men with whom he worked, however, were as clever as herd dogs in cutting out for themselves a few of the cattle of Alberto and Luis Terrazas, whose acres were numbered in the millions and livestock in the thousands of heads. And they did occasionally pounce like marauding cats on a pack train or stagecoach which carried a shipment of silver. From these swift hit-and-run raids, Pancho was able to give his mother enough money to pay her way out of debt, she being careful not to reveal the source of her funds.

He was only seventeen when he paid a visit to his mother's home one night, called by some subconscious force which his Indian forebears would have understood, to find his sister Martina shaking with sobs and his mother stiff in white-faced anger. Martina had been raped by the son of the *hacendado,* a bored young aristocrat with a well-known record of similar assaults. Pancho killed the man.

Months later, after he had taken on more of the leadership of the *banditos* in the "Dove's Nest," one of their enterprises ran into ambush and near-disaster. Pancho learned that one of the band, Felipe Reza, detailed to Chihuahua in advance of the raid, had been caught and had talked to save his own neck.

Villa rode into Chihuahua city early the next morning and went to a barbershop where he shaved off his mustache with one hand while he held a pistol on the barber with the other. Then, gently admonishing the man to a continued silence under pain of a lingering death, he went out into the street.

Pancho did not drink or smoke, but he was passionately fond of sweets. Ice cream he could not resist, nor candy, especially peanut brittle, which he ate by the pound when it was available. This morning he stood, clean-shaven, on a street corner by an ice cream vendor. The morning wore on but Pancho's appetite withstood the test and he was still eating ice cream when Reza, with two other men, walked by. Villa called softly, "Felipe," and as the three turned, he motioned the other men aside. Then he drew and fired. He paused for a moment, looked down at the informer, and made his way to his tethered horse. He mounted and rode out of town.

Emiliano Zapata was born on August 8, 1879, in the village of Anenecuilco, state of Morelos. His father was Joaquín and his mother Cleofas, both Guerrero Indians mixed with Spanish blood. He had one sister, Catarina, and a brother, Eufemio. The senior Zapata owned a small ranch and the family, while far from rich, was not poverty-stricken.

Emiliano and his brother grew up together, played, rode, hunted, fished, and later fought together. Eufemio was bigger and brawnier; the younger Emiliano was the brainier of the pair. In fact, Emiliano's reputation for intelligence and acumen was so great that he was chosen village *jefe* while he was still in his twenties and was regarded as the community leader. Like the farmers of the Durango village into which Pancho Villa was born, Zapata's friends had lost their lands when they were given away by the free-handed Díaz and they now worked on shares in the fields that had once been community property. Righting the plight of these people through agrarian reform became, in time, the cause for which Emiliano fought, first for Madero and then against him, and against other Presidents. It was the cause for which he gave his life.

The senior Zapata died in 1897 when Emiliano was eighteen. He continued farming but eventually bought mules and formed his own pack train, operating to Cuernavaca and Puebla. As it did for Villa, this gave young Zapata a detailed acquaintanceship with the countryside which was to be his battlefield for almost ten years after 1910. During his early twenties, Zapata also had the *charro* urge and became an expert roper and rider.

The stories, part fact, part legend, which surround Emiliano Zapata are as many and often as wild as those linked with the name of Pancho Villa. Certainly on one occasion he led an agrarian revolt of his villagers in an attempt to reclaim their land—an attempt which ended with Zapata being jailed. Most of the stories about the slight, wiry, mustachioed, and handsome 'Miliano (as he was called) were born and embel-

lished after the elections of 1910 when he turned revolutionist.

In the summer of 1910 the crusade of Francisco Madero
gathered force and grew into the Mexican Revolution of
1910. That autumn Don Abraham González, the Anti-reelectionist leader of Chihuahua, asked Pancho Villa to raise his
own army and gave him a commission as captain. It didn't
take too much persuasion. For some fifteen years Villa had
been marauding through the mountains of the state, stealing
cattle and any loose silver, gold, or guns left unguarded. But
Pancho had really little interest in the money he stole except
in the pleasure it brought him to give it away, some to his
family, but much more to the poor peons of Chihuahua and
Durango. During these years he had seen much of the *rurales*
and *soldados* of President Porfirio Díaz, had seen men lashed
for the smallest of wrong doing, killed for protesting the loss
of their land. He himself had been shot at too often and spent
too many weary hours and days dodging the Díaz enforcers.

He accepted his commission and sent his fifteen *bandidos*
through the hills of his two home states and a month later reported back with a respectable army of 350 mounted and
armed men.

By late fall of 1910, Villa had joined forces with his old
mentor, the wagon master and *arriero* Pascual Orozco, and
both were part of the Madero revolutionary army. Villa never
liked Orozco, who had pretensions to being an aristocrat, but
he was willing to fight on the same side with him.

They cut the railroad between Chihuahua city and Juárez
and by the end of the year, after several small victorious battles, they were pretty well in control of the southern end of
the state and looking northward. And while they were campaigning there, the revolution had caught fire in other states,

principally in Morelos. There, Zapata had started fighting the *hacendados* and had ended up with a force of irregulars which controlled a sizable chunk of the state very close to Mexico City and parts of neighboring Guerrero. The victories of Zapata and Villa inspired other guerrilla leaders and soon there were uprisings and battles in half a dozen states—Sonora, Guerrero, Veracruz, Tabasco, Oaxaca, and Yucatán. The people of Mexico were thoroughly sick of Porfirio Díaz after thirty-odd years.

In March of 1911, Madero grouped his generals, his advisors, and his forces a few miles south of Juárez. Besides the Madero brothers, the meeting was attended by Abraham González, the political leader of Chihuahua, by Governor José María Maytorena of Sonora, Venustiano Carranza, governor of Coahuila (and who was to become the bitter enemy of both Villa and Zapata), and by Orozco and Villa.

Violent arguments ensued between Villa and Carranza as to whether it was best to assault Juárez or lay siege to Chihuahua city, and Madero made no decision. Meantime, 1,500 government troops, led by General Juan J. Navarro, stationed themselves in a ring around Juárez.

Madero called upon Navarro to surrender and Navarro refused. Not wanting to risk his entire force in an encounter at this point, Madero gave strict orders to Villa and Orozco not to attack. But he failed to credit Pancho Villa with the natively innocent deceit which had made him such a great bandit in his earlier years.

Filling old tin cans, bottles, and leather bags with dynamite, nails, screws, bolts—any small pieces of metal they could find—Villa's men literally blew the federal forces out of the first line of defense. Orozco, fearing that Villa would capture the city and thus the glory, moved in on the flanks. After a day's fighting, the two joined forces and, using the same kind of homemade bombs, blew out Juárez homes and public buildings and took the city. On May 10, 1911, Navarro surrendered and Madero held Juárez. Two weeks later Díaz resigned and the government was placed in the hands of a caretaker until Madero could be legally elected.

When Madero was installed as President and named his cabinet, it was one of aristocrats. Pancho Villa felt that the men who had fought and risked their lives for Madero, the men who had fought with him, with Zapata and the other guerrilla leaders, should have had a voice in the new government which would replace the tyranny of Díaz. In the fury and frustration of the moment, Pancho accepted a 10,000 peso payment for his services, turned his men over to Raoul Madero, and resigned.

Emiliano Zapata's cause, which he came by early and never gave up, was to force the return of public and Indian lands which had been given away by Díaz. When Madero pronounced the Plan of San Luis Potosí, he had dwelt long on political freedom, open elections, and no reelections. He had also included one paragraph promising the return of the Indian lands and espousing agrarian reform in general. So Zapata had immediately declared for Madero and against Díaz.

Zapata, like other revolutionaries who had been fighting for the same ideal of land reform, expected Madero to act immediately after Díaz fled the country. But Madero seemed to forget, after his arrival before cheering thousands in Mexico City in June, 1911. His cabinet, half of them old Porfiristas for harmony's sake, convinced him to go slowly. For Zapata this was not good enough. He met with Madero, but there were no assurances and no moves toward agrarian reform. After Madero's election, when he still took no action, Zapata declared the hero of the revolution was a traitor to the people who had supported him, and he resumed the revolution. Victoriano Huerta, the Porfirista general who was to prove himself the most treacherous figure in Mexican history, was sent to subdue Zapata. Huerta just missed capturing him and for several months harried his forces, but in the end he could not pacify the states where Zapata's guerrilla forces operated and he was recalled.

Though both made sincere efforts, Madero and Zapata were never reconciled. Madero sent out half a dozen expeditions, some punitive and some with promises of amnesty and even action on land reform if Zapata would disarm his men. Zapata finally exploded in anger: "I have been Señor Madero's most faithful partisan. But no more. Madero has betrayed me as well as the army and the people of Morelos and the nation."

Meanwhile, Pancho Villa had gone into retirement, but was called back into action by Madero, who asked him to raise an army and take the field against his old *compañero* (though no friend), Pascual Orozco. Orozco had turned against Madero and was attempting to overthrow his government. Villa, always ready for a fight, accepted.

After a few weeks—and a few victories—Madero asked Villa to place himself under General Huerta, who was in overall command of the federal forces. Villa reported to Huerta at his headquarters in Torreón. The two disliked each other on sight and had constant trouble, but Villa was willing to fight under Huerta's command—and did, heroically.

For several weeks Villa's men led every attack on the Orozco forces, wherever they could be found. Finally, on May 24, 1911, the main bodies of the Huerta and the Orozco armies met at Rellano, a small town on the railroad between Torreón and Ciudad Camargo. Given the assignment of blocking a reinforcement force of some 2,000 men, Villa ambushed them, cut them up badly and then circled around and fell on their camp to effect a complete rout.

For his action here, highly contributory to the Huerta victory, Villa was promoted again. This probably was just one of the events which led Huerta to decide that in addition to being an insolent inferior, Villa was also a dangerous threat. So when Pancho refused to give up a beautiful mare he had "liberated" and fancied, and when he contemptuously ignored a Huerta command to report to him that moment and explain, Huerta wrote out a death sentence for insubordination. He sent a squad of armed men to roust Pancho out of bed, placed him in a cell with the execution order to be carried out at dawn. Learning of it, Raoul Madero frantically telegraphed his brother in Mexico City. The reprieve, which Huerta dared not ignore, reached headquarters while Villa was being marched to the execution wall. Instead, he was taken to Mexico City and tossed into jail.

On July 30, 1911, General Huerta made his triumphant entry into Mexico City. Pancho Villa was still in jail, but in November, he bribed a clerk into sawing his prison bars and permitting him to escape to El Paso in the United States.

In February, 1913, Huerta had Madero murdered and assumed the presidency. Of all his enmities—and Villa had many—his hatred for Victoriano Huerta was paramount and after brooding for several weeks he, with eight companions, swam their horses across the Río Grande on March 13, 1913, and began his "conquest" of Mexico.

Summoning his old troops took only a few weeks and during the summer Pancho trounced the federal forces in at least six battles, collecting men and arms as he won. His army grew to ten, then twenty thousand, and his personal brigade acquired the name of the *Dorados*—the "Golden Ones"—as he conquered more and more of Mexico.

Meanwhile, in the south, Emiliano Zapata was gradually pushing the boundaries of his control to the seacoasts in both directions. Whereas Villa robbed, killed, and took wives where he found them available without benefit of divorce, Zapata was not casually immoral nor casual about killing. He fought mainly to regain land which he immediately turned over to his peasant followers. Neither Zapata nor Villa sought to amass riches and neither really wished to plunder the nation.

The third revolutionary force in the field against Huerta was the white-bearded former governor of Coahuila, Venustiano Carranza, and his able lieutenant, Alvaro Obregón. Huerta foresaw defeat and fled the country, a convention was held to select an interim President, and Eulalio Gutiérrez, a general from San Luis Potosí, was named.

Obregón's army had been first into Mexico City, followed by Zapata and in turn by Pancho Villa and his forces, including the superbly armed and mounted *Dorados*.

The general of the south and the general of the north agreed to a meeting on neutral ground, and they found each other *simpático* and their aims the same—a free government and land for the peons. They arranged a parade of their armies for the following Sunday, December 6.

It was the greatest array of military might Mexico City had ever seen, possibly 50,000 men, forming into columns and marching down the Paseo de la Reforma to the National Palace. For the occasion Villa put aside his fighting clothes and wore a dark blue uniform with high leather leggings. Zapata was in a heavily embroidered *charro* costume, all gold and silver and Mexican eagles. They later posed with Gutiérrez for pictures.

Mexican history would be more pleasant if it could be written that the country then became orderly and peaceful and that soldiers returned to their homes to stay. It didn't happen that way. Though Zapata returned to his native Morelos, Villa remained in Mexico City creating trouble for the government. Eventually Gutiérrez fled the capital and joined Carranza, who did want the presidency and who had gone to Veracruz with Obregón and their forces. Villa took his forces into the field and in a series of bloody battles he was defeated by General Obregón.

In 1916, Villa staged an ill-conceived and ill-starred raid on Columbus, New Mexico, with some 400 men. His mission was repulsed by the army post there and Villa retired in some disorder. This served as an excuse for President Woodrow Wilson to send Brigadier General John J. Pershing to Mexico, where his cavalry chased Villa through the hills of Chihuahua fruitlessly for almost a year, never really coming close.

In the meantime, the Mexican capital saw frequent changes. In 1916, Carranza finally claimed the presidency, but he was assassinated two years later, and Adolfo de la Huerta succeeded him, followed by Alvaro Obregón in 1920. Both de la Huerta and Obregón tried repeatedly to make peace with Villa, and on July 28, 1920, he finally accepted a government gift of several thousand acres in Durango, near Parral, to which he and several of his chief lieutenants and their families retired to live a peaceful life. It lasted, for Pancho Villa, just three years.

At eight o'clock in the morning on July 23, 1923, Villa and five companions were leaving Parral in a new Dodge automobile. Villa was driving and two of the men were riding the running boards as bodyguards. A barrage of gunfire, followed by a running charge of several armed men, killed all five. Only Villa drew a gun. He killed one of his assassins.

There are varied reports as to the "why" of Villa's murder.

It could have been vengeance or politics, or a combination of both. Old fears die hard, and in the minds of some there must have been the picture of Pancho Villa always riding his *Dorados* through the hills.

With Villa retired, Obregón had returned to Mexico City at the head of Carranza's forces, and the two armies were able to send Zapata back to the hills of Morelos. There he was invincible to military forces but was not, however, invincible against treachery.

In March of 1919, a Carranza officer, Colonel Jesús María Guajardo conceived and carried out an elaborate plot against the hero of the south. Zapata was normally the wariest of the wary, but tricked by a show of good will, an ambuscade was carried out and he was shot to death along with his closest friends.

No one knows for certain where Emiliano Zapata is buried. There are some stories that on the clearest of nights he can still be seen, an elegant vaquero in a *charro* costume, riding a fine white horse over the hills of Morelos.

ALVARO OBREGÓN AND
LÁZARO CÁRDENAS

ALVARO OBREGÓN was forty years old on the November 30, 1920, when he draped himself in the three-colored sash of office and was inaugurated as President. As a Carranza general, he had defeated Pancho Villa and he had been by far the most popular candidate in the election. He was a sturdy, rather handsome man, more than ordinarily honest and much more than ordinarily inclined to remember and retain old friends. His advent in office was the signal for literally hundreds of old guerrilla leaders to invade the capital. They had started with the gun; now they had big cars and big cigars, bodyguards, gold, and pretty consorts. Obregón once remarked that there were no more bandits in the hills. "I've brought them all to Mexico City," he said.

His inauguration marked the ten-year milestone of the revolution and the end, too, of its most bloody phase. Although there were to be minor uprisings for a number of years, the Mexican civil war was over.

After three years in office Obregón made peace with both the government and business establishments of the United States, finally obtaining the recognition which had been withheld so long. The three phases of Mexican life which made the greatest strides during his administration were labor, land reform, and education. In establishing his policies, Obregón set a course for Mexico which it would follow for a number of years. The course was neither radical nor socialistic. Much of it was simply a process of catching up.

During the period of 1920-24 about three million acres of land were returned to their original owners, some 625 villages. But Obregón's greatest accomplishment during his presidency was in appointing José Vasconcelos as his Minister of Education and giving him support and room to act.

Vasconcelos was a man of deep and varied culture. He wrote and spoke brilliantly, and appreciated art in every form—writing, painting, sculpture, architecture—and almost single-handedly was responsible for the outburst of creative talent which followed the revolution. He created normal schools where hundreds of teachers were trained and sent out into the remote Indian villages. He restored old missions and monasteries, hiring Mexican painters to decorate the walls.

But peace—peace could not last in Mexico even yet. As the end of his term grew near, Obregón threw his support to Plutarco Elías Calles, a cabinet member and old military friend. After a rather reluctant rebellion led by Adolfo de la Huerta was crushed by Obregón, Calles was elected President in 1924. Four years later he attempted to pass the presidency back to Obregón and the Mexican people could foresee a perpetual shuffle of the office between the two men. There were beginnings of rebellion, but those plotting to overthrow the government were quickly disposed of via the execution squad. Obregón was left as the only candidate.

He was elected in the summer of 1928. Three weeks later, he was approached in a cafe in San Angel by a young man carrying a sketch pad. He was a cartoonist, José de León

Toral. After sketching the President-elect for a few minutes, Toral drew a pistol and shot him dead.

The six years of what would have been the assassinated Alvaro Obregón's second term as President saw three different men fill the office—Emilio Portes Gil as interim President 1928-29, Pascual Ortiz Rubio, 1929-32, and Abelardo Rodríguez, 1932-1934. The selection of all three was engineered by Plutarco Elías Calles, who at that time exercised such political power behind the throne that he was known as *El Jefe Máximo,* "the Big Boss." He controlled all three Presidents completely. Ortiz Rubio so obviously danced to any tune which Calles played that he was known derisively as "Pascaulito." When Ortiz Rubio made some appointments Calles didn't like, *El Jefe Máximo* announced that the President was resigning; Ortiz Rubio could only confirm the fact.

In 1934, Calles selected as his candidate General Lázaro Cárdenas, but Cárdenas proved to be nobody's man but his own. He also was a superstar in the game of practical politics. Within two years after Cárdenas took office, Calles was no longer "the Big Boss." He was no boss at all.

Lázaro Cárdenas was born May 1, 1895, in the isolated Michoacán village of Jiquilpan, almost due west of Mexico City and about midway from there to the Pacific coast. He was the first son and one of eight children born to Damaso and Felicitas del Río Cárdenas. Damaso Cárdenas ran a pool hall around whose one table and small bar most of the male villagers collected when they had time and a few centavos to spare. He named it the "Reunion of Friends." Through his friendship with a doctor who visited the town occasionally, and through remembering the old Indian remedies, Damaso had acquired a fund of healing lore in which the villagers had a blind faith. His fee was usually a scrawny chicken or a mess of vegetables.

Lázaro's grandfather, Francisco Cárdenas, tilled a few acres of farm land and was a weaver, enjoying considerable local reputation for the excellence in design and in the quality of his blankets and *rebozos*.

There were two elementary schools in Jiquilpan, one for girls and one for boys, and both went as far as the sixth grade. Lázaro completed the local course of study and probably could have gotten a scholarship to a higher school in the state capital of Morelia had he chosen. The only course of study available, however, was for the priesthood. Lázaro had no leanings in that direction and none of the family pushed him, so he remained in Jiquilpan and went to work in the office of the town tax collector. His duties included keeping the tax records and files, and he also became jailer because the post was vacant. This was in 1910; Lázaro was fifteen years old.

It was also the year Francisco Madero began to challenge the seemingly endless dictatorship of Porfirio Díaz. The man for whom Cárdenas worked was an avid reader, a liberal, and an admirer of Madero. He loaned many of his books to Lázaro, including eventually the one written by Madero which started the revolution. The books, and his talks with his employer, influenced the boy's thinking. He came to hate the Díaz tyranny, which reached even into the tiny village of Jiquilpan in the form of federal troops. Lázaro had watched once while the Díaz men quelled a minor protest against lost community lands by firing point-blank into the crowd.

In that year, 1910, Lázaro's father died and as the elder son he became head of the family. They gave up the pool hall and Lázaro went to work as a hand-set printer, while his mother and sisters took in sewing.

Since his earliest boyhood Lázaro had wanted to be a soldier—or thought he did—and finally in 1913, when he was eighteen and after Huerta had overthrown Lázaro's idol, Madero, the boy told his mother he was going to work for an uncle who owned a small ranch near Apatzingán. There, however, he offered his services to General García Aragón, one of Zapata's erstwhile lieutenants, who was fighting Huerta.

Aragón detested book work and as soon as he learned of young Cárdenas' experience in the tax collector's office he made him his paymaster with the rank of captain. The "paymaster" in a guerrilla army was actually the man trusted with both guarding and dividing the loot. Cárdenas could be trusted and the general recognized the fact.

His career with Aragón, however, was short. It was his misfortune to be assigned on a minor mission which ran into a federal ambush. His detachment was wiped out. Cárdenas escaped by the skin of his teeth, evaded the pursuit, and finally made his way back to Jiquilpan where friends hid him until Carranza troops came through and he could join them.

It was near the end of the campaign and Huerta's forces were disintegrating rapidly under the combined assaults of Villa, Obregón, and Zapata. Cárdenas distinguished himself in one battle and participated in the triumphal march into Mexico City as an uneasy peace descended on the country.

Cárdenas stayed in the army for twelve years, the latter few simply because he was awaiting the right moment to get into politics. By the time of the Carranza-Villa civil warfare, he had risen to the rank of lieutenant colonel and was supporting Carranza simply because he thought the white-bearded leader of the constitutionalists was operating legally while Villa was not. His immediate commander at the time was General Plutarco Elías Calles, who formed a quick affection for the young officer, calling him *El Chamaco,* "The Kid." After Carranza became President, Cárdenas knew the life normal to an army officer in those days. He chased and sometimes caught bandits, was available to help suppress minor rebellions, and generally made himself useful.

When de la Huerta became interim President in 1920, after the flight and murder of Carranza, he promoted Cárdenas to the rank of general, probably at the urging of Calles, whose protegé Cárdenas had become. Cárdenas was only twenty-five at the time, young for such a high rank, but he was also unusual in other ways for a Mexican military man. On the battlefield he was inclined to be rash and to take extraordinary chances, both personally and with his men, but frequently this over-boldness paid off in victories against great odds. (Once, at Teocuitlán, he was defeated, wounded, captured, and barely escaped execution.) Aside from these faults—or talents—he was quiet, sober, abstemious, and almost painfully honest. Once given a million pesos to conduct a campaign, he startled everyone concerned by returning 700,000 of it to the national treasury. (Three other generals given similar advances at the same time did nothing of the sort.) His personal bravery and supreme self-confidence extended in other ways. On at least two occasions, rather than annihilate a foe when he had overwhelming strength, he walked alone into the enemy camp and persuaded his adversary to give up. And, unlike most other Mexican commanders, he never shot prisoners.

The young general was unreachable through bribery or gifts. During a tour as commander at Tampico, heart of the oil industry, he astounded the local barons by refusing the gift of a new automobile, although his own was falling apart. He did, however, note with keen interest the activities of the foreign oil operations. At the same time he was made a general officer, he filled in for three months as interim governor of his home state of Michoacán. It was his first taste of the life political, and he liked it. Eight years later, with the blessing of Calles, he ran for a full term of the Michoacán office and was elected. It was 1928, the same year that Alvaro Obregón won his short-lived second term as President.

Here, except for occasional military assignments from the national capital, Governor Cárdenas devoted his time and considerable energies to social and economic reform projects. Michoacán was his home state and he knew it well; he also knew its history. Father Hidalgo had issued the famous *Grito de Dolores* from near there and the condition of the peasants more than a century later was little different than it had been in Hidalgo's day. The state was almost totally agricultural in production, but less than 3 per cent of its farmers owned the land on which they labored, lived, and died. Some sixty *hacendados* owned the remainder, great estates ranging in size from five thousand acres to almost half a million.

Almost immediately after taking office, Cárdenas began a program of building roads and schools (a total of 47 per cent of the budget went to education) and of land reform. In many cases he was able to extract tillable acres from the *hacendados*. In others, he drained lowlands or created access roads to thousands of acres of mountain land which were government-owned but had always been operated by the big land proprietors simply because they controlled the only way in to them. He also learned at firsthand that the peons had been so long subjugated they were almost incapable of thinking or acting for themselves. He had to browbeat them into accepting the land and then he had to send in agents and loan money to help them with their own farm programs. It was a lesson he carried with him into the office of the presidency some years later.

In 1930, Cárdenas was chosen chairman of the Partido Nacional Revolucionario (PNR), Mexico's first permanent political party. Heretofore political parties had been formed to serve a purpose in one election campaign and were abandoned after the election. Calles, *El Jefe Máximo,* saw the need for a party which would have a continuous life and continuous professed principles—and also continuous support from majority factions in the country.

The PNR has survived, although its name has been changed twice—to the Partido de la Revolución Mexicana in 1938 and to the Partido Revolucionario Institucional in 1946—and although there have been other parties which have come and gone, PNR (now PRI) has and continues to dominate Mexican politics. In that sense, Mexico is a one-party nation.

Cárdenas remained as PNR chairman for ten months and the position served to place him in the national spotlight more than he had ever been before. From that post he went to the cabinet of Ortiz Rubio as Minister of Interior, found the setup between "Pascualito" and *El Jefe Máximo* not to his liking, politely made his manners, and returned to the governorship of Michoacán.

A few months after his return home to the Michoacán capital of Morelia, Cárdenas met, wooed, and married Amalia Solórzano, the daughter of a well-to-do Tacámbaro family. Despite the fact the Cárdenas held the office of governor and had become a national figure, it was an uneasy courtship. Amalia's parents were staunch Catholics and the federal government at that time was very much at odds with the Church, a quarrel which had led to a three-year strike of Catholic priests. Some of the more religiously ardent became militant under the banner of *Cristo Rey,* or Christ is King, and banded together as the *cristeros.* Both as a general and as a governor, it had been Cárdenas' duty on several occasions to enforce the stand of the government. He had always avoided open warfare and bloodshed, but he was not regarded favorably by the "good Catholics."

So the Solórzanos sent their daughter, who was still in her teens, to a convent school (which was forbidden and operating clandestinely) in Mexico City. Here Cárdenas showered her with letters and small gifts and Amalia showed a remarkable talent for mischieviously contesting the will of the school authorities, until in desperation they asked her parents to please take her back. Once at home, a suit for the hand of their daughter from the governor of the state was very hard to deny. The couple married in the fall of 1932, though the parents did not attend the very simple ceremony.

The governor's term and his honeymoon ended almost simultaneously, and he took his bride to his new post at Puebla where he was commander of the military zone. According to his biographers, Cárdenas, although he was a general officer and had just completed a term as state governor—both traditionally the routes to wealth—had to borrow money to move his household goods.

After only a few months in Puebla, Cárdenas was named Minister of War in the cabinet of President Rodríguez. He was, by this time, one of the best known and most popular figures in the country. Although Calles was aware that Cárdenas held beliefs regarding social and economic reforms which were far more liberal than his own, he apparently felt that once in office, Cárdenas would need him and become another shadow President. So *El Jefe Máximo* backed him for the top office, and at the PNR convention in Querétaro in December, 1933, the nomination was duly conferred.

Cárdenas proceeded to confound the country by conducting an active, tough political campaign. It was something Mexico had never seen before. He traveled almost 18,000 miles and visited all twenty-eight states. He spoke in the state capitals at organized rallies, but he also visited the desert and mountain villages where no candidate had ever dreamed of going before. He was simple and unassuming and convincing. He listened to farmers and to laborers. He became so fascinated with the things he was learning from his own countrymen that he kept on campaigning even after the election was over—an election he won by more than 98 per cent of the votes.

The Cárdenas honeymoon with *El Jefe Máximo* lasted less than a year. The new President was elected in July, 1934, took office in November of that year, and broke with Calles in the summer of 1935. Cárdenas, biding his time, had permitted Calles to have a strong voice in naming the cabinet, but then almost immediately angered *El Jefe* by some of his presidential acts. Cárdenas declined to live at Chapultepec Castle, reduced his own salary by half, and cut off the customary entertainment allowance given to the First Lady, his own new wife. Gambling establishments, mostly owned by the old Callistas, had flourished for years. Cárdenas closed them down. He established a system whereby the national telegraph lines would accept free for one hour each day any message from any Mexican to the President.

Like Benito Juárez, when he was governor of Oaxaca and turned the governor's palace over to his brother Zapotec Indians, Cárdenas opened the presidential palace to the *campesinos,* were they barefoot Indians or laborers in khaki, and he listened to their troubles and their grievances—while generals and politicians cooled their heels in the anterooms. He had been inaugurated in a plain, dark business suit and he worked in the same costume; the uniform of the general was laid aside. He silenced the buglers who were accustomed to blowing a fanfare on the arrival of the President. He banned presidential portraits in public buildings and quietly destroyed half a hundred busts of himself presented by some over-eager supporter.

Calles duly noted these oddities and felt that he was losing control of the situation, so he invited a number of old-line senators to his home in Cuernavaca where he called attention to the recent epidemic of strikes which had broken out. (In many instances Cárdenas had expressed his sympathy for the strikers.) The situation was deplorable, Calles told the senators, and he harked back to Pascual Ortiz Rubio. Certain weaknesses of his regime, said Calles, had made his resignation necessary. He feared Cárdenas was showing the same tendencies.

Calles couldn't have achieved a greater effect with a lighted skyrocket. Cárdenas moved instantly. He dismissed his entire cabinet, which Calles had virtually named. He installed former interim President Portes Gil as head of the PNR, where together they formed a left-wing coalition that was strongly anti-Callista, and which almost immediately dominated the party. He let religious leaders know that he was inclined to soften the official attitude toward the Church; since Calles had been the author of the anticlerical laws, *El Jefe Máximo* now lost any support he might have had in that direction. The new Cárdenas cabinet was of both the left and the right— but not of Callistas. In a few weeks even the senators who had gone to Cuernavaca climbed on the bandwagon and the Cárdenas control of Mexico was complete and as secure as that of Calles ever had been. Calles rapidly became very unpopular and when, in 1936, a mass labor meeting demanded his execution, Cárdenas quietly had *El Jefe* flown over the border into California. Calles took with him one book, the one he had been reading when he was arrested—a Spanish-language copy of Hitler's *Mein Kampf.*

After Calles had left Mexico, Cárdenas was to all extents and purposes an absolute dictator, but he was a dictator like Mexico had never seen before. The press was free and could and did criticize. Labor could strike; in fact, strikes gradually replaced revolutions as a national exercise in venting emotions. Cárdenas encouraged unions but he carefully offset their power by organizing the peons and seeing that their delegates were given full representation and voice in union affairs. He also gave the *campesinos* weapons and organized them into district militias as a safety measure against the military.

The quality of leadership and the esteem in which the people of Mexico held their President could not have been more dramatically demonstrated than in the expropriation of the oil companies, largely owned in the United States and in England. In 1935 some twenty-one oil workers' organizations had merged into one union. Two years later, partly due to a sharp increase in living costs, the new syndicate presented demands to the oil companies for a hefty raise in pay, along with additional benefits, including paid vacations and the training of Mexican nationals to fill administrative positions. The oil companies refused and a strike followed. An arbitration board recommended wage and other benefit increases of about one-fourth those originally asked.

The union accepted; the oil companies did not. They appealed to the Supreme Court, which sided with the unions. Again the oil companies refused, this time either to accept the terms or to consider further arbitration.

Cárdenas, after going on the national radio to explain the situation and to call for support, expelled the oil officials from the country and seized their properties. It was a bold act, but it was enormously popular. Of all the foreign companies operating in Mexico, the oil barons had been the most disliked. They were obviously getting rich off Mexican natural resources which could never be replaced. They had long opposed any kind of government regulation, were arrogant, and charged more for their oil in Mexico than they did abroad.

There was an international storm, of course. The British protested so loudly that Cárdenas broke off diplomatic relations. In the United States, President Roosevelt took a sympathetic stand. Mexico had a right, he said, to expropriate the companies; he asked only that a reasonable compensation be made.

Mexico's financial situation was desperately shaky for the next two or three years, and the entire people of Mexico, united by a common enemy for once, rallied around the government and actually gave millions of pesos in personal contributions to keep the treasury going. Eventually the national company, Petróleos Mexicanos, acquired the skill to operate the companies. An agreed price for the property was reached and the oil of Mexico became oil *for* Mexico and not oil *from* Mexico.

Other programs of the revolution were also carried on by the Cárdenas administration. Under his agrarian program he had redistributed more than forty-five million acres of land by 1940, more than twice that returned to the peasants by all previous governments combined. Cárdenas instituted the first experiments in cooperative farming, starting them off with loans for fertilizers, seed, and machinery. Not all of the agrarian program worked and it took years to untangle the complications, but it was effective enough that it raised the standard of living of the peon farmers; such a thing had only been a dream before.

The presidential term of Lázaro Cárdenas ended in 1940. During his six years in office he had spent more than one-third of the time out of Mexico City in his quest for knowledge of what the people of Mexico felt and wanted and needed. Many of his projects were initiated under his personal supervision; he would spend weeks in the countryside, trusting his cabinet to handle the decisions of their departments. And he obviously had selected them well. He had opposition and strikes and problems, but there was never a scandal; no one tried to abscond with the national treasury.

He promised a free and honest election for 1940 and he did his best, although there may have been abberations. His successor was his own Secretary of Defense, General Manuel Avila Camacho, whose own administration was middle-of-the-road and dedicated to stabilizing the economy. In April, 1943, Franklin D. Roosevelt and Avila Camacho met in conference in Monterrey. It was the first visit of any United States President to Mexico.

When his term expired, Cárdenas, with his wife and son, Cuauhtémoc, named for the Aztec chieftain, returned to Michoacán where the former President had bought an experimental farm. In 1942, when German U-boats sank two Mexican ships and Mexico declared war, President Camacho organized two defense zones, one on the Pacific coast and the other on the Gulf of Mexico. Avila Camacho asked Cárdenas to take command of the Pacific zone and as General Cárdenas, he did so. When war was over, he again retired to Michoacán and the country life he preferred. He died on October 19, 1970.

THE CONTINUING REVOLUTION

THE MEXICAN REVOLUTION, from the fall of General Porfirio Díaz to the present day, has been a vast social and economic movement. It was violent and bloody at first, then peaceful and orderly in succeeding years. It has always been dynamic. It has constantly endeavored and finally, today, has succeeded in building a bridge across a broad and bitterly defended caste system which had hindered economic development.

Initiated by Francisco Madero in 1910, the revolution began as a convulsive movement against dictatorship and for representative government. Later, and after many false starts, it was transformed into a struggle for social justice and for economic advancement.

In Querétaro, where Padre Hidalgo and his followers had plotted the first moves to free Mexico from the rule of the Spanish, a new constitution was adopted on February 5, 1917. It gave order to the revolution and it gave the nation a structure on which to build. The new constitution kept the strong federal control features of the old, which had been adopted in 1857, but it introduced new principles; they in turn permitted the innovation of the social and economic reforms which have made remarkable Mexico's progress since. Some of the reforms:

Private ownership must be subordinate to public interest.

The *ejidos*—the common lands held by every village for tillage by the villagers—were restored as was the perpetual right of every village to have those lands.

Subsoil mineral, petroleum, and gas deposits were declared to be unalienable national property.

The rights of labor were enunciated.

The rights of the Church to own property and to interfere in politics were limited.

With the blood-stained years of Santa Anna, Huerta, Díaz, and, more recently, of Villa and Zapata over, and with the realization of political reform, Mexico entered a new era.

A powerful nationalistic feeling swept the nation and with it came a realization of true identity. The man, the woman, the child was not an Indian or a *mestizo,* a *criollo* or a Spaniard—just a Mexican. The revolution was psychological as well as physical.

With the surge of nationalism came a parallel emancipation of the arts. Under Díaz and before, architecture, painting, and sculpture had been copies of European work, mostly French and Italian; writing has never thrived under any dictatorship. Under the enthusiastic guidance of José Vasconcelos, himself a revolutionist and former exile, a new ethic of art evolved. As Minister of Education, Vasconcelos urged artists to express their ideas and, for the first time in Mexican history, they were permitted by the government to do so, with government sanction and on government buildings. Every phase of cultural life in Mexico felt the impact of a new ideology which was neither Indian nor Spanish but true Mexican. It was the birth of a new and authentic development, a cultural renaissance and one of the most brilliant of the twentieth century throughout the world.

Painting emerged first and the great leaders of the Mexican Schools created a new movement which was echoed by painters everywhere. The message transmitted by their dramatic murals had its origin in Mexico's remote Indian past, in the tyranny and oppression of the years just past, and of the emergence of labor, whether in the cities or on the soil, as a national force. Even the technique of the artists was innovative because the revival of mural painting in Mexico was a protest against the easel. The easel was bourgeois.

The novels of the revolution, both from its battles and the peace which followed, were genuine expressions of a people who had made up their minds to abandon the old, and now unacceptable, clichés.

It has been said that during the first twenty violent years of the revolution Mexico was searching for her soul, and since then, for meaning. She sought and sometimes found it in her poets, who combined the earthiness of the Mexican Revolution with the modern movements for change which are common to much of the world.

With the revolution, young composers began to appear, abandoning tradition to seek their inspiration in the forgotten reed and drum themes of the Olmecs, the Toltecs, the Aztecs, and the Mayas. They were determined to do for Mexican music what the muralists had done for Mexican painting. They succeeded. The great music of Mexico today carries with it the strength and vitality of the earliest aboriginal barbaric rhythms—and dissonance.

Architects and builders stopped aping the cultured forms of Paris and Rome and looked instead to the mountains and deserts and jungles for inspiration—and found it in the primitive lines and vivid colors of all three.

And this new Mexico bought back, and paid for, the vast natural resources it had given away. It produced economists and bankers and statesmen who were wise enough to put the land back in the hands of the people where it belonged; and to pass laws which said that never again would the great natural beauty of Mexico, neither its shores nor mountains nor plains, become the targets of foreign exploitation.

JOSÉ VASCONCELOS

THE BIRTH OF education for the poorer children of Mexico dates from the year 1920 when the newly elected President, Alvaro Obregón, appointed José Vasconcelos director of the National University of Mexico.

Vasconcelos was a liberal, a pacifist, and an equalitarian. All humans have souls, he said, and all are equal. While he was Secretary of Education he coined the motto of the National University of Mexico, "Through my race the spirit will speak," in which the word *race* referred to the "cosmic race" that he envisioned as the outcome of the blending of European, Asiatic (Indian), and African ethnic elements and cultures taking place in Latin America. His two famous books of this period, *The Cosmic Race* and *Indology,* were widely acclaimed throughout Latin America, where he was given the title of "Teacher of America."

Vasconcelos was doubtless one of the most complex and even contradictory men of modern Mexico. As a politician his fiery idealism and intransigence prevented him from attaining his highest ambition—the presidency of his country. The same traits in later years led him to devote himself to the glorification of the civilization that Spain had brought to this hemisphere and to incessant attacks on the policies of the United States. In his *History of Mexico* he derided the achievements of some of Mexico's most revered leaders and painted with dark colors what had been done by the revolutionary regimes which succeeded Obregón.

Vasconcelos was probably also the best educated man in Mexico. He was born in Oaxaca on February 28, 1882, the son of Ygnacio and Carmen Calderón Vasconcelos. He received his LL.B. degree at the National University of Mexico in 1905 and later did postgraduate work in Puerto Rico, El Salvador, and Guatemala. In addition to teaching and heading the university, he later caused to be created the government cabinet office of the Ministry of Education and became its first Minister. He was a candidate for President, a revolutionary, an exile, and a voluminous writer. He was a deeply versed student of the ancient Greek philosopher Pythagoras, whose theories stressed astronomy, mathematics, and the mystical significance of numbers. He was, in fact, a disciple of all of the ancient classics and once proclaimed to Obregón: "What this country needs is to sit down and read the *Iliad*. I am going to distribute a hundred thousand Homers in the schools."

Vasconcelos began his involvement in Mexican politics with the beginning of the revolution against Porfirio Díaz in 1910, supporting Madero and actually serving as a confidential agent in the United States during the latter's brief administration as President. During the years after the assassination of Madero, Vasconcelos was both in exile and associated at times, though never in any military capacity, with the revolutionary leader, Pancho Villa. It was not until Obregón took over the presidency after the death of Carranza, however, that Vasconcelos found a leader with whom he could work.

He was also fortunate that his boss, Obregón, not only believed strongly in education but, in his association with Vasconcelos, had come to both admire and trust him. He had been in office only a few months when he created the Ministry of Education, at cabinet level for the first time. He not only named Vasconcelos as Minister but gave him both money and freedom to work.

It was a little like loosing a damned mountain stream. Vasconcelos established training academies which turned out hundreds of teachers. Fired by the infectious zeal of their mentor, they poured out into the towns and villages of rural Mexico. Here, serving with little or no pay, they contrived to build schools and for the first time taught the children of Mexico's great *mestizo* class something besides the dull and rather fearsome dogma they had been getting from the local padres for generations. The children responded and the result was that the teacher frequently supplanted the priest as the man in town to be consulted when wise counsel was needed. The Church objected violently, but Obregón stood by his Minister and his work.

The concentration of education under the new regime was on the thousands and thousands of children who had gone virtually unschooled before. "We don't help Mexico by teaching French in the university," said Vasconcelos. "For the thousand pesos it costs to teach one man French in the university, I can teach fifty Mexican boys and girls to read and write Spanish." He emphasized crafts, music, the ancient dances and customs, and he organized hundreds of festivals in towns and villages to promote them, all through the aid of his ubiquitous and enthusiastic teachers. Carried away by his enthusiasm for the classics, he bought inexpensive editions of Plato, Dante, Virgil, Homer, and other philosophers. He sent them out by the hundreds; actually, he planned on a never-ending stream, but when his library of classics reached fifteen or sixteen the teachers protested that other books would be more practical for the task at hand, so Vasconcelos reluctantly withdrew his head from the clouds.

In 1922 he brought Diego Rivera back from France where the great muralist had spent too many years away from his native land—or so Vasconcelos thought—and this was the beginning of a great surge of art which captured the spirit of Mexico and the Mexican Revolution.

Rivera, with the other great muralists of his day—Siqueiros and Orozco—covered most of the walls of most of the public buildings in Mexico and also carried their work to other nations of the world. To prove they were part of the revolution, they worked on their scaffolds with pistols strapped to their belts. Vasconcelos encouraged Mexican architects—Jesús Acevedo and Federico Mariscál, among others—to quit copying the traditional arches and columns of France and Rome and to create their own reflections of Mexico, and they did. He encouraged composers, notably Manuel Ponce, the great teacher, and Carlos Chávez, both composer and conductor. Among his disciples was Jaime Torres Bodét, the poet who later became Secretary-General of UNESCO.

Vasconcelos himself was a man of medium height and weight, of olive complexion and dark hair. He was very intense and voluble, an accomplished conversationalist who could and practically always did take charge of the conversation at any dinner table. It was a mark of his ability in this factor of his character that no one resented his assumption of conversational leadership; he was unfailingly interesting. During his middle years Vasconcelos met and became great and good friends with many women, but married only one— Serafina Miranda, who gave him two children, José, Jr. and Carmen.

Throughout his entire life Vasconcelos found himself suffering from mild to intense disgust at the spectacle of Mexican politics. In 1929 when Plutarco Elías Calles, by this time *El Jefe Máximo* of the current political system, put forward the obviously incompetent and subservient Pascual Ortiz Rubio as his presidential candidate, Vasconcelos decided to take a fling at the office himself. There were, actually, three candidates—Ortiz Rubio running under the auspices of the National Revolutionary Party (PNR), which Calles had set up; Vasconcelos, who campaigned as the candidate of the Anti-reelectionist Party; and General Pedro Rodríguez Triana, the Communist candidate.

Many Mexicans at the time believed that Vasconcelos won the election, which was held on November 17, 1929. The Congress, however, announced, as expected, that Ortiz Rubio had received a great majority of the ballots.

Vasconcelos immediately denounced the election as fraudulent and issued a call for the overthrow of the government. Those days of armed revolt, however, were gone from the Mexican scene, and the only result of the call to rebellion was that Vasconcelos had to spend the next seven years in exile in the United States and Europe. Like other exiles, he did not find it safe to return until the administration of Lázaro Cárdenas.

After his final return to Mexico in 1939, Vasconcelos continued to write and to lecture. He was appointed director of the National Library, and was given honorary awards and degrees by the Academy of Letters, the National Historical Society, and the National College. Upon his death in 1959 he was buried, by decree of the government, at the National Cemetery of Illustrious Mexicans.

DIEGO RIVERA

DIEGO RIVERA, the first of Mexico's great muralists, was a painter of genius. He was also a revolutionary and, through his paintings, an eloquent and impassioned defender of justice everywhere. During his lifetime he mastered nearly every known art process, but he created his own style. Of him an admirer wrote: "Almost all of his painting seems to have been accomplished on some clear immortal morning. All is invested with the radiant joy of living."

Rivera was an affiliate of the Communist Party and had little respect for the dignity of established tradition, entrenched wealth and power or the formal trappings of religion. He was a most controversial man and wanted it no other way.

Diego Rivera was born on December 6, 1886, in Guanajuata, an old and history-touched city north of Mexico City. His family had lived there since colonial times and had been wealthy, before the silver mines on which they depended for a living had petered out.

Diego's father, quite a liberal for those days, moved the family to Mexico City in 1891 and a few years later, when the youngster showed signs of artistic talent, sent him immediately to the National School of Fine Arts. There Diego studied drawing and other art mediums, and by 1905, when he was nineteen, he was studying under the famous romantic landscape painter, José María Velasco.

In 1907 he went to Spain on a scholarship to study and spent the next three years there, with some traveling through-out Europe—France, Belgium, the Netherlands, and Britain. Of this period he later wrote: "The clash between what I had been taught and the Spanish painting of that period produced a disastrous effect in my mind. The result was that I painted some of the worst works of my life." He might have added that he was very young at the time, with an unformed talent. Bad or good, the works of that period are much in demand today.

During the years between 1911 and 1920, Rivera followed the custom of the times. Like all artists who could, he lived in or near Paris. His work of those years shows the influence of the neoimpressionists who followed Cézanne, Renoir, Monet, and Pissarro. He became a close friend of Picasso, who was in his cubist period, and became a convert to the great Spanish painter's far left political ideals. He traveled through Italy in 1920-22 and studied and sketched the work of the Byzantine, early Christian, and other pre-Renaissance schools. It was in Italy, too, that he became interested in fresco painting.

By 1922, Rivera was being talked about and acclaimed. He was achieving an international reputation. And, at this time, a man who probably appreciated artistic talent as no one else in Mexico did was rector of the University of Mexico. The man was José Vasconcelos, later to become Minister of Edu-cation. Vasconcelos could not bear the thought that a Mexi-can artist as gifted as Rivera was living the life of an expa-triot; so he sent him money to come home. Almost immedi-ately after his arrival Rivera told Vasconcelos that he wanted to paint a mural, and the two of them chose the interior of the Bolívar Amphitheater in the National Preparatory College. There Rivera painted his gigantic composition on the religious theme of the Creation. The mural, which was done in encaustic—paint mixed with wax and then held firm by the application of heat—was immediately acclaimed. He followed this with other murals on other public buildings. In 1929 the United States Ambassador to Mexico, Dwight W. Morrow (whose daughter, Anne, married Charles Lindbergh, the first man to fly alone across the Atlantic), himself a passionate friend of Mexico, commissioned Rivera for the work which gained him international fame. It was, and is, the beautiful and moving idealized scenes of the conquest and settlement of Mexico by Cortés and his followers. The murals were done on the Cortés Palace in Cuernavaca.

Later that same year Rivera began his work on the great stairway of the National Palace, the theme of which was the social and political evolution of Mexico. This task was interrupted when he received two invitations from the United States. One was from the Detroit Institute of Fine Arts, the other from the Rockefeller family to create a mural for the entrance to the newly begun Rockefeller Center in New York.

Both works created storms of controversy. The Detroit mural, which dealt with the theme of the Creation, was strongly criticized as irreligious and aroused the wrath of the churches in the city.

The Rockefeller Center work included portraits of Lenin, the father of Russian Communism, and of John D. Rockefeller, the father and grandfather of the creators of the Center. In his heroic mural, Rivera presented Lenin, the patron saint of the worker, as a noble figure. Rockefeller, possibly the world's richest man in his day, was caricatured and not so nobly.

The storm over the two murals raged for months. The Detroit Institute of Fine Arts defended its work and it remained, but the fury over the Rockefeller Center concept became in time a national controversy over principles and morals; it had to go. The Spanish painter, Sert, was commissioned to do the substitute mural which adorns the entrance to Rockefeller Center today. Rivera remained in the United States long enough to complete several frescoes in San Francisco and then returned to Mexico City where he reconstituted his Rockefeller Center mural at the Palace of Fine Arts where it is admired by hundreds of viewers daily. He also completed the work at the National Palace in 1935.

It is usually the destiny of skilled painters to achieve fame after their deaths. Diego Rivera arrived at his international acclaim while he was still alive. His politics, his personal life, and his great works were all controversial. Although he was a Communist and assailed for so being, he was also attacked by the party for his friendship with the Russian Communist leader, Leon Trotsky. It was, indeed, through Rivera's influence that President Cárdenas granted Trotsky asylum after his quarrel with Stalin. (Trotsky was murdered in Mexico City in 1940, presumably on Stalin's orders).

Rivera had a tremendous personal charm and magnetism for all who knew him and especially for several colorful and talented women of his day, two of whom became his wives. The others were simply great and good friends. One wife, Frida Kahlo, was herself a leading Mexican surrealist. The other, Lupe Marín, presented him with a daughter, Lupe Rivera Marín, who has been elected to the Mexican Congress and has held other important political positions. Rivera was unable to live long with any one women but he did have the faculty of remaining life-long friends with them all.

If Mexican mural painting is the harvest of the Mexican Revolution, as has been said, than certainly Rivera was the greatest of the reapers. He died on December 3, 1957.

CARLOS CHÁVEZ

EVEN AS the Mexican muralists drew their inspirations from the impassioned colors of the mountains and deserts and valleys of Mexico's land, so Carlos Chávez, the greatest of the country's musicians, recreated in his music the harmonies and rhythms of Mexico's Indian tradition by adapting them to contemporary musical expression.

During the years when he was producing the compositions which established him as Mexico's greatest musical genius—one of them the incomparable *Sinfonía India* which employs melodies of the Yaqui, Seri, and Huichole tribes in scores available for native Indian instruments as well as for the conventional orchestra—he was also Director of the National Conservatory of Music and, for a time, head of Mexico's Department of Fine Arts.

In 1928, Chávez received and accepted an invitation of the musicians' union of Mexico City to conduct their orchestra. The group was, according to their own appraisal at the time, "completely unschooled in symphonic routine." Chávez worked with the group for nine years and at the end of that time had welded its ninety musicians into an orchestra which toured the country under government subsidy. It performed native, modern, and classic subjects and won equal acclaim in all fields.

Carlos Antonio de Padua Chávez was born on June 13, 1899, near Mexico City. He was the seventh child of Agustín Chávez and Juvencia Ramírez Chávez, both of mixed Spanish and Indian blood. One of Carlos' ancestors had been a publisher, soldier, and politician of some renown. He was José María Chávez who fought against the French invasion which placed Maximilian on the Mexican throne. Later, while governor of Aguascalientes, the early-day Chávez was executed by a French firing squad.

Chávez started his study of music when he was eleven, his brother being his first teacher, and then came under the tutorship of two of Mexico's better known musicians, Manuel M. Ponce and Pedro Luis Ogazón. They found him sufficiently advanced even at that age to study harmony, theory, and counterpoint, and the composition of the symphony.

Manuel Ponce, who gained international and everlasting fame through his composition of *Estrellita* or "Little Star," wrote of his most famous pupil: "Carlos Chávez is a rare example of ability conjoined with industry. . . . The first thing one notices in his compositions is a striving for originality. Debussy, with his intensely personal mannerisms, fascinates our young composer whose aspiration goes beyond a mere imitation of the classics and romantics . . . Beneath certain procedures in his music, characteristic of the composer of a work like *Pelléas,* is discernible a latent streak of romanticism that the immoderate use of dissonances and the persistent rhythmic intricacies cannot hide. Carlos Chávez is a very serious young man, in fact a trifle on the melancholy side. He has talent and bears watching."

Señor Ponce was infinitely correct.

Chávez wrote his first symphony when he was eighteen and followed it with works for the piano, orchestra, and voice. At this same time he was organizing string quartets and composing pieces for them. In 1921, José Vasconcelos, who figures so large in all of Mexico's cultural revolution, and who was then Minister of Public Education, commissioned Chávez to produce a ballet which would be based on themes of the ancient Aztec culture, including their wars and religion and human sacrifice, and which would incorporate an interpretation of native Indian melodies. It became *El fuego nuevo* (*The New Fire*), a remarkable work for a thirty-two-year-old composer.

In 1922, Chávez married Otelia Ortiz, herself a pianist and a woman of great musical perceptivity. The two of them went to Europe the following year where they found the German and French schools both stereotyped and colorless, and they fled briefly to New York where they remained just long enough to promise themselves they would return when Chávez' position in the international music field was more secure. Over the next few years, Otilia Ortiz presented her husband with three children, Anita, Agustín, and Juanita.

Chávez' work as conductor of the *Orquesta Sinfónica de Mexico,* and for a short time of the orchestra of the Philharmonic Union, while mostly praised, occasionally brought storms of outraged criticism around his head for his daring innovations. In 1928 he introduced John Alden Carpenter's *Skyscraper Suite*, a strident work whose unusual dissonance caused such an uproar there were threats of removing him from his post. In spite of the storm at the time, he was requested to give a repeat performance some months later and it was widely acclaimed.

Chávez visited the United States frequently in the 1930s and 1940s where he conducted the symphony orchestras of Philadelphia and Boston, and the Brooklyn WPA orchestra. He also conducted the Cleveland and Los Angeles philharmonic orchestras, the San Francisco, St. Louis, the National, the Chicago, and the NBC symphonies. At this time he wrote in *Nuestra Música* a detailed article outlining his theories on both composition and conducting. Most notable of his thoughts, perhaps, was the one often quoted line: "The conductor must not command but convince."

During one visit to New York in 1940 the Museum of Modern Art invited him to present a program of music based on pre-Columbian themes. The performance was a brilliant success and included his own composition *Xochipilli Macuilxochitl*. In 1944 he conducted the Mexican Harmonic Orchestra over an international radio network. Somewhat earlier Leopold Stokowski conducted, in New York, the Chávez modern ballet *Horse Power* with programs designed by Diego Rivera. The critics received the work with mixed emotions and reviews. It was followed by his *Sinfonía de Antígona,* a short (eleven-minute) composition which one critic called "too astringent" but which enhanced Chávez' reputation enormously.

Chávez is, and will be historically, remembered for his compositions, particularly as they have captured both the wild, untamed spirit of ancient Mexico and the color and ambience of the nation today. It is equally, however, for his skill as a conductor that he has made his very solid niche in the musical world of the twentieth century.

The famous critic Olin Downes, in 1937, wrote that Chávez' direction of the New York Philharmonic Symphony "surpassed any achievement since that of Toscanini." Downes also compared Chávez to Stravinsky, likening some of the parts of *Sinfonía India* to "savage wood carvings full of barbaric rhythms."

Carlos Chávez is a solidly built man of medium height with features which show a possible trace of Indian ancestry. His eyes light up, particularly at the sight of a pretty face or figure, for he is a gallant man with Old World courtesy and charm, and he greets a feminine acquaintance by kissing her hand.

He likes to eat and to drink, though both in moderation, and he is an avid conversationalist on almost any subject—music, art, and literature, but politics as well. He holds strong opinions and is quite relaxed about expressing them, either in his native Spanish or in English, which he also speaks fluently.

Today, although his compositions number in the scores—*Sinfonia de Baile, Soli, Cantós de Mexico, Llamadas,* among others—most of his work is limited to conducting, in Mexico, Europe, and often in New York. He lives comfortably in a home near Mexico City, which also contains his enormous record collection, including many modern recordings—from Art Tatum to Burt Bacharach.

CANTINFLAS

TWO GENERATIONS OF film-goers have compared Mexico's great comedian, Cantinflas, to Charlie Chaplin. Chaplin himself called Cantinflas the greatest comedian the film world had ever known. When Diego Rivera decorated Mexico City's largest theater with a monumental mural, the central figure of the work was the little, bedraggled *pelado,* the underdog of the Mexican slums who has delighted audiences throughout the Spanish-speaking world for thirty years. And his performance as the valet in *Around the World in Eighty Days* won him the plaudits of English-speaking audiences as well.

Cantinflas was born Mario Moreno on August 12, 1917, on Santa María Redonda, in Mexico City in what one account calls "a poor but respectable" neighborhood, to José and María Guizar Moreno. He was the sixth in a family of twelve sons and three daughters. José Moreno, the father, was a postal employee, eminently respectable and god-fearing, as was his wife, and they tried their best to give Mario an education, first in the Bartolomé de las Casas School and then in the national agricultural school at Chapingo. It was a valiant effort but it didn't work. Mario had little taste for formal learning and a growing dislike of the poverty which enveloped his world like a smothering miasma. Forsaking school, he ran away and joined a *carpa,* a traveling tent show, as a dancer.

The audiences which attended the *carpa* were the men and women from Mario's own world, the workers and their wives, soldiers and their girls and household drudges, out for an evening's entertainment when they could scrape up the three or four cents admission. The shows they saw were slapstick, broad political parody and broader jokes, the sharp, slanted humor of the slum and the street.

Mario began with the *carpa* as one of the group of dancers who entertained between other performances. He stumbled onto the talent which has characterized his performances since, and also to his name, purely by accident. One evening an announcer failed to show up and the show's manager told Mario to go out on the stage and fill in for him.

Dancing before an audience was one thing. To step out on the boards, look out at the sea of faces, and speak coherently was quite another. With Mario's first sentence came a spell of stage fright. And when he spoke, the words were garbled into a mishmash of nonsense. He tried to correct and simply dug himself into a deeper verbal mire. In a matter of seconds he found himself hopelessly entangled in a frenzied combination of gibberish and pantomine.

The audience was convulsed and someone yelled *"Cantinflas,"* a meaningless word which bore some relation to one of Mario's utterances. And then the man cried again, *"Collate* (shut up) *Cantinflas"* and the name of Mexico's newest comedian was born.

Cantinflas' style has been imitated by a dozen lesser performers, just as Chaplin's has, but no one else has approached the success of either. The costume Cantinflas wears is that of the day laborer, the hodcarrier or porter. The trousers are baggy and drape loosely from the hips, held up from the imminent disaster of falling by a piece of tattered rope. He wears a long shirt (which may really be an undershirt) and a bruised felt hat. A handkerchief, whose color identity has long since disappeared, is knotted around his throat. He carries a ragged, frayed, unbelievably disreputable jacket which he treats with such care it might be made of Russian sable.

When he talks, and that may not happen until he has been on the screen for several minutes and his audience is keyed up to an almost uncontrollable pitch of anticipation, it is with the earnestness of a used car salesman. His words, however, transcribe a circle of absolute, meaningless nonsense. It is double-talk pronounced with wide-eyed, straight-faced sincerity. *The New York Herald Tribune* described it as a "madcap, gibberish delivered in solemn earnestness. It is a hash of ad-libs, double-talk, innuendoes, words that don't exist or are mispronounced."

While Cantinflas and Chaplin relate to each other in many ways, they differed greatly in one sense. Chaplin was always the victim of his own frustration; Chaplin never won the battle or even the girl. He may have brought discomfort to his enemies and righted great wrongs, but at the end he was always shuffling off into the sunset, swinging his cane, a jaunty figure but always alone. Cantinflas, on the other hand, rises from the gutter (or below it, if possible) and through sheer effrontery and gall triumphs in the end. He scorns authority and drowns pomposity in the volume of his meaningless but unbelieveably funny conversation. When Hollywood came out with Ibáñez's *Blood and Sand,* starring Tyrone Power, Cantinflas (and it could have been coincidental) made his own *Ni Sangre Ni Arena (Neither Blood nor Sand),* in which he stumbled and fumbled his way through a bullfight and managed to win despite himself. *Ni Sangre Ni Arena* was such a success in Mexico that it outgrossed by 75 per cent any of the North American imports, usually so successful, including such milestone pictures as *Gone with the Wind* and *The Great Dictator*.

Cantinflas is, incidentally, an expert *matador*, a factor which probably enabled him to burlesque the filmed bullfight with such success.

Cantinflas is slender and of medium height, inclined to be almost dapper off the screen. He is quiet and unostentatious, rarely goes to parties, lives almost as a recluse. He was married in 1937 to Valentina Zubareff (or Zubariova) and they adopted a son, Mario, in 1960. Valentina died in 1965.

In the 1940s Cantinflas formed a partnership with Santiago Reachi, an advertising executive, and together they formed Posa Film Company in conjunction with Columbia Pictures, which both furnishes the capital and handles world-wide distribution except in the United States. Cantinflas has taken an active part in union activities of the Mexican film industry and in 1944 helped organize the Cinema Production Workers Union. This resulted in a bitter fight with a rival union and at one point the government stepped in to mediate in favor of Cantinflas. He had threatened to leave the country when the rival union refused to permit his films to be shown at theaters they controlled. The Mexican film industry is in effect Cantinflas, said the government, and so dependent on him that there could be no question of letting internecine battles drive him from the country.

In recent years the Cantinflas films have been leaning more and more toward carrying the message of social reform; it is as though he is now trying to help the very *pelado* character he made famous on the screen. He has been making one, sometimes two, films a year and they have come invariably to carry, in one form or another, the Cantinflas dedication to helping the poor of his country. The parts he plays in the pictures reflect the hundreds of anonymous people in Mexico who Cantinflas believes spend their lives as unheralded benefactors of the less fortunate.

In *El Señor Doctor* he is a traveling rural general practitioner who cares for the peasants of his mountain towns and villages, almost as poor as his patients, loving and beloved. In *Un Quixote sin Mancha* he is a lawyer who is not quite a lawyer, that is, who never really passed the bar, but his kindliness and his wise, and often wily, advice save dozens of his friends from the grasping and unscrupulous land owners. Cantinflas in *His Excellency* plays the part of an ambassador who is very undiplomatic in getting himself involved in all sorts of ambigious but helpful situations. *Por Mi Pistoles* is a parody of a Western. Cantinflas crosses the Northern American border to rustle cattle but somehow gets involved in good deeds instead. *El Professor* is always lecturing, often in the famous Cantinflas double-talk, against the local *cacique* or political boss and, of course, completely confounding him.

In the autumn of 1972 Cantinflas was in Spain making *Don Quixote Cabalga de Nuevo—Don Quixote Rides Again*— in which he plays Sancho Panza, Don Quixote's faithful companion. The emphasis of the picture is set on that portion of the Cervantes book wherein Sancho Panza is made governor of the *Ínsula Barataria,* and here again he will be in a position to dispense a typical Sancho Panza—or Cantinflas— brand of justice, always protecting the small man from the rich and powerful.

During his stay in Spain, Cantinflas found himself almost as popular and well known in Madrid as he is in Mexico City. When he stepped out of a restaurant or from his hotel, the Grand Via on the Avenida José Antonio, he was surrounded by scores of admirers and autograph seekers. He was also the target of newspapermen but, in these crowds they found him almost impossible to interview because Mario Moreno, facing an audience, invariably slipped into his other self and became Cantinflas. He was performing, delighting his audience with meaningless double-talk.

Cantinflas did, however, find time occasionally to talk about the film he is making, which will cost about two million dollars, and about his work and the future.

Does he think this will be his best picture?

"I always think that my best picture is yet to come, that which I have not made yet and which perhaps I will die before making. I have a long road to go before reaching the goal—my supreme ambition—which is to make my best picture."

You have changed your style and your ideas in the last twenty years?

"Of course I have changed, otherwise I would be obsolete. The true artist has to evolve. The characters must adapt themselves to Cantinflas. In this new picture Sancho Panza is in a sense the ideal Cantinflas."

The Mexican film star said that he was tremendously interested in making this picture, *Don Quixote Cabalga de Nuevo,* in such a way that it could easily be adapted for use in other countries and other languages.

"Because Don Quixote and Sancho Panza are universal characters that everybody knows around the world. I was able to bridge the gap of language in the picture *Around the World in Eighty Days* and now I am trying to bridge a wider gap of understanding even if I do speak my own language in this film."

What will be your next picture?

"I think that it will be one called *Conserje en Condominio* *(Doorman of the Apartment)*. In it I will depict the new urbanized Mexico."

Have you thought of retiring? There was a smile in considering this question. Mario Moreno was obviously resisting a temptation to slip into the character of Cantinflas for his reply. But he gave a straight answer.

"When you give me a good reason to retire perhaps I will do it."

MARTÍN LUIS GUZMÁN

THE REVOLUTION produced a number of notable writers: Ruben Romero, who wrote of everyday life in Mexico; López y Fuentes, whose style is as polished as obsidian stone; or Mauricio Magdaleno, whose forte is logic, though his works are intense and full of movement. But the best known of Mexican authors, both within his own country and internationally, is Martín Luis Guzmán. And Guzmán's best known book by all odds is *The Eagle and the Serpent,* dealing mostly with the months and years that Guzmán spent as a civilian secretary to Pancho Villa.

Guzmán's output has not been extensive but it covers a considerable span of time, which continues as this is written. And it covers an unusual variety of experiences, ranging from his experiences with Villa as related in *The Eagle and the Serpent,* which he completed in 1928, to a collection of stories written in New York and published under the title of *By the Hudson (A Orillas del Hudson),* which he had written earlier.

Martín Guzmán was born in Chihuahua on October 6, 1887, and was taken by his parents to Mexico City two months after his birth. His father was an army colonel and the move was occasioned by his appointment as cavalry instructor at the National Military Academy. The senior Guzmán was wounded and died in 1910, the year the revolution began, and apparently had found his own military career unrewarding enough that on his deathbed he made his twenty-three-year-old son swear he would not follow in his father's footsteps; that he would never take up arms, in fact. It was a promise the younger Guzmán kept without much trouble; he was a liberal and an idealist and had no inclinations toward a military career.

After Guzmán was graduated from the National Preparatory School, which at that time had the status of a college, he started upon the study of law, another career which didn't interest him much. As early as 1902, when he was barely fifteen, his father's duties had taken the family to Veracruz and here Martín edited (and largely wrote) a monthly student magazine, *La Juventud*. At this age he had already become an inveterate reader, centering his attention on the classical works of Spain. The reading he did at this time and his choice of authors greatly influenced his own writings later.

Martín's study of the law, which was unenthusiastic at best, was frequently broken by his explorations in the literary fields of his day. His first commercial venture was a job as a reporter with *El Imparcial* which served as unofficial but accurate spokesman for the regime of President Porfirio Díaz. Martín soon found that he held political leanings he hadn't been fully aware of; he could no more adapt them to the reactionary dictates of the old *caudillo* than he could have born arms on his behalf.

So he left *El Imparcial* with his political views much clarified and in 1911 wrangled an appointment as a delegate to the convention of the Progressive Constitutional Party, which first nominated Madero as President of Mexico. After Madero's election, Guzmán served briefly—because Madero's term was brief—in the Department of Public Works, and after Madero's assassination, resigned, planning to go to the north of Mexico to join the revolutionary forces operating there. And thus began the experiences which are related in *The Eagle and the Serpent*. Of his departure from Mexico City Guzmán noted: "I had fifty dollars in my pocket and a burning indignation against Victoriana Huerta in my soul."

Since Huerta's armies controlled the routes to Chihuahua where Guzmán was headed, he went first to Veracruz and from there took a boat to New York. It was his first trip outside his native country and it gave him an insight to a new way of life, a different civilization. It also gave him an appetite for further travels.

After six days in New York he was unable to raise the money necessary to travel across the United States and into Mexico, but he was able to work his passage back to Veracruz and thence to Mexico City. Here he joined an old friend, Alberto Pani (who served in later governments as Minister of both Foreign Affairs and Treasury) and together they began printing and circulating handbill propaganda sheets against the Huerta regime. Within a few months the federal police were hot on their heels and they took off in some haste northward. It was the year 1913 and Carranza was out in front in the three-cornered battle against Huerta, that is, Zapata in the south, Villa in the north, and Carranza in the north central part of Mexico. Guzmán and Pani quite logically made contact with the first rebel forces they could reach, after dodging the Huerta troops, and these belonged to Carranza. Guzmán didn't like Carranza, and very quickly discovered he couldn't get along with the Carranzista staff, either. So, at the first opportunity he slipped away quietly to join Villa.

It was another step in the political evolution of Guzmán,

who was twenty-six at this time. He was undoubtedly attracted to Villa because of his stature as a revolutionary military leader. But he was also convinced, as he disclosed in later conversations and writings, that a rough, uncouth man like Villa more truly represented the common people of Mexico than did the conservative and sometimes pretentious Carranza and the upper-class Creoles who made up his staff and advisors. Guzmán was not sure if Villa could or should be tamed, but he was quite sure that Villa's rough crudities hid a tremendous elemental force that was both sincere and honest; and that this force could be directed into compassionate channels. Guzmán was proven both right and wrong in his beliefs, of course. There were times when Villa's driving force was simply uncontrollable.

Guzmán spent almost two years with Villa. He refused any military commission although he rode the deserts and mountains of northern Mexico with the great revolutionary as part of his personal staff, and the two found a mutual respect and became friends. In 1936 Guzmán published the first of six volumes of his *Memorias de Pancho Villa*, with the other volumes following. In the 1950s, when Guzmán was special Ambassador to the United Nations and used to go to New York frequently, he gave lectures, some formal and some informal, on Pancho Villa. His talks were on those two years he spent with Villa, of the terrible civil war, and his spoken word was used as he might have done in a novel, sometimes dramatic, sometimes humorous. Guzmán is an engaging man, a man who smiles easily and often, a man easy to like. He is short, about five-feet-four, a Creole born of Creoles, but more properly according to his own definition and liking—a Mexican.

When the first phase of the revolution ended, Guzmán preceded his chief into Mexico City, which was not very clever of him. Carranza's army was the first to reach the capital and the Carranzistas promptly tossed Guzmán into jail. When Villa (and Zapata from the south) arrived a week or so later he was released, but then, when the revolution split into its three fratricidal sections, the Carranzistas, the Zapatistas, and the Villistas, Martín Guzmán became disgusted with his own country and its politics. He exiled himself to Spain in February of 1916 and began to write for some of the weekly magazines published in Madrid, chiefly *España* under the pen name of *El Fósforo* (The Match).

He remained only a year and then went to New York where he became editor of *El Gráfico,* a Spanish-language weekly. A friend of his wrote of him: "Martín was an avid observer of life and customs in the United States, particularly the gigantic city of New York. He criticized as well as praised many of the things he observed. His style was both subtle and deep and he seemed obsessed with the idea that he must explain the local customs which were so alien to the Latin Americans. His subjects varied widely, from such concrete things as lawn tennis or boating in Central Park to such abstractions as 'the soul of New York.' "

In 1920, Guzmán returned to Mexico as editor of *El Mundo,* one of the earliest evening papers in Mexico City, and under his guidance it soon became widely read and politically influential. Guzmán himself was elected to Congress and became a member of the recently formed Cooperative National Party. In the election campaign of 1923 the party decided to support Adolfo de la Huerta against Plutarco Calles and Guzmán became thoroughly enmeshed in the minor revolution which accompanied the election. De la Huerta sent him to the United States as special ambassador, hoping to get both sympathy and financial support, but President Coolidge decided in favor of President Obregón, who was still in power and supporting Calles. The rebellion collapsed and a penniless Guzmán exiled himself once more to Spain. He remained there fourteen years this time, working as co-editor of two Madrid dailies, *El Sol* and *La Voz*. During these years he became much a part of the intellectual life of Spain, more than he had ever—up to that time—had time to do with his native Mexico. Oddly, perhaps, his closest friends were among the conservative Spanish Republican politicians, perhaps because they befriended him. He was especially intimate with Alcala Zamora, who had been elected President of Spain in 1931 and who offered Guzmán a post in his own secretariat along with Spanish citizenship. Guzmán declined both offers.

In 1926 he began writing his memoirs, which were eventually published in Madrid but not in Mexico. Then in 1927 news arrived in Spain of the execution, obviously at Calles' orders, of two rivals for the presidency of Mexico. The cold-blooded killings created an enormous stir in Spain and particularly aroused Guzmán. Putting aside his memoirs, he began what was to be his most gripping novel, *La Sombra de la Caudillo (The Shadow of the Leader)*. The book was an instant sensation in Spain, where it was first published, and in Buenos Aires shortly thereafter. It was not published in Mexico City until 1938.

In 1934, when Mexico's great Lázaro Cárdenas became President, it also became safe for Martín Guzmán to return to his native land. He immediately started two magazines, one a literary publication which he called *Romance*. The other was, and is, modelled after the North American *Time* magazine and also is called *Tiempo*. (*Tiempo* comes to the United States under the title of *Hispanoamerica*). In 1972 *Tiempo* devoted many pages to the one hundredth anniversary of the death of Benito Juárez, and to the other great liberal leaders of Mexico.

And, at long last, Martín Guzmán rejoined the country he loved but from which he spent so many years in exile. He also is or has held positions as an able servant of Mexico: as a Senator of the Republic, Special Ambassador to the United Nations, a member of the more important intellectual organizations and as director of a new government agency which is charged with free printing and distribution of millions of textbooks to school children.

And he has not, at this date, shown signs of relinquishing any of the vigorous enthusiasm he has always demonstrated toward Mexico's affairs, and toward the continued advance of the cultural, political, and doctrinal revolution to which he has contributed so much.

PEDRO RAMÍREZ VASQUEZ

PEDRO RAMÍREZ VASQUEZ, one of the foremost architects of Mexico, is best known throughout the architectural world as the designer and builder of the National Museum of Anthropology in Mexico City, which is considered to be the most striking and best organized museum of its kind in the world.

It was finished in 1964, the last year of the administration of President López Mateos. Its achievement of harmonizing pre-Columbian and futuristic styles has been hailed as an architectural feat of brilliance and originality. The entrance of the museum is marked by the celebrated fountain which contrives to give an impression of ethereal timelessness while at the same time convincing the onlooker of its strength and solidarity. It dwells, almost uncaring, on the inevitability of the decay of civilizations, the uncounted cultural eras of the past and our own as well.

His lasting fame for the average man or woman of Mexico, however, is probably due to his work as the president of the Organization Committee of the XIX Olympic Games held in Mexico City in 1968. The concept which Ramírez Vasquez developed and which held him a fascinated, tireless slave throughout the planning and construction of the

Olympic site, was much more than a simple group of buildings, graceful and functional though they might be. Ramírez Vasquez' Olympic Village was built on grounds which had been one of the cradles of ancient civilization, and in the construction he undertook successfully to build a link between the present and the far ancient past.

On the south side of Mexico City, where the stadium of the games was erected, stands the Pyramid of Cuicuilco, which had lain neglected for centuries, partially covered by lava, until archeologists restored its magnificence. Cuicuilco was a ceremonial center which flourished during the preclassic period, around 2000 B.C., probably at the heights of two great civilizations—the Greeks in the Mediterranean and the Mixtecs in Mexico. For Mexico that era must have been the great Mesoamerican period whose culture produced agriculture—including the corn which was to become the Mexican staff of life—and also saw the proliferation of modeled sculpture, the scores of graceful figurines in human form which were unearthed beneath the ancient lava beds. Cuicuilco was founded about four thousand years ago and destroyed by an eruption of the volcano Xitle probably in the first millenium before the birth of Christ. Part of the layer of lava the eruption left still lingers in the area of Mexico City and is known as the *pedregal,* or stone field.

An ancient legend relates that before abandoning Cuicuilco, the inhabitants who had survived the rain of lava and hot dust assembled on the pyramid and predicted that one day a great culture would arise on that very spot. To Ramírez Vasquez the gathering of the world's greatest athletes for the 1968 games, united by the Olympic ideal, was a symbolic fulfillment of the ancient prophesy.

Pedro Ramírez Vasquez was born in Mexico City and received his degree in architecture from the National University in 1943. Following his graduation he served on the staffs of several Mexican institutions where he specialized in the study of the problems of urbanization. He designed and oversaw the construction of some 35,000 Mexican schools which were so successful in their utility concept that they were copied in many countries of South America, Europe, and Asia. He projected the great Aztec Soccer Stadium, and has designed and overseen the construction of buildings in Brussels, Seattle, and New York. He served as president of the Mexican Society of Architects and received the grand Medallions of the XII Triennial of Milan, Italy, and the VII Biennial of Art in São Paulo, Brazil.

Ramírez Vasquez comes from a middle-class family of professional men, mostly lawyers and engineers. He is a man of medium height, olive skin, and expressive eyes and hands. He has the precise speech of the professional teacher. When not working on one of his vocations or avocations that he has built into his life, he devotes his time to his family and their Mexico City home.

When Ramírez Vasquez was engaged in building the vast complex which made up the Olympic site, it was essential that each of the buildings be completed within the time specified, so that its schedule could dovetail with the work on the other structures. There were a multitude of details, some idea of which can be gauged by the fact that hundreds of miles of roads, drainage systems, transportation facilities, parking spaces, and public facilities had to be created, all on a precise timing schedule. In addition, an immense amount of electrical wiring as well as radio and television facilities were built, for this was the first time that satellite broadcasting was used on such a large scale. Under the planning of Ramírez Vasquez, the major works of the games, the Aztec

Stadium, the spectacular Sports Palace, and others remain in continued use for spectator events.

Much of the Olympic Village, however—the quarters for the athletes, the dressing rooms, the apartment annex for distinguished visitors—all linked to Mexico City by the high-speed freeway circling the city, was converted after the games closed and sold as moderately priced condominiums for Mexican workers. This, too, had been part of the Ramírez Vasquez grand plan.

JORGE PASQUEL

In the late 1940s, when he was at the height of his power as
Mexico's organized baseball czar and making sporadic raids
on the American and National Leagues of the United States,
Jorge Pasquel was a spectacular figure—in any language, in
any setting. He was compactly built and of medium height.
Some said he resembled Thomas Dewey, the once Republican candidate for President of the United States. But he was
as flamboyant as Dewey was not.

Pasquel's watchband was a platinum strip and his tie clasp
a diamond-studded arrow. The light of his blue-tiled office
was softened by stained-glass windows. His home, which occupied the center of a grandly landscaped estate, had a gun
room with two score monogrammed hunting rifles. A .45 Colt
automatic tucked in his waistband was as much a part of his
daily costume as the tie clasp. "Self-defense," a friend explained, "and there had been occasions—" But there is so
much gossip mixed into stories of that kind that it is best to
pay no attention.

Jorge Pasquel was, actually, an ardent sportsman, at one
time owning a four-engine transport plane which he used to
ferry baseball players about and used also for private lion-
hunting safaris in Africa. He neither smoked nor drank (nor

permitted his five brothers to), and worked out daily in his private gymnasium. He spoke English well, slowly and deliberately. He was at one time married to the daughter of former President Plutarco Elías Calles, then divorced. He was on intimate terms with the Presidents who succeeded Calles.

Jorge Pasquel was the president and self-declared (but undisputed) dictator of the Mexican Baseball League. He was also the most dynamic member of the totally dynamic multimillionaire Pasquel family which had its money-making fingers into many pies in Mexico. Jorge was one of eight children, the eldest, and was born in 1907 in Veracruz. The elder Pasquel, Francisco, began his business life as the owner of a small cigar factory. He switched to become a customhouse broker (while still holding onto the cigar factory) and then branched out into a dozen other businesses and industries with the shrewd aid of his sons, particularly Jorge.

"My family is in everything," Jorge once remarked. "You name it, we own it—real estate, shipping, banking, pottery, mining, brokerage."

On another occasion when he was luring North American baseball players to his Mexican league with fabulous salaries, he said: "Money. People always think first about money. I have thirty, forty, or fifty million in American dollars. Why should I worry about money?" Why, indeed? Jorge's interest in *béisbol;* in fact, his baseball career dates from the days he played the game on the sandlots of Mexico while he was in his teens. From these days it was simply a matter of money and enthusiasm, and Jorge Pasquel, who was probably one of the shrewdest businessmen his country ever produced, had plenty of both. By 1940 he was owner and manager of the Mexico City team, which won the Mexico championship, and by 1945, with his brothers, was responsible for the "expansion league" of Mexico which included teams in Mexico City, Veracruz, Torreón, San Luis Potosí, Monterrey, Puebla, Tampico, and Nueva Laredo.

The Pasquel brothers owned stock in all of the teams, with the remaining interest in the hands of various wealthy local people who were quite content to permit the Pasquels to run the show as long as they got box seats and were able to throw out the first ball at the opening of the season. Don Jorge had often been heard to say, "I am the Mexican League," and no one was interested in contradicting him.

The Mexican League first came to the attention of North American baseball owners, players, and fans in the mid-1940s when Pasquel hired Rogers Hornsby. Hornsby had been, in the 1920s, one of baseball's immortals, a slugging second baseman for the St. Louis Cardinals (and other teams), but by the mid-forties was reduced to managing a team in the Texas League. During the next year or so Don Jorge angered and dismayed the two American leagues by raiding their rosters, signing up a total of eighteen major league players from New York, Cincinnati, and Chicago, not to mention a number of minor league stars and Negro players who at that time had not yet broken into the big time. Some of these players the team owners didn't miss much, but when the Pasquels pirated Luis Olmo of the Brooklyn Dodgers, an outfielder who had batted .313 the preceding year, it was too much. Something had to be done.

The American and National Leagues got together and first declared that any player who participated in Mexican baseball in any way whatsoever—exhibition, off season, or full time—would be suspended from playing with the big leagues in the United States. The Pasquels considered this sanction and countered with an invitation to "Happy" Chandler, the Commissioner of organized baseball of the day, to migrate south of the border and join their setup at an increased salary. He declined. They also proceeded to stage a couple of additional raids, this time picking up Vern Stephens of the St. Louis Browns and Mickey Owen, a popular and accomplished catcher of the Brooklyn Dodgers.

(Owen stayed in Mexico under a five-year playing-managing contract. Stephens came back complaining that he had trouble with the signals, which were problably in Spanish idiom, and with the random carrying of firearms on the playing field; everyone but the players lugged a pistol, he said. Stephens was eventually reinstated.)

The year after all of these gyrations, 1946, the North American baseball team owners sought injunctions restraining the Pasquels from inducing players to break theoretically binding contracts with United States teams. The Pasquels cried "monopoly" and "peonage" and, while the cases were pending in court, proceeded to deplete the Cardinal bench of four players.

About this time, however, Babe Ruth made an "exploratory" visit to Mexico and came back to report that there really wasn't much interest in baseball in Mexico and that most of the fans didn't know third base from the dugout, but that the whole country was delighted at the spectacle of Jorge Pasquel matching wits, guile, and bankroll with the North American baseball moguls—St. George tilting with the dragon, more or less. Baseball in Mexico at it best was about equal to the Class C leagues in the United States, the Babe said, and until Mexico set about the business of building its teams slowly, systematically, and with some regard to playing skills, no really first-class player could possibly be happy competing there.

Baseball continued in Mexico with Don Jorge shuffling his players around to the teams which needed them most.

Sometimes one team would have ten more players on its roster than another. Pasquel tried to keep the scores even. It made for better competition and a bigger gate.

But the great baseball war with the North American leagues gradually declined due to the obvious natural causes that Ruth had stated and probably because everyone concerned wearied of it. And then Jorge Pasquel died on March 7, 1955, still a young man—one who would liked to have stayed around longer because he had a great zest for living. Meantime, *béisbol* continues in Mexico, neither better nor worse than before—but more quietly.

ANTONIO ORTIZ MENA

FOR TWELVE YEARS as Mexico's Secretary of Finance, Antonio Ortiz Mena was architect and engineer of the financial program which gave his country a sustained annual economic growth of more than 6 per cent, placing its performance very high indeed among that of the world's nations.

He is today, as a more or less sequel to that accomplishment, president of the Inter-American Development Bank, the second largest international lending institution in the world. In Wall Street and in the financial capitals of Europe and Latin America, Antonio Ortiz Mena is widely known and respected as a financial expert, as a clear-headed economist, and as a man with a personal fortune in the millions, whether the addition is done in pesos or dollars.

These facts are so well documented that they usually get in the way of other and equally interesting sides to the life of Señor Ortiz Mena. For instance, as a younger man he was an expert at the difficult and dangerous game of jai alai and helped make up a family basketball team with four of his brothers; he is still quite an expert on the tennis court and in the swimming pool. He, his wife, and youngest daughter live sedately enough five days a week in Washington's slightly pretentious Watergate apartments; they spend every weekend at a fifty-acre *ranchito* a few miles out of the city where the Mexican banker plays *vaquero* to fifty head of cattle. The little ranch also makes a pleasant place for the nineteen Ortiz Mena grandchildren to frolic on frequent visits.

The history of Antonio Ortiz Mena's growth from youth to manhood is hardly a rags to riches saga. He was born in the state of Chihuahua, where his family had long held property.

"My father and his brothers were miners," Ortiz Mena has remarked.

Did he mean they actually worked in the mines with a pick and shovel, or were they engineers?

"I mean they owned the mines," said Ortiz Mena, "though they were engineers too, of course."

What kind of mines?

"Oh, silver, lead, zinc—lots of metals."

His father and brothers—and grandfather—also had long been involved in Mexican politics, and when Antonio was three years old and the revolution was getting warm, they left the town of Parral, where he had been born on April 16, 1909, and moved to Mexico City. They settled there on a substantial estate in the Colonia Roma section of the southeastern part of the city. Antonio was one of ten children (five brothers and four sisters) and, with the other males of the family, grew up with a love of sports of all kinds.

The estate had its own *frontón* for jai alai as well as its own swimming pool, which were unusual on private estates in those days, Ortiz Mena admits. In addition to playing on the family basketball team, Antonio also played on the school team and competed in both tennis and swimming.

"I loved sports of all kinds," he said. "I still do." That fact is reflected in his appearance—the slim, muscular figure and the lightness of his movements, despite his sixty-plus years.

School in Mexico City was fairly rigorous. Classes began at

eight in the morning and continued until noon when the break came for the traditional substantial midday meal and *siesta,* and were resumed at three o'clock and went on until either five or six, depending on the grade. For as long as Antonio can remember he had physics and chemistry and math daily (two hours), and of course there were the basic languages. These, however, he perfected later at the University.

"I studied economics in English," he said, "philosophy in German, and law in French. The native tongue is always better than a translation." He can also handle Italian with reasonable competence.

Ortiz Mena graduated from the National University of Mexico in 1932 with a doctor of law degree, but his favorite subjects, both in school and later, were economics and banking, with more than a touch of politics on the side. Both of his grandfathers were Mexican congressmen, and his father held many federal offices. Antonio Ortiz Mena tends to follow in their footsteps.

Actually, his entire career since leaving school has been in government. He began in the Legal Office of the Federal District, became chief of the Consulting Department of the Attorney General's office, moved into the Mexican Social Security Institute and then, in 1958, became Secretary of Finance and Public Credit. The Mexican banker-economist-lawyer is very much aware that politics plays a major part in his life. (He was seriously considered as a candidate for President of Mexico by the country's governing Revolutionary Institutional Party in 1970.)

"It would be unrealistic in the extreme," he said, "for anyone who has taken part in public life in Mexico for as many years as I have not to consider himself a politician, no matter what his other vocations might be."

The political acumen which he has displayed throughout

his career was very necessary when Ortiz Mena took over as president of the Inter-American Development Bank. His predecessor, Filipe Herrera, had resigned the post after ten years and considerable criticism near the end of his regime. Herrera is a Chilean and was a close friend of Chile's President Salvador Allende, whose rather far left socialism and policies of expropriating foreign properties have led to criticism throughout the rest of the world. His first few months in the job Ortiz Mena spent trying to allay fears of Latin-American nationalism and checking what had become a spreading policy of expropriation (that is, taking over—"nationalizing" —foreign-owned mines, oil wells, manufacturing plants, or other property at prices usually established by the government and not always considered adequate by the owner), and of reestablishing Latin America in the good graces of possible foreign investors.

The Inter-American Development Bank was established December 30, 1959, to promote development among its Latin-American member countries. It has twenty-three members at present—the United States and twenty-two Latin American countries. Canada has indicated its willingness to become the twenty-fourth member, and Ortiz Mena sees no reason why European nations should not become members also.

The IDB operates both the same as other banks—and differently. Basically, of course, the member nations deposit money into the bank according to their means, the richer nations depositing the most. Certain banking institutions in each nation, then, are authorized to borrow funds from the IDB at a much lower rate than they would have to pay the depositors who normally make up their reserves. This means they can then lend the money in turn at lower rates than they ordinarily could, and do it without upsetting the normal economy of their nations. It is "outside" money created for this purpose.

The IDB was originally created with resources of less than $1 billion. Those resources are now more than $6 billion and members are in the process of raising the figures to $10 billion. The United States is by far the largest "depositor" in the IDB. Argentina and Brazil share second place with identical amounts, and Mexico occupies the third position. During its years of operation the bank has invested in the neighborhood of $5 billion in Latin America in development loans in the fields of agriculture, industry, electric power, roads and transportation, communications, water supply, housing, and education.

These loans have brought—or are bringing—some nine million acres of farmland into production and supplying the necessary credit to farmers to make them productive; have built or expanded 4,475 industrial enterprises; installed seven million kilowatts of electric power and 43,200 miles of transmission lines; built 25,000 miles of roads, provided 414,000 homes for low-income families, built 4,000 water and sewage systems, and added or improved 600 school centers—vocational, technical, and university.

These are just figures—dry and dull statistics which have meaning only to the men and women who live in the world of banking and finance. True, but only partially. These figures, these statistics, come to life and pulse with excitement when you trace the flow of money from the seven floors of the Spanish-speaking citadel the IDB occupies on Seventeenth Street in Washington to the ultimate borrower—to the man who gets the money in pesos or bolivars or quetzals, to the farmer in Peru who gets a road over which he can take his crops to market, to the cafe owner in Venezuela who is able to modernize his kitchen, to the cooperative along the Amazon in Brazil which can buy a tractor for the harvests, or to the rancher in Mexico who can buy a bull to improve his herd and his milk production. To these people the statistics translate themselves into gifts from heaven.

It is possible, if one digs a little beneath the figures, to come up with stories that are warm and human. Take the case of the Peruvian Indian village of Layo. For centuries the farmer citizens of Layo lived at a level very near the bare subsistence point, raising their crops primatively, working at handicrafts, bartering with each other—the same life they had lived for a thousand years.

Layo's transformation is part of a program typical of the Inter-American Bank under the direction of Antonio Ortiz Mena. In negotiations with the Peruvian government, loans totaling $20 million in sols were made to be used in aiding development programs in seven scattered and isolated communities in the high Andes. In each case, the people in the communities—the Peruvian Indians themselves—decided what should be done to develop their towns or areas. For some places it was a bridge; for others a market or school. One, where water had always been carried in stone jars for two miles, asked for and got a water system. Layo chose a road.

A four-centuries old road led to the village and stopped there. The fertile valley, then a mountain pass, and then a densely populated plain were impassable. Today that twenty-five miles has become an avenue of trade traveled by families from fifty miles and more away, who come to the weekly market in the ancient square, where vegetables, fruit, lace-trimmed *hupiles,* blankets, handcrafted artifacts, and even transistor radios are bought and sold. The road has lifted the town of Layo out of the past and into the twentieth century.

This is only one example. There has been help for Mexico too, of course, under the IDB loan program. In 1971 a credit of $32 million was extended to Nacional Financiera S.A., Mexico's national credit agency, which channeled the money to some 47,000 low-income landowners and farmers to improve the productivity of Mexican agriculture. A smaller loan helped develop the nation's fishing industry, and another went toward a massive irrigation program to aid disadvantaged farmers.

Antonio Ortiz Mena can be proud of his achievements in the world of finance and economics. It is fortunate—for his own country and other nations—that his interests went beyond law and politics, or a love of sports.

AMALIA LEDÓN

✳

MEXICO, ALONG WITH the rest of Latin America, has undergone striking changes in the changing status of women since
the beginning of the revolution. Up until the early part of
the twentieth century, women had few educational opportunities, could neither vote nor hold office, and were barred
at least by tradition from most of the professions. Their lives
were relegated to matrimony, child bearing, and household
duties. With the revolution came changes, though slowly, in
Mexico. By the end of the 1930s women were admitted to
the universities. Law, medicine, teaching, and even engineering became acceptable careers. The vote for women in Mexico
came state by state and was not made universal until the
time of the election of President Adolfo Ruiz Cortines in
1952.

One of today's most notable examples of the career woman
in Mexico is Señora Amalia González Caballero de Castillo
Ledón. She was born Amalia González Caballero in the early
part of the century in the town of Santander Jiminez in the
state of Tamaulipas. She was a nationally known beauty by
the time she was fifteen, and at seventeen she married the
prominent historian and statesman, Luis Castillo Ledón, then
governor of the state of Nayarit. Amalia was a gracious and

charming hostess as First Lady of Nayarit, and she fulfilled her public duties as the governor's wife, but she also became active in the movement sweeping Mexico which today would be known as Women's Lib. Her husband's death in 1935 was the signal for her own rise to national prominence in public life.

The career of Amalia Ledón for the next thirty-five years is simply a recitation of one public assignment after another, all of them handled successfully. Less than a year after the death of her husband, President Portes Gil asked her to help with the organization of a national association for the protection of children, which she did and which still operates under the auspices of the presidential office. That same year she established a Department of Education office for public recreation. In that connection she founded the *Comedia Mexicana* for the performance of plays written by Mexican authors, and the *Guiñol Teatro* (Puppet Theater). In 1937 she established the Mexican Athenaeum of Women, which she directed for twelve years, and the International Club for Women.

Amalia continued her activities in public affairs as delegate to a dozen national and international conferences for some twenty years. As a member of the Mexican delegation to the United Nations she took part in the work of the General Assembly. In 1948-50 she served as vice president of the World Commission of Women, presiding at meetings in New York and Lebanon.

In 1953 she was appointed Minister Plenipotentiary to Sweden and Finland, later assuming the rank of Ambassador to these countries. After a stint as Under Secretary of Education (the first woman to become a member of a presidential cabinet), she was appointed Ambassador to Switzerland, thence to Austria, and finally was named permanent Representative of Mexico to the International Organization of Atomic Energy in Vienna.

Amalia Ledón came home to Mexico in 1971, a tall beautiful woman with darkly graying hair and the same smooth lovely skin she had at twenty. After nearly twenty years of traveling, sometimes on lecture tours but more often representing her country, she was tired and homesick.

"A steel cable could not bind me more strongly to Mexico than the nostalgia I feel," she said. "I have missed my country, my Mexico City, my friends, my children, my grandchildren —everything about Mexico.

"And not the least—Mexican food and music. I always had a good cook and stacks of Mexican records—but it is not the same. Mexican food has to be grown in Mexico, and no record can capture the spirit of the live performance, whether it is symphony or *mariache*."

On her return to Mexico, the magazine *Mujeres* devoted the major part of one issue to Señora Ledón and her career. There is a picture of her in her bridal gown with her new husband; she looks like a movie starlet and has the undeniable flapper air of the day. Another picture, in another era, shows her with Eleanor Roosevelt and, of course, there are innumerable shots of her in this conference and that, presenting her credentials to the President of Finland and then Sweden and Austria, of her at her desk, at home, and with her grandchildren.

From her vantage point of living outside the country for two decades, Amalia Ledón had fresh and lively comments on her country and the progress it had made in the time of her own memory (and her own participation in its affairs, though she did not mention that).

"Now that I am back, and back for good," she said, "it is

not hard to pick out the changes in Mexico which have struck me most forcibly.

"The civic spirit has developed notably. Economic progress is evident; there are more schools, more teachers, newer professions, more technicians. The scientific community of Mexico today is better qualified and more diversified.

"In my life abroad I was able to confirm my own feelings about how the image of Mexico among the world's nations has changed. The Olympics had something to do with this, of course, and we were fortunate that there were no serious incidents or tragedies to mar the games.

"But also, our music, our writers and painters, our ballet and other expressions of artistic talent have helped very much. The Treaty of Tlaltelolco (the nonproliferation of atomic weapons in Latin America), in which Mexico played a leading part, made a lasting impact in diplomatic circles around the world.

"Do you remember," she continued, "our struggles in the late 1940s to get the vote for women? Many important men said no, and the principal reason they gave was that—heaven knows why—it would be dangerous to the country; the clergy would again get the upper hand. The influence of the Mexican clergy on Mexican women, they said, is so strong that all of the reforms which have been won since the time of Juárez will be lost.

"Well, women got the vote and the position of the Church hasn't changed much. Since 1952 many women have been elected to Congress and to state and municipal offices. Without an exception that I know of they have all been shining examples of honesty, hard work, and efficiency."

Amalia Ledón has retired—officially. But listening to her and watching the expressions which move across the handsome, mobile face, and catching the quick eagerness of her mental attitudes, it is difficult to believe that she will not participate again in the national affairs of her country in some way—as long as it does not involve her leaving home.

LUIS ECHEVERRÍA

THERE HAVE BEEN six Presidents of Mexico since the administration of Lázaro Cárdenas. The first five were Manuel Avila Camacho (1940-46), Miguel Alemán (1946-52), Adolfo Ruiz Cortines (1952-58), Adolfo López Mateos (1958-64), and Gustavo Díaz Ordaz (1964-70). They were all good men and good for Mexico, with politics which ranged from conservative to middle-of-the-road, mostly the latter. At times during their thirty years there were laments for "the lost spirit" of the revolution. Actually, the spirit of the revolution wasn't lost; it had simply gone peaceful. Most of the leaders of Mexico today, the leaders in every field, cannot remember, or were not born, when the last volley of shots was fired in Mexico in political anger.

The sixth President to be elected after Cárdenas was Luis Echeverría Alvarez who, like his several predecessors, finds all the fighting he can handle in the battles of economic stability for his country, for better education and housing, agricultural progress, and higher incomes.

In October of 1969 all three divisions of Mexico's Revolutionary Institutional Party—the laborers, farmers, and white-collar workers—named Echeverría as their choice for the presidential nomination.

Echeverría accepted the nomination on November 15 and the following day launched a record-breaking campaign that lasted eight months and carried him 34,000 miles from city to town to village across the face of Mexico.

It was a campaign patterned after that of Cárdenas, who himself had done much the same thing thirty years earlier. In his 226 days of campaigning Echeverría was up before seven every morning and rarely found a bed before midnight. A big touring bus became his office, study, and home as well as a means of transportation—although he used helicopter, train, boats, rafts, horses, small airplanes, and his own two feet at times. His first stop on the political tour was Querétaro, the scene of so much Mexican history since Hidalgo in 1810. From there he abandoned paved highways and threaded his way into the back country, the desert and mountain trails, where he found tiny villages where no candidate had appeared before. He crossed the Sea of Cortés to Baja California and traveled the length of its frequently uninhabited wilderness. He visited the jungles of Tabasco, Campeche, Chiapas, and Quintana Roo (still a territory), the tropical regions of Veracruz, and the arid deserts of northern Mexico. In the course of his campaign and of probably the most enthusiastic reception ever given a Mexican candidate, he visited over a thousand towns, villages, and cities. He made more than nine hundred speeches, but there were thousands of times when he simply listened. In his case it was a man discovering his own country. To Mexico it was a people discovering a future President.

They found him, these constituents, taller than average, balding and bronzed by the many suns of Mexico, wearing large, modern, steel-rimmed glasses. He dressed conservatively in dark business suits for the scores of luncheon, breakfast, and dinner meetings, but when he was away from the formality of tradition he wore the open-throated, outside-the-trousers white shirt (often pleated) which is the native costume of rural Mexico. They also found him *simpático,* a friendly, easy listener who could comprehend that a two-mile road over the mountains to market, a new water well, or the occasional visit of a doctor to the village was vastly more important to them than such things as Mexico's gross national product or balance of payments.

President Echeverría has never dropped his affection for the man on the street, the man on the farm, the man in the silver mine. He frequently quits the national capital to spend weeks in the byways of his country. And in the capital he will often walk from his office in the National Palace the considerable distance to the building housing Mexico's Congress, stopping to chat with people he meets. His speeches and his conversations frequently repeat the theme: "We are a *mestizo* people, and our country is also *mestizo.* We are proud of the two great fountainheads of our nationality. Every Mexican, whatever his nationality, is our brother. There is no racial prejudice in our country."

Luis Echeverría was born in Mexico City on January 17, 1922. His father was Rodolfo Echeverría, a government employee. His mother was Catalina Alvarez Echeverría. After grammar and high school, Luis entered the National Preparatory School in 1938 where he majored in social sciences. Two years later he entered Mexico's National University for the study of law. His early bent was in the direction of both journalism and politics. While in law school he edited the magazine *Mexico and the University,* and devoted his other extracurricular time to organizing conferences and seminars and to founding the anti-Fascist "Free Youth of Mexico" organization. His thesis for his Master of Laws degree in 1945 was entitled "The System of Balance of Power and the Society of Nations" and in it Echeverría analyzed the new pattern of forces which had assumed control of world politics following World War II. He himself was basically a pacifist. He favored international cooperation—a fact he emphasizes today—and the free determination of all people. Many years after writing his thesis, he was to say:

"No nation or group of nations, however powerful they might be, may assume as their exclusive task the management of world affairs, much less the tutelage of all other nations. Our [Mexico's] doctrine neither permits nor justifies the dominion of one people over another. It condemns any sort of international pressure tactic, rejects tacitly all forms of colonialism, and maintains that all peoples are equal and deserve the same right to the free integration of their political personality."

After getting his law degree Echeverría side-stepped into journalism, becoming an editorial writer for the Mexico City daily newspaper, *El Nacional*. Not long after, he received an offer from the University of Santiago de Chile of a scholarship to study sociology and political science in Chile. He took advantage of the opportunity to visit other nations of Latin America and to familarize himself with the political and social problems of them all.

Something over a year later he had definitely decided on a career of government service and politics, and he went to work implementing the decision, moving up in the system, from position to position: assistant to the president of the National Executive Committee of the Revolutionary Institutional Party (RPI) ; Director of Administration for the Navy Department; back to the RPI in 1957; as Chief Administrator and thence to become Under Secretary of Interior in the Lopez Mateos administration. In 1964 he was named Secretary of the Interior in the cabinet of President Diaz Ordaz and in 1969 became the candidate for President.

He won by a landslide in the first Mexican election in which eighteen-year-olds were permitted to vote. Some fourteen million persons went to the polls and almost twelve million cast their ballots for Echeverría against two million for his opponent, Ephrain González Morfin of the National Action Party.

Echeverría took office on January 1, 1971. Attending the ceremonies in Mexico City were his wife, María Esther Zuno de Echeverría, a native of Guadalajara, and their eight children—Luis Vicente, María del Carmen, Alvaro, María Esther, Rodolfo, Pablo, Benito, and Adolfo, ranging in age from twenty-five down to five years—and one grandchild.

During the time that he has been in office Luis Echeverría has been a strong President. He visited the United States in 1972 and both charmed and impressed the North American people with his candor and frankness. He had nothing but respect and affection for the United States, he said, but there were problems which existed between the two nations and until they were solved neither he nor his people could be content with relations between the countries. He returned to Mexico City with at least a promise of complete cooperation from United States President Richard Nixon. While in the States he also participated in a ceremony during which a portrait of Benito Juárez was presented to the Organization of the American States. It was the occasion, of course, of the one hundredth anniversary of Juárez' death.

There are many more concrete yardsticks to the strength of Mexico which appear in economic statistics—the dull figures which mean power or weakness to any nation. In recent years Mexico's economic development has shown two basic characteristics: a high overall growth rate and, at the same time, an industrial and agricultural production which is oriented toward the needs of the consumer—the Mexican people—and not toward the state.

Today when a Central American speaks of the "Colossus of the North," he is not referring to the United States; he means Mexico. Today the Mexican market is larger than that of Argentina, Chile, Peru, and Ecuador together. It is almost as large as the market of Brazil, which has double the population of Mexico.

As another measuring rod, production in Mexico has moved up from about $300 per person in 1950 to almost $600 per person today—just about double. The Mexican peso's rate of exchange has not varied since 1954 when the present rate of twelve and a half pesos to the American dollar was set.

In his first State of the Union address in September, 1971, President Echeverría announced several goals for his 1970-76 administration:

A 7 per cent rise in production, with emphasis in the agricultural sector.

A strict maintenance of law and order through legally established channels. "In the final analysis," he said, "democratic systems are characterized by the legitimacy of the procedures they employ to safeguard their institutions."

The delegation of civil programs to the Army, Navy, and Air Force; from carrying out the national census to providing aid to the civilian populace in times of national disaster.

A program of low-cost housing.

Prevention and control of pollution.

Educational reforms; strengthening the position of the teacher.

And, social security, better roads, minimum wages, higher standards of living.

President Echeverría is quite conscious of foreign trade and its values, and of foreign investment as a double-edged sword; it is welcome, but Echeverrían policy advocates that foreign investors reinvest an adequate share of their profits in Mexico. "We look upon foreign capital as being complementary to our own financial resources."

And: "Mexico has a clear awareness of its history and of its position in the world. We were born to independence when the collapse of modern colonialism had scarcely commenced. For over a century we suffered the political and economic ambitions of powerful nations. We bore, in periods now relegated to the past, abuse, misunderstanding, and violence. We now demand respect for our independence and seek, for all countries, justice and peace."

After his election in 1969, a news correspondent asked the new President how he felt about this personal triumph of receiving some 86 per cent of all the votes cast. Echeverría replied: "I'll talk of triumph six years from now when I'm convinced that I have served my country well."

A SELECTED BIBLIOGRAPHY

Alba, Victor. *Mexicans: The Making of a Nation*. New York: Praeger, 1967.

Arrangoiz y Berzabal, Francisco de Paula de. *México Desde 1808 Hasta 1867*. Mexico, 1968.

Beals, Carleton. *Porfirio Díaz, Dictator of Mexico*. Westport, Conn.: Greenwood Press, 1932.

Bustillos Carrillo, Antonio. *Apuntes Históricos y Biográficas*. Mexico, 1953.

Caruso, J. A. *Liberators of Mexico*. Gloucester, Mass.: Peter Smith, 1967.

Cline, Howard F. *Mexico: From Revolution to Evolution*. Oxford: Oxford University Press, 1962.

Creel, George. *The People Next Door*. New York: John Day Co., 1926.

Creelman, James. *Porfirio Díaz, Master of Mexico*. New York: D. Appleton & Co., 1911.

Díaz del Castillo, Bernal. *The Conquest of New Spain*. New York: Penguin Books, 1970.

Dulles, John W. *Yesterday in Mexico*. Austin, Texas: University of Texas Press, 1968.

Dunn, Harry H. *The Crimson Jester, Zapata of Mexico*. New York: R. M. McBride, 1933.

Durán, Diego. *Mexico—History to 1519*. Mexico City: University of Mexico, 1942.

Educational Systems Corporation. *Series on Mexican Heroes*. Washington, D.C., 1970.

Gibson, Charles. *The Aztecs Under Spanish Rule*. Stanford, Ca.: Stanford University Press, 1964.

González Obregón, Luis. *Historia de México*. Mexico, 1930.

Guzmán, Martín L. *The Eagle and the Serpent*. New York: Dolphin Books, 1965.

———. *Memoirs of Pancho Villa*. Austin, Texas: University of Texas Press, 1965.

Hamill, Hugh M. *The Hidalgo Revolt*. Gainesville, Fla.: University of Florida Press, 1966.

Hannay, David. *Díaz*. New York: Kennikat Press, 1970. Reprint of 1917 edition.

Harding, Bertita. *The Phantom Crown*. Mexico: Ediciones Tolteca, 1960.

Ibarra, Carlos M. *Historia de México*. Puebla, Mexico, 1963.

Johnson, William W. *Heroic Mexico*. New York: Doubleday, 1968.

Jones, O. L., Jr. *Santa Anna*. New York: Twayne Publishers, 1968.

Lansford, William Douglas. *Pancho Villa*. Los Angeles: Sherbourne Press, 1965.

Lansing, Marion Florence. *Liberators and Heroes of Mexico and Central America*. New York: L. C. Page & Co., 1940.

Lieberman, Mark. *Hidalgo: Mexican Revolutionary*. New York: Praeger, 1970.

O'Connor, Richard. *The Cactus Throne*. New York: Putnam, 1971.

O'Shaunessy, Edith. *Intimate Pages of Mexican History*. New York: George H. Doran Co., 1920.

Padden, R. C. *The Hummingbird and the Hawk*. Columbus, Ohio: Ohio State University Press, 1967.

Parkes, Henry Bamford. *History of Mexico*. Boston: Houghton Mifflin Co., 1950.

Pinchon, Edgecumb. *Viva Villa*. New York: Arno, 1970. Reprint of 1933 edition.

――――. *Zapata*. New York: Doubleday, 1935.

Poinsett, Joel. *Notes on Mexico Made in the Autumn of 1882*. New York: Praeger, 1969.

Poncelot, Victor. *Francisco Villa, Candidate for a Nobel Peace Prize*. Unpublished. Library of Congress, Washington, D.C., 1914.

Prescott, William H. *Conquest of Mexico*. New York: Modern Library, 1969.

Priestly, H. I. *The Mexican Nation*. New York: Cooper Square Publishers, 1969. Reprint of 1926 edition.

Reed, John. *Insurgent Mexico*. New York: International Publishers, 1969. Reprint of 1914 edition.

Robertson, William S. *Iturbide of Mexico*. Durham, N.C.: Duke University Press, 1968. Reprint of 1952 edition.

Ross, Stanley R. *Francisco I. Madero, Apostle of Mexican Democracy*. New York: Columbia University Press, 1955.

Santa Anna, Antonio López de. *The Eagle, An Autobiography*. Austin, Texas: Pemberton Press, 1967.

―――― (and Associated Generals). *The Mexican Side of the Texas Revolution*. Dallas, Texas: P. L. Turner, 1928.

Simpson, Lesley Byrd. *Many Mexicos*. Berkeley, Ca.: University of California Press, 1964.

Tannenbaum, Frank. *Peace by Revolution*. New York: Columbia University Press, 1933.

Timmons, Wilbert H. *Morelos of Mexico*. El Paso, Texas: Texas Western College Press, 1970.

Townsend, William Cameron. *Lázaro Cárdenas*. Ann Arbor, Mich.: Wahr Publishing Co., 1952.

Turner, John K. *Barbarous Mexico*. Austin, Texas: University of Texas Press, 1969.

Vasconcelos, José. *Breve Historia de México*. Mexico: Editiones Botas, 1938.

Von Hagen, Victor Wolfgang. *The Ancient Sun Kingdoms of the Americas*. New York: World Publishing Co., 1960.

Womack, John, Jr. *Zapata and the Mexican Revolution*. New York: Alfred A. Knopf, 1969.

INDEX

THE AUTHOR

Clarke Newlon is a former Southwestern United States newspaperman, magazine writer and editor, and the author of adult and juvenile books. His most recent volume was about outstanding Mexican-Americans. In the last years he has spent a great deal of time in Mexico and other parts of Latin America. He lives and works in Washington, D. C.